The Political
History of Finland
1809–1966

L.A. PUNTILA

The Political History of Finland 1809-1966

Translated by
DAVID MILLER

THE OTAVA PUBLISHING CO.
HELSINKI

The Finnish original
Suomen poliittinen historia 1809–1966

Second printing

ISBN 951-1-01366-1

Kustannusosakeyhtiö Otavan painolaitokset Keuruu 1975
Printed in Finland

Contents

FINLAND AND SCANDINAVIA

B A R E N T S   S E A

North Cape

Murmansk

K o l a
P e n i n s u l a

Kandalaksha

N O R W E G I A N   S E A

Vesterålen

Lofoten Is.
Vest Fjord

Arctic Circle

WHITE SEA

Onega
Peninsula

Oulu

S c a n d i n a v i a n

Gulf of Bothnia

FINLAND

NORWAY   SWEDEN

Vaasa

L. Onega

P e n i n s u l a

Tampere

L. Ladoga

OSLO

Turku HELSINKI

Vyborg

Åland
Islands

Gulf of Finland

Leningrad (St. Petersburg)

STOCKHOLM

Tallinn

Novgorod

Hiiumaa

ESTONIA

B A L T I C   S E A

Saaremaa

Skagerrak

Gotland

Riga

Kalmar

Öland

R U S S I A

Jutland

DENMARK

COPENHAGEN   Malmö

Kiel

Rostock

Gdansk

Hamburg

0 100 200 300 400 500 600 700 800 900 1000 kms

0   100   200   300   400   500 miles

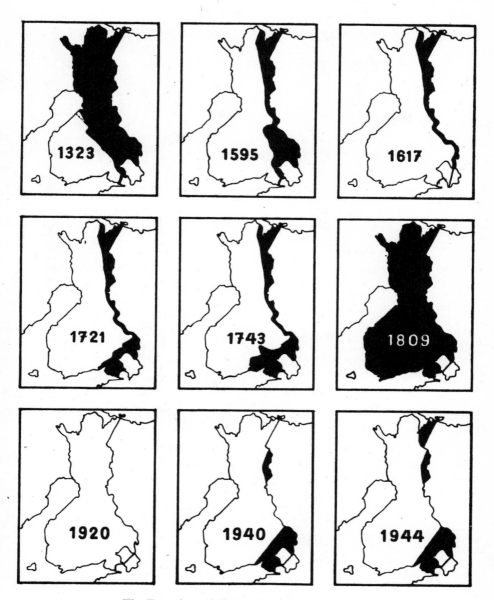

The Frontiers of Finland from 1323 to 1944

Areas shaded in black ceded to Russia/USSR.

Development before 1809

1. The Foundations of the Political History of Finland

Geographical location, physical conditions and natural resources, population, economic and cultural progress, and the efforts of groups and individuals with political responsibility – all these have contributed to the political history of Finland. Location has determined the manner in which the situation in the world at large affects the fate of the Finnish nation.

Situated in the northernmost part of Europe, Finland has generally remained outside the mainstream of European politics. In periods of great historic change, struggles for power involving neighbouring states or churches and conflicts caused by individuals or ideologies seeking world dominance have drawn Finland into European politics. Relations between Sweden and Russia and the role these states played in European and world politics – these are the external factors affecting the development of Finland's political history. Finland has not enjoyed the isolation and protection of the sea as has England, which created a powerful navy to ward off attacks from the outside and then proceeded to improve conditions at home and concentrate on the achievement of world supremacy. Nor has Finland served as the stage for major conflicts as Germany has – divided and powerless until the end of the 19th century and then as a force feared by others. Finland has not suffered directly from changes in European power politics as have small, weak countries like Belgium and the Netherlands in recent times. Neither is Finland, like Switzerland, located at the intersection of the boundaries of great powers whose rivalry and mutual envy have prevented any one of them from seeking Swiss territory. Until the beginning of the 18th century Swedish ambitions, and thereafter Russian, determined Finland's position. Finland suffered severely in the ebb and flow of conflict between these two states. Although independent Finland achieved general recognition of her Scandinavian status, she was generally regarded as a buffer state for Sweden immediately before and during the Second World War.

Migrating peoples found little in the topography, climate, and soil in the eastern, peninsula-like part of Fennoscandia to attract them. Knowledgeable Europeans first knew Finland as a land of ice and snow, forests and wild animals – a place where only the very hardy could live. Even in more recent times, when industrialization has forced national governments to seek out and take control of new sources of raw materials, no rare natural resources have been discovered in Finland – resources that might have focused the eyes of the world on this remote country in the north. Game from the forests and fish from the lakes provided a meagre harvest for the sparse population, the barren soil was poorly suited for cultivation and there was little likelihood it could sustain a large population. Systematic prospecting for minerals – except for iron ore – was unknown until the beginning of the 20th century. Finns did take advantage of water power and build mills, but the low fall potential of Finland's rapids boded ill for any large-scale exploitation. Tar production, based on Finland's forest wealth, became the most important export in the 17th century. Industrial use of timber did not begin until the end of the 19th century, and even then no foreign investors – to say nothing of foreign powers – took any interest. By the time the true worth of her forests was generally recognized and deposits of ore had been discovered, Finland was already independent and capable of defending her own resources.

Severe natural conditions and scanty resources, and to some extent wars and emigration, have kept Finland's population sparse. The population density in 1969 was only 14 people per square kilometre. The corresponding figure for the world was 26, for Europe 93, and for Europe's most densely populated country, the Netherlands, 315. Finland, with four and a half million inhabitants, is one of the smallest countries in Europe despite its areal size. In times of war it has not even been able to determine its own fate in northern Europe.

When the Finns began to settle their peninsula they had advanced beyond the stage of nomadic economy and mastered the skills of primitive agriculture. But centuries elapsed before any really advanced cultural or political life appeared. Unreliable harvests caused by the severe climate slowed economic development. Under Swedish rule the peasantry was taxed heavily – the revenues obtained benefited the Swedish kingdom and the individuals and institutions that served it. Half of these revenues went directly to Sweden. The loss of first-class manpower in Sweden's wars delayed the expansion and intensification of agriculture.

In the 19th century the value of the forests was understood, although stands of timber located on land owned by peasants were in poor condition due to cut-and-burn farming and tar-burning. Systematic forestry was possible only on large estates. Such forests provided the basis for the budding wood-processing industry. But recognition of the significance of forests for Finland's national economy was delayed until the 20th century. From then on systematic methods based on research and legislation (e.g. an act on the establishment of forestry boards and compulsory reforestation) encouraged forestry. The foundations for an internationally competitive wood-processing industry were created simultaneously.

There has been an iron industry in Finland based on domestic raw materials since the beginning of the Modern Age. Exploitation of bog ore began as early as the Middle Ages and the first seam of iron ore was discovered in the middle of the 16th century. Until the end of the 19th century, however, production was maintained with ores extracted from lakes and marshland and to some extent with ore imported from Sweden. Efforts to achieve self-sufficiency in raw materials led to the discovery of new iron deposits during the 19th century. These sources eventually proved to be of poor quality. In this respect, however, nothing of any significance for Finland's economy as a whole was achieved during either Swedish or Russian rule.

Independence stimulated domestic mining activity and made the industry based on it competitive. But efforts in agriculture and industry in the last few decades of the 19th century provided the real economic foundations for independence.

The level of popular education has been of great importance in the development of political history in the recent period. The man responsible for Finland's national awakening, the scholar and journalist J.V. Snellman (1806–1881), pointed out the interrelation between political goals and the level of education; only an educated people could demand political rights. The church spent centuries creating the necessary basis for the development of a multifarious national culture – a culture rooted in the work done by the church. Once this national culture had taken shape, it would provide shelter for further political development. Snellman's view proved correct. Finland's own rocky road to independence – and to an even greater extent the course of events in those nations born after the Second World War – provides abundant evidence of Snellman's foresight. As the concept of nationalism spread and gained acceptance, an increasing number of nations demanded independence. Where cultural development had not reached the level Snellman had in mind, the formation of independent states was difficult. These difficulties include a weak political system and executive and an inability to cooperate.

The advent of the influence of the western Church in Finland – an event that took place at the end of the first millennium of our era – was of extreme importance in the development of a society that had already travelled a great distance along its own path. Equally important was the development of a social system similar to that in the rest of Scandinavia. Finnish society was able to maintain continuity with its past in this community and although union with Sweden delayed Finland's national development in many ways, association with the rest of Scandinavia was fundamental to the preparation of the Finnish people for the foundation of an independent state.

The spread of the Protestant Reformation to Finland was also crucial to Finland's political development and the foundation of a national state. The principles of the Finnish Lutheran church favoured the use of Finnish, and thus laid the groundwork for cultural life in the language spoken by the majority of Finland's population. The pioneering work of Michael Agricola (1510–1557) – his translations and his efforts to advance the Finnish language – paved the way for further political development. Cultural life in Finland had also progressed in the Middle Ages – the period of Roman Catholic dominance – due to the relative independence of the national church. The Lutheran church, which is a state church, continued this work and also took charge of temporal matters. It furthered local self-government and made the parishes into local administrative centres.

The foundation of Finland's first university in Turku in 1640 was a milestone in national development. Sweden supplied most of the teachers for the Turku Academy in the beginning. Although the Academy – along with its printing press – might have formed an eastern bastion for propagating the ideals of a greater Sweden, it instead succeeded in a few decades in training a group of Finns in the spirit typical of European universities in that period. This group gradually took over positions in the university and eventually assumed control of the institution itself. Since professorships in remote Turku did not attract the best talent in Sweden, Finns competed for them successfully and thus gave the Academy a national character as early as the 17th century. Sweden's desire for great power status and the partisanship which arose when these hopes were dashed at the beginning of the 18th century suppressed Finnish separatism and disrupted intellectual activity. Despite these events, Finnish academic life retained its individuality. A political awakening at the end of the century encouraged this trend.

Following the peace treaty of 1809 in which Sweden ceded Finland to Russia, Turku Academy maintained the intellectual heritage of the Swedish period and became the centre for those who wanted to create a national state. In 1828 the Academy was renamed the Imperial Alexander University and moved to Helsinki, the new capital. Here the university produced an educated class and became the centre of national ideals, owing to a new generation of teachers who were influenced by cultural trends in Europe.

The political, economic, and social ideas which have affected the development of Finland's political history are of European origin. But Finland was situated far from the centres of culture and the journey there was long and arduous. Finnish youth rarely had the opportunity to study at the leading universities of Europe. After 1809 – during the period of autonomy – the authorities hampered Finland's contact with western thought considered dangerous to the Russian autocracy by limiting foreign travel. In the 19th century Finland was at least 25 years behind western Europe in intellectual development. Gradually nationalism, liberalism and socialism, along with variations of all three, gained currency in Finland. The general public learned of these new concepts through literature, the lecture hall, and other media.

Advocates of these ideas sought to convey them to the average man by word of mouth or print or by forming societies, both large and small. Political parties made their appearance at the end of the 19th century. No single line of thought gained enough support to remould society in its own image. Developments followed the path of compromise. Apart from peasant uprisings during Swedish rule, obstacles to revolutionary activity permitted politically significant activity on only two occasions: in conjunction with the general strike in 1905 and at the time of the March Revolution in 1917 in Russia. Two attempts were made to overthrow the existing social order by force: in southern Finland in 1918 and in a single locality in 1932.

2. From Sweden's "Eastland" to Autonomy

A European influence – that of Sweden – was apparent along the eastern shore of the Gulf of Bothnia and the northern shore of the Gulf of Finland by the end of the first millennium A.D. Sweden's trade route to the east ran along the Finnish coast which was protected by the archipelago. After entering an alliance with the Finns, the Swedes founded a number of colonies along this route in order to trade with the interior. As Finnish settlement expanded deeper into the interior, Sweden strengthened its position in the south either by restoring the old Finnish fortifications or by building new ones. By the end of the 14th century Swedish rule was secure in the most important parts of Finland.

Sweden's influence on Finland's political development was both that of a stronger ally and a social architect. The influence of the central government in Sweden on conditions in Finland depended on the power it had at its disposal. As a result, governors in Finland were personally in charge of the country's affairs during times of internal struggle in Sweden. The most independent phase occurred during the Kalmar Union period (1389–1523) when the central administration lay in distant Denmark and had to contend with Swedish aspirations for independence. Finland's ties with Sweden in this period were weak. Powerful bishops were able to develop Finland's administration independently, concentrating on her own special interests. After

Gustavus Vasa, king of Sweden from 1523 to 1560, succeeded in establishing an order of succession favouring his own descendants and concentrated power in the hands of the monarch, systematic efforts were made to develop the country's administration and economy and to settle new areas. The guiding hand of the sovereign was felt all over Finland and his officials tightened their control. The subsequent "great power" period meant economic control, heavy taxation, and a continuous drain of manpower for Sweden's frequent military objectives.

The participation of Finns in political life during the Swedish period was based on an independent tradition from former pagan times – a tradition that originated in the prehistoric era. When Finland came under Sweden's economic and political influence, the Roman Catholic church created an official system of provinces based on traditional boundaries. The importance of provincial rights was stressed in 1326 when the representatives of the Finnish provinces concluded a peace treaty with Tallinn side by side with representatives of the central government of Sweden, observing the diplomatic procedure of the time. In 1362, when a representative of Finland gained the right to participate in the election of the king in the same way as the representatives of the other Swedish provinces, Finland achieved similar political recognition. Provisions for this right were included in the law of the land in the middle of the 15th century. In principle, Finns participated in elections from then on, although many factors – weather conditions for example – might prevent the voyage to Sweden. Finland's importance received further recognition when it was considered necessary to hold elections there. When the crown became hereditary the question of elections arose only if there were no heirs.

Finnish involvement in Swedish politics was not limited to royal elections. Finns had the right to take part in decisions concerning the entire realm just as the other inhabitants did. Little advantage of this right was taken during the Middle Ages. The realm was governed on a provincial basis, and the Finns, like the Swedes, were legally able to settle matters concerning both Finland and the whole kingdom at their own provincial meetings. When Gustavus Vasa and his immediate successors concentrated political authority in Stockholm in an effort to create an absolute monarchy and a uniform kingdom, consultations became less frequent. Decisions were now made outside Finland. In connection with the struggles for the throne at the end of the 16th century, however, the Finns overcame their isolation and regained their rights. A meeting of the Finnish Estates occurred in Turku in the early spring of 1593. Sigismund, king of Poland from 1566 to 1632, was the heir to the Swedish throne. As John III's (1568–1592) son, he requested an oath of loyalty through his envoy. Without consulting the Swedes, the Finnish Estates gave their oath in Turku and Finland's fleet supported Sigismund in his attempt to ascend the throne of a refractory Sweden.

Leaders in Finland and Sweden arrived at different views of the situation. New meetings of the Estates were called and conflicting decisions were made. Relations between Finland and Sweden continued to deteriorate and in the end a civil war was necessary before Finland would submit to the mother country. The Swedish branch of the House of Vasa emerged the victor in these power struggles at the end of the 16th century. The establishment of a hereditary monarch meant the concentration of power. The Riksdag in Stockholm decided on affairs concerning the entire country and provincial assemblies of the Estates lost their influence. A significant exception for Finland's political development took place during the reign of Gustavus II Adolphus (1611–1632). On ascending the throne he was forced to promise not to impose any new taxes nor organize any further military conscription without the consent of the people. Sweden had just waged a victorious war against Russia and was now negotiating the peace. In 1616 the king called the Estates in Finland to a provincial diet in Helsinki in order to prevent a recurrence of the stand taken in the 1590s. The Estates were requested to explain how Finland could be protected from potential attacks by King Sigismund of Poland – who was seeking the Swedish crown – and from the Russians. These consultations may not have been the real reason for convening the Estates. The king obtained the approval of the Estates for an additional war tax. At the Diet in Helsinki, the Estates swore their loyalty to the king and to lay down their lives in the fight against Sigismund and the Russians. But Finnish participation in the Riksdag in Stockholm remained minimal.

Sweden's great power policy did, however, mark a turning point in Finnish political activity. Sweden sought hegemony in the Baltic region and the necessary preparations had to be made. In order to secure supplies and troops and to pay those who served the king, taxes collected by the crown were transferred to noblemen. Reduced taxation and conscription for the tenants of noblemen at a time when the crown needed more money and men meant increased pressure on those Finnish peasants who were directly under the crown. Those representing these peasants in the Riksdag became increasingly insistent in their demand that the grants be repealed. Some nobles who had received grants themselves understood Finland's interests and joined in these demands. When the king considered it necessary to curb the power of the nobility, the Finns were united in their support of the sovereign. The grants were withdrawn at the 1680 session of the Riksdag. In supporting the king, the majority of the Finns helped consolidate absolute rule, transfer the powers of the Estates to the king, and limit the hereditary political rights which had been enjoyed in Finland.

Sweden emerged from the Great Northern War (1700–1721) weak and stripped of her great power status. Concentration of power in the hands of the king was blamed for the misfortunes that had befallen the entire country. The Estates took complete control. But the resultant "Age of Freedom" (1719–1772) by no means meant an improvement in Finland's position, and valuable areas in the southeast were ceded to Russia according to the terms of the Peace of Uusikaupunki. Finns recognized the threat posed by a great power bent on expansion and adopted a flexible, conciliatory policy toward Russia, as did the "Caps" faction in the Riksdag. Another faction, the "Hats," dominated the Riksdag during the Age of Freedom. They were pro-French and pursued an anti-Russian policy. The Hats considered the situation in Europe favourable and launched a war against Russia, relying on help promised by France. The result was the so-called "Lesser Wrath" (1741–1743) and the turning point in Finnish attitudes toward union with Sweden. During the Great Northern War, or the "Great Wrath," most officials fled to Sweden; this time they remained in Finland. Finns gathered in provincial assemblies in an attempt to work out relations with the Russian army of occupation. They also discussed a Russian proposal which would permit Finland to choose her own sovereign – a prince whom the Russians could approve. The Peace of Turku in 1743 ended talk of separation from Sweden, although Finns in the Riksdag continued their efforts to win acceptance for the prince favoured by the Russians. Their aim was to secure peaceful relations with Russia and thereby save Finland. Finnish efforts were also successful in the combined Diet, although this did not prevent Finland from losing those areas located east of the Kymi river according to the terms of the peace.

Confidence lost in Sweden during the Great Wrath and the split which developed during the Lesser Wrath proved permanent. Swedish ruling circles did recognize Finland as their most important remaining possession and they established several committees and commissions with the objective of improving Finland's status. Finns of course participated in the Riksdag and led efforts to improve conditions in Finland. Their activity resulted only in unkept promises and unfulfilled plans. The Swedes had a large majority in the Riksdag and strove consistently to protect Swedish interests while the improvements were being implemented; the Finns were again accused of separatist and secessionist aspirations.

The majority of the Finns opposed the policies of the Hats and operated in the Riksdag on the basis of a mutual understanding with the Caps. This meant continual trouble when the Hats were in power; the Finns were in the opposition and could not have their own way. As a result, Finnish opinion became increasingly radical. Many Finns – even some from the Peasant Estate – belonged to the Hats. But at the end of the 1760s the leading Finns had taken their position in the front ranks of the Caps, and the Hats were put down. A reform movement began and attempts were made with the aid of freedom of the press to start up newspapers and encourage the development of public opinion. An end to commercial dependence appeared to provide an opportunity for stimulating the economy; sailing rights held by the peasantry permitting them to carry on trade were of great importance for Finland. But the Finns were also a minority in the Cap Riksdag. They were unable to make their voices heard and there was general concensus that Finland was no better off with a Cap Riksdag than she had been under the absolute monarchy of the great power period. Gustavus III (1771–92) had Finnish backing when he made plans in 1772 to subdue the Estates.

Finns enjoyed the confidence of Gustavus III and some improvements in conditions in Finland were made; this was particularly true in the case of defence. Finland came into her own during the reign of Gustavus III. She gained a measure of the recognition she sought, but it was too late for the cause of continued unity with Sweden.

Close cooperation among Finns brought out new points of view and furthered the belief that the country had its own special needs and status. The Finnish faction found itself more and more involved in disputes with the representatives of the mother country and acted with increasing frequency in the name of Finland in the Riksdag. Teaching and research that emphasized Finland's individuality took root at Turku Academy at approximately the same time, marking the beginnings of Finnish intellectual development. Politics abroad supported Finnish aspirations for separation. Russia – led energetically and ambitiously – was expanding her territory in both Europe and Asia. The balance of power between Sweden and Russia changed incessantly in the 18th century, to Sweden's detriment. The most observant Finns foresaw what this would mean for Finland's future. Certain accommodations would be necessary and preparations had to be made. Any deterioration in relations with Russia had to be avoided and Finland had to build up her own forces at the same time; training Finnish officers in a Finnish military school was an example. The same realistic view of the situation determined the action taken by certain Finnish officers. In 1788 when Gustavus III launched a fruitless war against Russia without the consent of the Estates and in violation of the constitution, the officers ignored their obligation to obey and opposed the king's plans with the aim of restoring peace. The advocates of independence attempted to exploit the spirit of opposition in the army, although the suppressive policies of the Russian government in Poland and in the Baltic countries boded ill for any rearrangement of Finland's status under Russian protection.

Efforts to improve Finland's special status made at Turku Academy developed out of a general European current that reached Sweden and Finland during the great power period. This current of thought tended to stress the historical significance of one's own people and thus also led to an exaggeration of its talents and accomplishments and an idealization of the past. Although they lacked any basis in fact, these ideas still had significance in instruction and in the selection of topics

20

for scholarly research. Under the direction of Henrik Gabriel Porthan (1739–1804), teachers at Turku Academy devoted themselves to research on Finnish conditions and the Finnish nation – its past, language, and intellectual heritage. Societies were formed in which Finland's special problems were considered. The results of these efforts were presented in the lecture halls of the Academy to a receptive audience. Finland's small educated class had adopted a primitive form of nationalism at the end of the 18th century when the series of major political events started by the French Revolution of 1789 made Finland the subject of talks between states deciding the fate of Europe.

Napoleon I, the child of the Great Revolution, strove to extend French influence with the ultimate goal of world dominance. Napoleon was an unequalled military commander and organizer in his time. A strong-willed statesman, he attracted ambitious soldiers and politicians in France and in those countries which either feared his growing power or joined him in order to exploit it. Napoleon took advantage of the feeling of strength the revolution produced and played upon French admiration of grandeur in order to inspire his people and his army to continual sacrifice. He also succeeded in organizing the resources of the countries he conquered to serve the ends of the empire. The rest of Europe was divided and ruled by rival houses and this prevented Napoleon's opponents from presenting a united front. Napoleon crushed one opponent after another. The victories he won as a relatively young officer in the revolutionary army secured his position in France and he met no opposition when he proclaimed himself emperor in 1804.

Britain was Napoleon's leading opponent. Relying on her powerful navy and the protection offered by the sea, Britain built up a world empire while the continental powers spent their strength in competing with one another. Britain has always sought to prevent any single power from achieving hegemony on the continent; she has been willing to enter alliances and go to war to preserve the balance of power. France achieved dominance on the continent under Napoleon I. Britain consequently joined forces with those European states that opposed Napoleon in order to preserve her own status as a great power.

Napoleon I fought incessantly to achieve his goals and aroused fear and resignation in the governments of Europe. But his tyranny also encouraged resistance and the desire for cooperation grew along with it. Alexander I of Russia (1801–1825) was aware of Napoleon's ultimate goals and Napoleon's success or failure was also of extreme importance to Russia. After Alexander and his allies suffered defeat in two wars with Napoleon a reappraisal of the situation was in order. Alexander accepted when Napoleon offered a settlement concerning spheres of influence at Tilsit in 1807; he needed to buy time and strengthen his country's defences.

Changes in Finland's eastern border have reflected shifts in the balance of power between Sweden and Russia. In periods of Russian weakness the border was pushed east and south by treaty and by force of arms. In 25 years of war with Russia (1570–1595) and when interfering in Russian internal affairs at the beginning of the 17th century, Sweden sought certain objectives. She wanted hegemony in the Baltic and strove to drive Russia from its shores. Sweden achieved these goals, and the provinces of Käkisalmi and Ingria were joined to Finland in 1617 by the Peace of Stolbova.

Once Russia had put her own house in order, her military strength began to increase her bargaining power in foreign affairs. The roles in northern Europe changed. Access to the sea and to shipping routes was a prerequisite for Russian recovery. Peter I (1689–1725), the ruler who made Russia a great power, made plans for expansion with this in mind. Russia had to dominate the Baltic and the Black seas. He exploited the defeat suffered at the beginning of the Great Northern War. While the ruler of Sweden was involved in military adventures in Europe, Peter founded a town at the mouth of the Neva river in an area ceded to Sweden in the Peace of Stolbova. As a demonstration of his determination to hold this area, Peter made the new town, St. Petersburg, his capital in 1712. Sweden ceded Ingria and the towns of Viipuri, Sortavala, and Käkisalmi according to the Peace of Uusikaupunki in 1721. In the Peace of Turku in 1743 at the end of the Lesser Wrath, Russia furthered her conquests; the border moved westward to the Kymi river and Finland lost the towns of Hamina, Lappeenranta, and Savonlinna. Security for the new capital determined Russia's policy toward Finland. The war Gustavus III started against Russia proved that the border stipulated in the Peace of Turku had not stabilized relations between Sweden and Russia.

In sizing up the situation when Napoleon I was at the height of his power, Alexander I considered it important to secure his northwestern border. At Tilsit he agreed to take part in the blockade against Britain in accordance with Napoleon's wishes, seeking to obtain a free hand in Finland.

Russia could have secured her defence in the tense situation existing in Europe by merely gaining control of the northern shore of the Gulf of Finland; she had no plans to conquer all of Finland or annex it. But in 1808, when the attack begun under pressure from Napoleon seemed to advance almost unopposed and when the whims of Gustavus IV Adolphus set Sweden's policy, Alexander I expanded his objective and sought to take all of Finland. This goal dovetailed neatly with the ideas of those who advocated Finnish independence, especially those of Y.M. Sprengtporten (1740–1819), who had moved to Russia in 1786. Sprengtporten was mainly interested in the separation of Finland from Sweden, the unification of all Finnish territories, and in securing either independence or as much autonomy as possible, with Russian cooperation. It was in Russia's interests to make men like Sprengtporten her allies.

Alexander I may have been ready to consent to Finnish wishes before war broke out and to grant Finland autonomy. But Russian attitudes toward the future of Finland were by no means clear. A proclamation convening the Estates in Turku was made as soon as hostilities began. But when the advance faced virtually no opposition, the orders of the commander-in-chief, F.W. von Buxhoevden (1750–1811), changed, and in the early summer Alexander I proclaimed his intention to join Finland to the Russian empire for ever. A crucial turn in favour of autonomy took place in the middle of the summer when the Finns themselves went to war. They were not nearly so eager for separation from Sweden as Russia had anticipated. Loyalty to the Swedish crown still bound the fighting men and the lower-ranking commanders. This immediately became apparent when more vigorous men took control of the Finnish forces. Both the unclarity of Russian attitudes toward Finnish autonomy and the violence of the Russian troops themselves increased Finnish mistrust of the invaders. The fighting was brutal in accordance with the practice of the time and the economic resources of the conquered areas were exploited thoroughly in order to maintain the army. The behaviour of the invaders, which Finnish guerillas made more severe, estranged Finns from the idea of closer cooperation. Plans announced by the commander-in-chief at the beginning of the war for an oath of loyalty from the Finns to the new ruler collapsed as the mood of the country changed. The stiffening of Finnish resistance, both military and civilian, forced Alexander I to reconsider the situation.

On the basis of the events in Europe occurring after Tilsit, Alexander expected Napoleon to settle accounts with Russia ahead of schedule. The war in Finland had to be ended as soon as possible. While Sweden concentrated on safeguarding her interests in Norway and the military leadership in Finland dawdled, failing to take advantage of the successes of the summer of 1808, Alexander sent substantial reinforcements to crush military resistance in Finland. The tsar encouraged the Finns to give up the fight by consenting to proposals for an autonomous Finland made by advocates of Finnish independence.

Those who supported autonomy for Finland had the backing of Alexander's trusted adviser, Mikael Speransky (1771–1839), who had risen to a position of influence after Tilsit. Speransky had plans to develop the Russian autocracy along the lines of a constitutional monarchy and worked on the basis of an understanding with the tsar. These plans coincided with those held by the Finns as did the constitution of Gustavus III of Sweden, which gave the monarch extensive powers. As Speransky brought Finnish affairs to the attention of the tsar after 1809, he was largely responsible for setting the course of political development in the conquered country.

In this way Finland's national defence, developments on the international scene, and contemporary constitutional ideals all had an effect on the position taken by the tsar. After the war took a favourable turn from the defenders' point of view, the Russians stopped talking about turning Finland into a province. In February 1809, the tsar issued a proclamation convening the Diet at Porvoo; there was some talk of Finland's elevation to nationhood. In a sense, the tsar had already recognized the existence of a Finnish nation. On November 30, 1808, the foreign minister introduced a delegation from Finland and the tsar received them as though they were representatives of a friendly state. Although later developments showed that Finland's "elevation to nationhood" was a good part wartime persuasion and although only limited autonomy was actually granted, this turn of events did pave the way for cooperation based on trust. Alexander guaranteed on his oath as tsar to maintain the constitution in effect under Swedish rule. Although otherwise shallow and vain, Alexander should be remembered for his personal liberalism when judging this act of state. Alexander extended this guarantee to his successors in 1816. Assurances were also given at Porvoo that Finland could maintain her religion and retain the other rights her citizens possessed. The Diet was to deal with proposals made to it and also make petitions according to the procedure used in the Swedish Riksdag. The Estates were convened in the manner required in the constitution of Gustavus II and the term "Diet" underscored Finland's status.

The meeting of the Estates held in Porvoo during the war considered Finland's separation from Sweden an accomplished fact. Legislative efforts concentrated on shaping a new political order. The most important of these was the establishment of a national governing body and the determination of its relationship to the Russian empire.

Finland was henceforth governed as a separate entity within the Russian empire. It had the status of a grand duchy, and Alexander, like the Swedish kings before him, included the appellation "Grand Duke of Finland" among his many other titles. A governing council was established in 1809 as the highest governmental body and supreme court, and Finns were appointed to serve on it. In 1816 it was renamed the Imperial Senate of Finland. The Senate was composed of two sections. The financial section functioned to some extent as a modern-day ministry. It also exercised the powers of a supreme court in administrative matters in a manner similar to that of the Supreme Administrative Court after Finnish independence. The judicial section was the highest court of appeal, similar to the Supreme Court of the more recent period. The tsar appointed and dismissed members of the Senate. The governor-general, the representative of the tsar in Finland, served as chairman of the Senate. Thus the governor-general was in the position to safeguard the interests of the empire in the highest administrative organs of the country. The vice chairman of the financial section resembled a modern-day prime minister and usually acted as chairman. Only on very special occasions did the governor-general preside at the meetings.

Although scholars are divided about the significance of the decisions made at the Diet in Porvoo for political development in Finland, practice until the end of the 19th century confirmed the Finnish analysis; the decisions of the Diet were valid. Participation in the work of the Diet was an indication of voluntary submission to the tsar. The peace treaty between Sweden and Russia was a formality; it merely acknowledged the new order which already existed.

In the talks between Sweden and Russia leading up to the peace concluded at Hamina on September 17, 1809, Sweden accepted the decisions made at the Porvoo Diet. The king of Sweden considered them an indication of the tsar's intention to govern his new subjects with justice; they also meant an effective end to Sweden's obligations in Finland. The most important difference of opinion concerned the border between Sweden and Finland. The Kaakamajoki river had served as the border and the Swedes argued that it should continue to do so. The Russians demanded that it be moved westward, to the Tornio and Muonio rivers. They were steadfast in this demand, and as a result, Finland expanded to fill out her "natural border" in the northwest according to the terms of the Peace of Hamina. An important river route now served as the border and an area inhabited by a Finnish-speaking population was united with the rest of Finland.

In 1812 the provinces east of the Kymi river – ceded to Russia in the treaties of Uusikaupunki and Turku – were reunited with the rest of Finland. The grand duchy thus included all the Finnish national areas.

CHAPTER I

The Period of Frozen Constitutionalism, 1809–63

Russia broke the back of Napoleon's eastern offensive in 1812 and thereby became the most important factor in the land war fought against the French. Alexander I exercised the authority due him by virtue of Russia's military achievements at the Congress of Vienna in 1814–1815. Decisions simply were not made without his consent. Britain, Napoleon's other major opponent, withdrew from European affairs for the next 40 years; this lent further strength to Russia's position as the major power on the European continent.

In 1809, while hostilities continued in Finland, a military coup in Sweden relieved Gustavus IV Adolphus of his crown. The Danish prince chosen to succeed the eccentric, head-strong Swedish ruler died and Napoleon's Marshal Bernadotte was elected. Bernadotte rapidly achieved a position of great influence in the government. Contrary to the expectations of his former commander, Bernadotte took a realistic stand in foreign policy. Belligerence soon proved futile in relations with a powerful Russia and Bernadotte sought to conciliate his recent enemy. Once he obtained assurances from Russia concerning union of Norway with Sweden – to be implemented along with a new political and economic order – he formed an alliance with Alexander I in 1812. In this way Russia consolidated her position in Finland and secured peace with Sweden.

1.

Finland began to feel the effect of Russia's position of strength in European politics after the Congress of Vienna in 1815. The great problems of Europe and Russian internal affairs occupied the tsar;

Russia's position in newly conquered Finland was secure and public opinion there provided no cause for concern. 1808 was an important year in the development of Finland's administrative system. It was then that the tsar proclaimed that matters concerning Finland should be referred directly to him. This act led to the formation of the Finnish state secretariat, headed by the minister secretary of state after 1834. Administration in Finland after 1809 continued along the lines laid down at the Porvoo Diet and in 1811 a committee was set up to deal with Finnish affairs.

Otherwise political life was at a standstill; this was a period of bureaucracy and "frozen" constitutionalism. The Diet was not convened and the hopes encouraged by the Diet at Porvoo waned. According to the constitution of 1772, legislation was the joint responsibility of the sovereign and the four Estates – the Nobility, the Clergy, the Burghers, and the Peasants. The sovereign was not entitled to enact new laws or repeal old ones without the consent and knowledge of the Estates. The right to propose new laws was reserved for the sovereign. Legislation concerning financial matters and the issuing of administrative ordinances was also in the sovereign's hands. Taxation did require the consent of the Estates. When tax revenues did not leave Finland – as was the case under Swedish rule – they were used to meet the country's own needs and public finances remained in equilibrium for years without any new taxes. As there was no mention of customs duties in the constitution, decisions on them were left up to the sovereign. As customs duties formed the major part of the state's income in Finland, finances could be handled for some time without consulting the Estates.

According to the constitution, the sovereign also had the right to convene the Diet. Failure to do so did not mean a formal breach of the constitution. On the other hand, the Estates could have played a significant role in Finnish political development. A single session of the Diet held during time of war could not settle the affairs of Finland and Russia after unification – nor could it determine the duties of the tsar-grand duke who ruled both. Neither did it reveal Finnish hopes for the future. The return of constitutional rights after peace was concluded – particularly those involving the Estates – was generally desired and even demanded. But censorship silenced public debate. It kept a close watch on the press and Finnish reformers felt the hostility of the authorities in the form of dismissals, discrimination, and even exile.

Alexander's rule took a reactionary turn due to reversals met in attempts at domestic reform and Russia's position of strength in international politics. Preservation of the status quo was the watchword of Alexander's successor, Nicholas I (1825–55). The Decembrist revolt, which occurred as Nicholas came to power, only confirmed his distrust of reform; the officers involved in the rebellion had contracted the contagion of liberalism on military campaigns in Europe. The autocrat of Russia was no more willing to permit public discussion in his own country than he was in any other territory now a part of the empire, including Finland. He was equally intolerant of the activity of any governmental institutions that limited his own absolute authority.

Reaction in Russia did not, however, put an end to progress in Finland after the Peace of Hamina. Finnish officials were by no means inactive. Even without the support of the Diet they adapted to the existing state of affairs and went on with their work. Differences of opinion later arose about what the changes brought about in the peace treaty really meant for Finland's future. Those who held fast to traditions carried over from the Swedish period and those who favoured the Swedish language, culture, and customs, considered separation a catastrophe. Finland lost cultural ties that had grown strong over the centuries and joined a great power whose social system, religion, and entire outlook on life were alien. And Russia was also a European great power – it had to maintain a constant watch on affairs in Europe and take a position in every conflict. There were fears that Finland would be involved in war, particularly against Sweden. Some participants in the Porvoo Diet argued that Finland's military force should be disbanded and not recalled for the next 50 years. Rapid Russification was also feared. Reunion with Sweden was considered the only salvation for the Finnish nation by those who idealized the traditions of the Swedish period. A widespread desire for revenge in Sweden fed this hope, although the government continued the policy of conciliation with Russia it had begun in 1812.

There were also those who considered union with a great power advantageous. Russia's position looked unassailable and individuals in these circles held that the expression "ex oriente lux" would hold true in the future. Finns had the rights of Russian subjects throughout the empire, although Russians did not have the corresponding privileges in Finland. Russia offered Finns, particularly the nobility, an opportunity to advance in the hierarchy of a large state and participate actively in European politics. With this in mind, families trained their sons for, service in Russia. Many achieved positions of considerable significance in the bureaucracy, the army, and particularly in the navy. Russia of course was not a seafaring nation. There were around 3,000 Finns in the Russian officer corps from the 1830s up to the end of the First World War. One-tenth of them rose to the rank of general and 70 to that of admiral.

Those officials whom the Russians trusted naturally advanced to the top after the Peace of Hamina. They soon acquired many of those features characteristic of Russian bureaucrats; they disparaged representative institutions and paid no heed to public opinion. Some of the most extreme expressed outright admiration for the Russian system. They sought to ward off reform efforts that originated in the west and were especially opposed to nationalism, democracy, and demands for individual freedom and freedom of the press.

The most alert members of the educated class discerned a third alternative after the conclusion of Peace at Hamina. The status of Finns and the Finnish language had grown increasingly difficult during the Swedish period. Discrimination led the Finns to increased criticism of Sweden and when the reforms they demanded and expected were not forthcoming, they joined those who desired a change in European politics. Those who supported this line of thought feared that continued union with Sweden would mean that everything characteristically Finnish would gradually wither away. The outcome of the war fought from 1808–09 opened new perspectives. The national patriotic circles were no less aware of the dangers involved in union with Russia than were those who longed for union with Sweden. Russification was clearly possible. But Russian nationalism was dormant for many years and once aroused, its major objective until the 1860s was the unification of the Slavs. As for Finland, Russia's rulers were primarily concerned with defence and power politics in Europe. As long as the Finns remained loyal and appreciated the advantages of union with Russia, little attention was paid to the national awakening. In fact,

Russian leaders were favourably inclined towards the rise of national sentiment in Finland in the first few decades after unification because it furthered estrangement from Sweden.

Teachers at Turku Academy – under the influence of German romanticism – launched a national movement in the 1810s. The contribution of the historian A.I. Arwidsson (1791–1858) to the awakening was particularly important. The slogan, "Swedes we are not, Russians we will not be, therefore let us be Finns", summed up his ideology. He boldly began to publish articles in the press that were sharply critical of conditions in Finland and directed them at readers in both Sweden and Finland. He paid for his efforts; he was dismissed permanently from the university in 1822. His livelihood lost, he moved to Sweden the following year. But Finnish nationalism had gained a firm foothold. It grew stronger – both at Turku Academy and at the university after the move to Helsinki.

According to the national patriotic point of view, Finland had suffered enough in the long struggle for power between Sweden and Russia. Now part of the most powerful nation in Europe, Finland ought to be able to live in peace and use her intellectual and economic resources for constructive purposes. Defence was Russia's principal concern on her northwestern frontier after the conquest of Finland. She sought to maintain the status quo. Swedish foreign policy since 1812 provided further evidence that years of constructive internal development lay ahead.

Russia offered Finland's nascent industry an extensive duty-free market which would also remain open should war break out in Europe. Both domestic and foreign trade were now free from the dependence of the Swedish period – as long as the Russians did not attempt to establish a similar system. Such perspectives were consoling, although the dangers confronting a great power were appreciated. War between Russia and a naval power would attract an enemy fleet to Finnish territorial waters. Shipping – so vital to the development of the national economy – would undoubtedly suffer. At the end of the 19th century Finnish merchant tonnage still exceeded that of Russia. But these disadvantages to union with Russia were not felt until the second half of the 19th century.

2.

The French Revolution and the Napoleonic Era that followed it caused a thorough upheaval in Europe. Monarchs who had fought both revolutionaries and Napoleon had been under particular pressure. Alexander planned a fraternal order of the rulers of Europe to save the world from a similar fate. After the downfall of Napoleon, Austria and Prussia joined Russia in forming the Holy Alliance. All Europe – with the exception of Britain, Turkey, and the Vatican – took part. Although the alliance itself was of limited importance in international relations, opposition to reform – one of its major tenets – gained ascendancy in each country.

But the tradition of the French Revolution went on. Despite all the action taken against them, new national movements formed in Europe. Revolutionary movements and those that strove for national independence posed a threat to the entire existing system. A revolutionary outbreak in one tended to spread throughout Europe; if one throne tottered, reverberations were felt in every capital. Ruling circles were on constant alert, and when revolutionary stirrings developed in one country, precautionary measures were taken everywhere.

The effects of the July Revolution in France in 1830 spread to different parts of Europe. Forewarned by the Decembrist revolt, Nicholas I tightened his grip even further. He was still unsuccessful. Inspired by the July Revolution, the Poles revolted and fought for their independence. Nicholas crushed the rebellion in November of the same year. In Finland, students were particularly susceptible to the revolutionary contagion. In the 1820s the struggle for Greek independence aroused them. They were caught up by the ideal of liberty and the struggle for national independence. Instruction in the schools and the university had portrayed ancient Greece as the ideal state and the struggle of the Greeks against invading Persian hordes served as a model for all small nations. Finnish students also sympathized with the Poles, and made no secret of it. Danger threatened both the university and Finnish autonomy itself when the tsar became aware of this. Nicholas believed that sympathy for the Poles was directed against the autocracy and made plans to close the university. Although the worst was avoided, Nicholas resorted to stricter censorship and internal controls. His suspicions were aroused.

The consequences of the revolution that broke out in France in 1848 were even more significant. The upheaval there led to the formation of the Second Republic and the shock wave it caused spread throughout Europe, shaking the very foundations of autocracy. Limitations were placed on absolute rule, civil rights were extended, and parliaments on the continent gained their first authority.

Strict controls and the espionage system imposed in Russia after the July Revolution and the Polish revolt prevented the wave of discontent caused by the revolution in February 1848 from wreaking havoc there. But the conflagration did rage in neighbouring states. In Austria the Hungarians believed they could exploit the turmoil in Europe and rose to fight for their independence. In Germany the constitutional empire born in the upheaval there offered the Imperial German Crown to the king of Prussia at the Frankfurt Assembly in 1849. But peaceful unification of Germany was prevented. The king did not want to accept a crown offered him by representatives chosen by the people and demanded the consent of the German governments. The latter refused, and once they had gained the upper hand from those who had started the insurrection, the wave of revolution subsided.

Dissatisfaction with the House of Hapsburg during the turmoil of 1848 led to the Hungarian struggle for independence. The rising was initially successful; the Hapsburgs were in the process of losing the Crown of St. Stephen in Hungary. But Nicholas I recognized the joint responsibility of Europe's monarchs and dispatched Russian troops. His intervention put an end to the struggle for Hungarian independence in 1849. Loyal to the principles of the Holy Alliance, Nicholas I did not demand compensation for his intervention. He was content to return the Hapsburgs to power.

The revolution in February also had repercussions in Finland. The first news from France rekindled enthusiasm, mainly in student circles. Student associations were hotbeds of support for liberty and sympathy for those struggling against tyranny. The students made no attempt to conceal it. On May 3, 1848, they held their annual spring celebration at Kumtähti meadow near Helsinki. Members of the student union marched there with banners. Runeberg's "Our Country" was sung for the first time to the music of Fredrik Pacius, and Fredrik Cygnaeus

(1807–1881), senior history lecturer at the University of Helsinki and curator of the Ostrobothnian student union, made an inspiring speech in honour of the name "Finland". This youthful demonstration was essentially harmless. But it did attract attention in ruling circles in St. Petersburg where it was considered another indication of the susceptibility of Finnish students and the educated class to western influences and an affront to the existing order. Once more the university became the object of close surveillance. In 1852 St. Petersburg decided the student unions were dangerous breeding grounds for revolutionary sentiment and dissolved them. Suspicion of the national movement had already led in 1850 to a ban on all publication in Finnish with the exception of religious and economic literature. The objective was to strike a fatal blow at the budding national literature and also at the national patriotic circles which both the Russians and Finland's own bureaucracy considered revolutionary. While Russia stood at the peak of its influence in Europe, Finland was experiencing a period of dark reaction.

3.

Nicholas I recognized the joint responsibility of Europe's monarchs when he suppressed the Hungarian rising and supported the Hapsburgs. This was the last expression of the "ideology" behind the Holy Alliance. A new phase of power politics was beginning. Nothing was done, as the saying went, "for the sake of blue eyes". Governments existed solely to preserve and pursue their own interests as great powers. This led to military and economic competition between states, to an arms race, to diplomatic manœuvring, and to increasingly destructive wars.

The Second French Republic, founded in 1848, was followed by the Second Empire in 1852. The hardships of the era of Napoleon I were forgotten. Memories of France's greatness were still alive and influenced public opinion. The restoration was not particularly successful; the monarchy was powerless and France enjoyed scant respect. The French were prepared to support a government that seemed capable of restoring order at home and regaining status as a great power abroad.

Louis Napoleon Bonaparte, the nephew of Napoleon I, was able to exploit this sentiment. He tried to take power by force of arms on several occasions. After the revolution in February he entered the National Assembly. He was elected President in 1848 and made emperor by a plebiscite held in 1852. Napoleon III sought to re-establish France's status as a great power; the realization of this goal was also a prerequisite for the consolidation and maintenance of his own power. France's neighbours were exhausted from the revolution of 1848 and were incapable of interfering in the internal affairs of France. Napoleon won the time he needed to strengthen his grip at home.

Hereditary monarchs maintained that they ruled by divine right. Napoleon III was elected Emperor by the people and attempted to preserve his power by observing the principles of nationalism and liberalism and by carrying out a vigorous foreign policy. An opportunity arose when Russia's traditional aspirations in the Mediterranean became the guiding principle of the foreign policy of Nicholas I. Napoleon I saw both the interests of France and those of his own throne in opposing the growing power of Russia. He obtained support in this endeavour from Britain. Britain sought to prevent any single power from gaining hegemony in the Mediterranean in order to preserve her own status as a great power.

Britain joined forces with France in order to prevent Russian territorial expansion at the expense of Turkey; the result was the Crimean War of 1854–56. There was fierce fighting on the Crimean Peninsula. The combined British and French fleets controlled the seas, shelling and seizing merchant vessels with the aim of disrupting Russian operations. In the summers of 1854 and 1855 Finland also found herself in the theatre of war. Coastal towns were shelled and damaged and landings were attempted with rather limited forces. When Sweden formed a military alliance in 1855 with Britain and France to win back Finland, there seemed to be justification for Alexander I's conquest of the entire country; Finland did appear to act as a buffer state.

The fighting, however, was largely restricted to the Crimea and ended without victory for either side. Russia's internal weakness and lack of organization became evident during the war as did dissatisfaction with the existing system. Although the allies were hampered by long naval supply lines and waged war with little enthusiasm, the Russians were unable to drive them out of the Crimea. A good indication of the state of the Russian fleet was its failure to provide the Finnish coast any protection against allied shelling. Russian dominance – which had lasted for several decades – proved deceptive and France emerged as the leading power on the continent. The new balance of power in Europe appeared at the Congress of Paris in 1856. Napoleon III was in command. Russia went to war seeking control of the Turkish straits but was forced to accept the neutralization of the Black Sea, open it to all merchant vessels, and refrain from either building fortifications or maintaining military bases on the Åland islands.

Russia's isolation and the decline of her influence in Europe were soon felt in Finland's internal affairs. The person of the ruler in a genuine autocracy is of great importance; his will is decisive. After the death of Nicholas I – while war still raged in the Crimea – Alexander II (1855–1881) ascended the throne. Alexander was more flexible than his predecessor. Nicholas had held stubbornly to his status and rights as autocrat. The former knew western conditions and viewed them with considerable understanding. His rule foretold change in Russian domestic policy. But still more important was the fact that the new tsar recognized the weaknesses of the empire he inherited. As long as international tension continued, Russia had to prepare for future conflicts by carrying out reforms at home.

Finland was able to take advantage of the collapse of Russian hegemony and the tsar's favourable attitude toward reform and toward Finland, which had remained loyal during the Crimean War. The university arranged a celebration in honour of the coronation of the new tsar on September 20, 1856. F.L. Schauman (1810–77), professor of practical theology, was chosen to speak. Schauman expressed hope that the Finnish people would have an opportunity to develop their nationality freely and that "the Estates of our country would be convened soon and thereafter convened more often in accordance with the constitutional order", to consult about matters of importance for Finland. Although this hope had previously been expressed publicly – in Snellman's writings for example – Schauman's bold presentation and the publication of the speech by the university provided new emphasis. It aroused resentment both in ruling circles in St. Petersburg and in

Finland's own bureaucracy. The latter feared the cause would suffer a setback. But a return to constitutional rule through the convocation of the Diet was in accordance with Alexander's way of thinking and discussion on improvements in Finnish conditions continued without interference from the censor. Finland's wartime loyalty and the more relaxed atmosphere after the death of Nicholas I encouraged both the tsar and the empire at large to adopt a more favourable attitude toward Finland.

Conflicting views of Finland's future became acute during the Crimean War. Those who adhered to the traditions of the Swedish period hoped that Sweden would join Russia's enemies in a future European war and achieve reunification with Finland. These aspirations received strong support from anti-Russian public opinion in Sweden, which demanded preparations for a war of revenge. The anti-Russian orientation in Sweden also coincided with western military interests. Agents of the western powers tried to arouse public opinion by promising reunion with Finland.

The policies of Nicholas I toward Finland resulted in anti-Russian sentiment which grew more intense during the Crimean War. Students and young scholars with a Scandinavian orientation were the principal supporters of this point of view. Efforts to suppress freedom of expression and the national movement such as the edict of 1850 which prohibited the use of Finnish, strengthened resolve, particularly among students, to oppose the autocracy. As the autocracy seemed unshakeable in Russia itself, separation from the empire offered the only hope for an improvement in Finnish conditions. But Finland's status after separation was the subject of considerable debate. Finns professing nationalist sentiments who lived in Sweden, such as the poet Emil von Qvanten (1827–1903), author of the "Song of Finland", envisaged Finland as an equal of Sweden, or as the fourth member of a united Scandinavia. Public opinion in Sweden was nationalistic, however, and demanded that Finland be content with the restoration of the status she enjoyed under Swedish rule. Those who had fostered the traditions of the Swedish period took the same position. They sided with those in Sweden who felt that Finland was not yet ready for equality with the former mother country.

The discussion that went on during the war threatened to harm relations between Finland and Russia and forced Finnish nationalists to present their own analysis of the situation. J.V. Snellman and Zacharias Topelius (1818–98) opposed any change in Finland's political status. They argued that union with Russia had afforded Finland a chance to further national development in peace. Except for the disruption caused by the enemy fleet in her territorial waters, Finland had remained basically unharmed during the war. Finland's status within the Russian empire still seemed secure and appeared to offer the only opportunity for future national development. Foreign policy was another factor of extreme importance. Finland had to remain outside conflicts between the great powers, and contrary to reports circulating in Sweden, she was not prepared to rise against Russia. Although Finns had never considered Russia their "fatherland" they were loyal to the grand duke. Defensive measures taken against the British attack and the favourable response to the visit of Nicholas I in 1854 were reliable indicators of sentiment in Finland.

Although subject to strict censorship, public discussion of Finland's rights was not entirely suppressed. J.V. Snellman was particularly active. Snellman's thorough study of philosophy had prepared him for an academic career. His views, however, were not acceptable and he found the doors of the university closed. He was forced to take a position as rector of a school in the remote town of Kuopio. In the 1840s Snellman edited the newspaper *Saima* where he boldly criticized conditions in Finland, demanded an end to censorship and the establishment of freedom of the press, kept abreast of developments in European social and economic thought, and applied what he learned to Finland. He also pointed out the necessity of convening the Estates. But the brunt of his efforts was directed toward journalists and the educated class; he urged them to stop dreaming and take a long look at public affairs. A lively, biting style created considerable stir in the press; a great deal was written, both pro and con. He succeeded in stimulating his readers to discuss the issues of the day, and this was probably his primary achievement. People began to look at Finland's status in a new light. Systematic criticism of existing shortcomings and attempts to outline the course of future development began after the coronation of Alexander II. Demands for the convocation of the Diet, progress in legislation and education, the implementation of the principles of economic liberalism, and for freedom of speech were made with ever increasing frequency. The debate which began in the mid 1850s was both open and constructive; it proceeded without interference from the censor. From 1865 to 1866 discussion enjoyed the added benefit of the interim act on freedom of speech which the Diet had approved.

Alexander II, autocrat of an empire whose internal weaknesses were all too clear, recognized the importance of public opinion in Finland. As heir apparent, Alexander visited Finland frequently and from 1826 onward he served as chancellor of the university. He knew Finnish conditions; he was also decisive and sympathetic toward Finland. Evidence of Alexander's disposition appeared as early as 1856 in the programme he presented in Helsinki at a session of the Senate. The programme stressed the development of industry and transport, assistance for trade and seafaring, and the foundation of elementary schools. Alexander took on a considerable burden when he set out to improve conditions in Finland. Nationalistic Russians watched the progress of minority nationalities with envy – especially those like Finland which enjoyed a special status. War was necessary before constitutional rule was restored. At the beginning of the 1860s Russia did not participate in European affairs and France remained the leading nation on the continent. Napoleon III clung to his belief that a successful foreign policy was crucial to the consolidation of his rule. In 1862 he interfered in Mexico's internal affairs with the hope of gaining influence in America and failed. He attempted to enhance his reputation as a defender of national self-determination by assisting the struggle for Italian unification. The Poles relied on France's traditional friendship when they prepared to fight once more for their independence. Geography had provided the two nations with a certain community of interests. French policy in the east suffered a considerable setback when Poland lost its independence through the partitions of 1772, 1793, and 1795. Prussia, under Bismarck's leadership, was now becoming a great power. Thus Napoleon III regarded the foundation of an independent Poland as an essential element of French foreign policy. When revolt flared up in Russian Poland in 1863, Napoleon offered diplomatic support. The situation was hopeless; Russian strength was overwhelming and both Prussia and Austria were already in the process of dividing Poland. They merely awaited the suppression of the revolt. France wavered; she was still embroiled in the Mexican adventure. In the autumn of the same year Russia succeeded once more in crushing the Poles.

The restoration of constitutional rule in Finland during the reign of Alexander II was rapid, but by no means hasty. Preparations for a Diet had been made since 1856, although the situation in Russia led to postponement or a search for some other means to make the will of the nation known, such as the foundation of the January Committee in 1861. But the Finns rejected all efforts to avoid convening the Diet and dissatisfaction grew.

Considerable interest in the Polish struggle existed in Sweden. Anti-Russian sentiment grew stronger as Sweden sided firmly with the Poles. Later, as was the case during the Crimean War, there were many in Sweden who believed Finland would rise in rebellion once she was certain that landings would be made and that aid from the outside was forthcoming. In Finland, press reports of this sort were condemned even more forcefully than similar ones eight years previously. Any invader would be treated as an enemy and "he will see that our loyalty to the monarchy is unshakeable", wrote Snellman. In addition, the Finnish battalion participating in the suppression of the Polish struggle for independence distinguished itself in the eyes of the tsar.

Discussion of foreign policy in the press did not affect the decision of Alexander II to convene the Diet. But along with the Polish struggle for independence it did create an atmosphere conducive to improvement in Finnish conditions. By meeting Finnish demands, Russia could ease tension and also show how she treated a loyal minority nationality within the empire. The Estates were convened and the Diet was scheduled to begin work in Helsinki on September 15, 1863.

Alexander himself was present at the opening of the session, thus stressing the importance of the occasion. In his speech from the throne he removed any doubts about his intentions. He did not plan to rule without the consent of the Estates as his predecessor had and promised to reconvene the Diet in three years. Autonomous Finland enjoyed its first taste of genuine constitutional rule. Throughout this period efforts were made – with the tsar's assistance – to implement the liberal principles of mid-19th century Europe.

CHAPTER II

From National Division to the
First Era of Oppression

The development of the ideological foundations for Finnish nationalism that began with the Peace of Hamina continued after the transfer
of the university to Helsinki. Romanticism in Turku was succeeded by
a similar movement in Helsinki, where J.V. Snellman and J.L.
Runeberg (1804–77) were the leading exponents. According to the
Hegelian principles Snellman espoused, national spirit was the basis of
national existence. Snellman emphasized the importance of national
literature in the development of national spirit. At the outset,
everything written in Finland during the Swedish period was in Latin
and then in Swedish. The Finnish nation had produced religious works
and psalmody; there was also folklore, although there was no real
national literature. As a young man Snellman studied Hegelian
philosophy and a sojourn in Germany furthered his understanding.
Snellman first influenced public opinion as the leader of a student circle
and later by publishing scholarly works. The most important of these
was his *Läran om Staten* (Principles of the State, 1842). Snellman also
contributed articles to the newspaper *Saima* mentioned above. He
appealed to the educated classes with an excellent style and clear
presentation, independently applying Hegelian philosophy to Finnish
conditions. He demanded rights for the Finnish language and the
creation of a national culture. Beginning in 1844 he tried to reach the
Finnish-speaking readers with the newspaper *Maamiehen Ystävä* (The
Farmer's Friend).

Snellman was regarded as a revolutionary by his contemporaries. For
years he was the object of official disfavour and applied in vain for
professorships and other posts. He did not receive a position in the
university until after the system had changed in 1856; even then there
was little time left to concentrate on actual scholarship. He considered

journalism so important that he continued it for the rest of his life. Snellman's appointment to the Senate in 1863 provided him with a position in the highest administrative body in the land; he took advantage of the opportunity and worked to implement his programme for the next five years. He created the intellectual foundations for the Finnish party, although he never served as its leader.

J.L. Runeberg's life work was that of a patriotic poet. Like Snellman, Runeberg was active in journalism, although poetry was his main contribution to Finnish political development. He was not a nationalist in Snellman's sense of the word and he actually opposed many points in Snellman's language programme. Runeberg did consider himself a Finn, although he spoke Swedish. But the influence of Runeberg's works reached both the Swedish-speaking educated classes and the Finnish-speaking population in the form of translations. His poetry aroused enthusiasm; it fostered attachment to the "land of our fathers" and love for its people. Imbued with the spirit which gripped students in those days, Runeberg became acquainted with the Finnish population, received a profound and favourable impression of them, and warmly related his experiences in verse. In this way the educated classes learned about the conditions, thoughts, and shortcomings of the Finnish population. Runeberg thus complemented the influence of the Kalevala gathered by Elias Lönnrot (1802–84) and published in 1835.

The national awakening, which received its impetus from Turku romanticism and gathered strength in Helsinki, was patriotic in nature. The entire population considered itself Finnish, although some spoke Swedish and others Finnish. They were forging a national unity under the new circumstances in which Russian pressure was great. A Finnish national state seemed to be the common goal. It was generally accepted that the educated classes must learn Finnish and acquaint themselves with the common people. The result would be a single nation capable of resisting Russification. In a spirit of enthusiastic self-sacrifice, the educated classes made no effort to oppose the demand made previously by the Turku romantics; the Swedish language had to be abandoned in favour of Finnish.

Opinions began to change in the 1850s as Finns reassessed their country's foreign relations during the Crimean War and its aftermath. Since the separation of Finland from Russia had seemed possible, those who spoke Swedish at home and considered it the language of culture were forced to take stock. There were two explanations. Either they were part of the Finnish-speaking nation and had merely drifted away from the majority of the population through the use of Swedish in the schools and university or there were in effect two nationalities existing side by side in Finland – the Finnish and the Swedish.

1.

In the debate on the status of Finland that took place in Scandinavia in the 1850s, claims were repeatedly made that two nations lived in Finland, the Finns and the Swedes. Both linguistic and racial differences separated them. Concepts originating in France that stressed the differences between the races of man lent support to this division. The linguistic situation in Finland – a Swedish-speaking educated class and a Finnish-speaking majority – was a racial and not a historical phenomenon. The Finnish population was the inferior of the two and was uncultured; the Swedish-speaking educated classes were descendants of the Swedes who arrived during the period of national migration. The latter were creators of culture. The Scandinavian scholars concluded that everything accomplished in Finland to date was the work of the Swedish nationality. This included popular education and the creation of the Kalevala. Finland's future continued to rest with the Swedes, and not with the ungifted Finns.

These Scandinavian theories received most of their support from younger members of the educated classes and students who dreamed of reunification with Sweden during the Crimean War. Lines were drawn between speakers of Finnish and Swedish and between "Finnishness" and "Swedishness". At the end of the 1850s A.O. Freudenthal (1836–1911), a young student from the province of Uusimaa and the son of a pharmacist who had emigrated from Sweden, asked whether all people who lived in Finland were really "Finns". His answer was negative. Those who spoke Swedish were Swedes – both the Swedish-speaking population who lived along the coast and the educated classes. These ideas, based on Snellman's national philosophy, gained currency in a few years. In a few decades they had influenced the majority of the Swedish-speaking educated class. This class had been searching for an intellectual argument to refute Snellman. An educated class of Swedish nationality need not adopt Finnish as its language of culture much less as the language used at home, as Snellman had urged. It should preserve its mother tongue and dedicate itself to the cause of Swedish nationality and culture in Finland.

Freudenthal himself drew attention to the Swedish-speaking population on the coast and in the archipelago and in this way contributed to the Swedish national movement which he had begun. It was soon discovered that this population suffered from a lack of education and economic underdevelopment. Compensation for past neglect was demanded.

The national patriotic movement, which began when Finland entered the Russian empire and continued for many years as a single movement for national defence, split in the 1860s. Both branches operated on the basis of democratic principles. One set out to meet the educational, social, and economic needs of the Finnish population, the other those of the Swedish. A heated language conflict arose when the Finns began to feel their programme was advancing too slowly and the Swedes feared they were losing ground too rapidly; this in turn led to a political division.

The language factions – which existed in the 1860s although they were not formally organized – were soon joined by a liberal movement. Its programme for political reform was the most radical; it called for changes in the existing economic and social order in Finland in the spirit of western European liberalism. Participants in the movement discussed Finnish autonomy and made plans to develop it. They sought compromise in the language question. Unlike the nationalists, the liberals merely viewed language as the most important means of communication. The most complete bilingualism possible was their ideal. Liberalism flourished in the 1860s – a decade of energetic planning and open discussion. But it lost ground during the struggle between the nationalists. There was no room for compromise; the choice was either Finnish or Swedish. Most liberals joined the Swedish party at the beginning of the 1880s.

2.

Change in the administrative system improved the position of the Finnish language. The Language Edict of 1850 was not fully implemented in the beginning and lost all significance in a few years. The Finnish Literature Society, founded in 1831, worked to advance Finnish-language culture. The obstacles in the Language Edict did not render its activities more difficult; the society used Swedish as a working language and most of its publications were also in Swedish. Finnish did not become the society's working language until the 1850s. At this point Finnish scholarly literature got its start. The first two dissertations in Finnish appeared in 1858; Rietrikki Polén (1823–84) defended a thesis on Finnish literature and Yrjö Koskinen (1830–1903) presented his study of the Club War. Intended as a devastating blow against Finnish, the Language Edict simply broke down in practice.

Application was made for the establishment of a Finnish-language secondary school in Joensuu at the height of the discrimination against Finnish under the 1850 Edict. It was rejected. No new efforts were made until after Alexander II had presented his reform programme to the Senate in 1856. Volmari Schildt-Kilpinen (1810–93), a district physician, obtained statements from 14 parishes located around Jyväskylä in support of a proposal to establish a secondary school in Jyväskylä. Yrjö Koskinen was determined to support these efforts on the following condition: "A Finnish-language secondary school or none at all." Permission was granted despite the opposition of a minority in the Senate, and Finland's first Finnish-language secondary school opened on October 1, 1858. The first class of students matriculated in 1865. A bilingual secondary school was then founded in Tampere and a Finnish-language secondary school in Joensuu. But this also marked the end of administrative favour for Finnish-language secondary schools.

Snellman supported bilingual secondary schools; until an educated stratum had been Finnicized by means of increased Finnish-language instruction, teaching should be carried out in Swedish as well. Snellman also promoted this position while he served in the Senate.

The removal of educational institutions from the jurisdiction of the church was also a part of the liberal reform programme implemented in the 1860s. The Diet passed a bill on separation in 1867. But there was no reform of the legislation concerning schools and their status later proved fatefully dependent on administrative fiat. Kasimir von Kothen (1807–80), who had been promoted to the rank of lieutenant general in the Russian Army, was appointed director-in-chief of the national board of education, which was founded at the beginning of the 1870s. Von Kothen was already well known for the measures he took against the Finnish language as governor of the Province of Viipuri and in his capacity as Senator. He believed that every effort was necessary to maintain the leadership of the Swedish-speaking population; Finnish-speakers were destined to work in the practical trades. Ties with Russia were to be advanced through instruction in the Russian language. He began to carry out these principles when he became director of the board of education. Since supporters of the Finnish movement considered Finnish-language secondary schools the only means for achieving national equality, a fierce struggle broke out.

In the opinion of von Kothen and the board of education he headed, the Finnish language remained at such a low level of development that its use as the language of higher education was not "in the interests of true culture". The majority of the Senate agreed with him. The decision to transfer the Finnish section of the Helsinki Normal Lyceum to Hämeenlinna and to reduce the scope of the school in Jyväskylä to that of a four-year institution marked the end of the positive approach taken in the 1860s.

Von Kothen carried out his policies by administrative order and immediately aroused the opposition of the Finnish-speaking faction and some of the liberals as well. Money was collected to found Finnish-language secondary schools and teachers in Swedish-language schools who enthusiastically supported these efforts offered to assist with instruction. The press condemned von Kothen's policy and attacks were made against it in the Diet. Numerous petitions were made for founding new Finnish-language schools. Statistics pointing out the disparity in educational opportunities were shown. There was one state secondary school for every 750 Swedish-speaking children but only one for every 7,000 Finnish-speakers. Every tenth Swedish speaker was able to attend a Swedish-language secondary school; only one in 176 Finnish-speakers had a similar opportunity.

The public uproar caused by these educational policies forced the government to dismiss von Kothen in 1873. But educational reform cannot be achieved overnight and it was not until the 1880s that Finnish-language secondary schools began to fare better. This change occurred after supporters of the Finnish language and liberals entered the Senate and Yrjö Koskinen (Y.S. Yrjö Koskinen) became director of the Senate's ecclesiastical committee in 1885. Efforts by the bureaucracy to stifle the development of the Finnish-language secondary school led to a rapid growth in the desire to learn and encouraged a great deal of voluntary work and self-sacrifice for the sake of these schools. The growth of interest in learning among the peasantry was striking.

Swedish was provisionally declared the official language of Finland at the Porvoo Diet in 1809. Official recognition for the Finnish language was also an objective of the national movement. The common people suffered most from discrimination against Finnish; peasants petitioned for the use of Finnish in courts of law and government offices. Snellman stressed this defect in his manifesto and was persistent in his efforts to achieve recognition for Finnish as an official language. Alexander II visited Finland in 1863 to open the Diet and wished to show that his attitude toward Finland was generally sympathetic. Snellman worked closely with the minister secretary of state, Alexander Armfelt (1794–1876), and prepared a manifesto which the grand duke signed on July 30, 1863 in Hämeenlinna. According to this manifesto Finnish was to obtain equality with Swedish as an official language in all matters directly concerning the Finnish-speaking population. The change was to take place in the course of two decades.

Although those officials who were accustomed to using Swedish and those who knew no Finnish or had only a limited command of it tried to block this change, Snellman was correct in considering this Language Edict the cornerstone of the Finnish people's future. An important change in the status of the Finnish language occurred and at the same time Finnish political life emerged from over a half-century of stagnation.

Foreign models and Finnish imagination were the dominant factors in the development of the practical side of Finnish politics in the 1860s. A realistic appraisal of the situation was generally missing. There were reform proposals among those discussed publicly that had not taken the position of the grand duke as tsar-autocrat into consideration; the reforms he had approved in Finland could never be realized in Russia proper, to say nothing of Poland, which had lost its autonomy after the suppression of the struggle for independence. Finnish liberals advocated far-reaching reforms which stressed Finnish neutrality. They called for the creation of a limited parliamentary system by making the Senate responsible to the Diet and proposed the establishment of a Finnish consular network and a national merchant flag. These proposals did not advance Finland's cause and they were the source of considerable concern in Russian nationalist circles. They also caused trouble for the tsar. How far did the Finns want to go and how much could public opinion be appeased without leading to Finnish separatism and without evoking similar demands from other minority nationalities and from forces opposing the autocracy? Nevertheless, many important reforms which strengthened Finland's special status were introduced after the convocation of the Diet in 1863.

The most important of these was the 1869 Edict on the Diet. Until this edict came into effect the tsar had no obligation to convene the Diet at regular intervals; this had resulted in the period of "frozen constitutionalism". This shortcoming was the source of the sharpest public criticism in the 1860s, and the Senate, in which Snellman represented the forces of cautious reform from 1863 to 1868, drafted a bill providing for regular sessions of the Diet. The Estates approved the measure and the tsar confirmed it in 1869. According to the new edict the Diet was to meet every five years; in this way the Estates would not be denied influence for any extended period of time. In 1882 the interval was shortened to three years and in 1886 the right of representatives to introduce legislation was expanded. The Diet had previously enjoyed the right to petition the tsar to propose new bills; now it could introduce its own legislation.

From 1865 to 1867 experiments were also made with freedom of the press – a freedom that both journalists and liberal politicians supported. Sweden had enjoyed freedom of the press and expression from 1772 until 1789, when censorship was introduced. A board of censorship was established in Finland in 1829 and local censors worked under its direction. Permission from the Senate was needed for printing newspapers and other periodical literature and also for the establishment of printing works. Prior censorship was required for all materials published privately. The obstacles these provisions presented were generally recognized and attempts were made to circumvent them. Criticism was also voiced. Public opinion did not begin to make an impression until the 1850s – then the censor loosened his grip. The 'Estates approved a bill drawn up by the Senate establishing freedom of the press. Since differences arose concerning the content of this act, it remained in effect only until the end of the next session of the Diet. Agreement on the content was still not reached and the system of permits and censorship was re-established by administrative ordinance in 1867. This ordinance remained in effect for forty years, legalizing administrative caprice and making it possible for the representatives of a foreign power to interfere with this basic right, a prerequisite for sound political development.

The rouble became legal tender alongside Swedish currency after the Peace of Hamina. The disadvantages of two currencies were immediately clear, although there was little need for cash in the barter economy that prevailed in those days. Since the value of money in both neighbouring countries fluctuated, Finns were uncertain of the rate of exchange. In 1840 the rouble became the only valid currency in Finland. The Bank of Finland was still required to redeem both its own and Russian rouble notes in silver; the stability of Finland's monetary standard thereby became dependent on variations in the value of the Russian rouble. As the Finnish economy developed more rapidly than the Russian, this drawback had an increasingly detrimental effect on economic activity and credit. It also provided opportunities for speculation, and Finland eventually began to demand her own currency.

In 1860 the Bank of Finland gained the right to issue its own money – the Finnish mark. This achievement was the result of the persistent efforts of Fabian Langenskiöld (1810–1863), the head of the financial section of the Senate. The Finnish mark remained tied to the value of the rouble and Langenskiöld continued his efforts to obtain an independent Finnish monetary unit. The nation backed him up. Consent in principle was obtained in 1862. Despite the stubborn resistance of the Russians, J.V. Snellman, Langenskiöld's successor, succeeded in completing the reform. In 1865 the silver mark became Finland's only legal medium of exchange and it was no longer compulsory to accept Russian notes in financial institutions. The success of the reform meant stability and local control over currency. In conjunction with the reform, Finland received the right to borrow from outside the Russian empire; this further emphasized her special status.

The Porvoo Diet of 1809 had expressed the hope that Finns would not be obliged to perform military service for fifty years. In this way a generation which had considerable attachment to Sweden would avoid involvement in war against a kindred people. Napoleon's attack and his advance to Moscow threatened Russia's position and Alexander issued a decree providing for the recruitment of three Finnish light infantry regiments, each composed of 1200 men. Officer training began the following year. Harassment of the coast by the English fleet during the Crimean War aroused enthusiasm for national defence. District conscription – nominally retained following the Peace of Hamina – was revived. Three rifle battalions were formed on this basis. The practical significance of a national military force – alongside the Russian or as a substitute for it – was the subject of political debate in subsequent years. The realization spread that the creation of a national military force would underscore the country's autonomy. But it was simpler said than done. The Russians were hesitant to let the Finns have arms and the rifle battalions were disbanded before 1867. The Finns themselves were reluctant to expose Finnish youth to the possibility of fighting somewhere on the borders of the vast Russian empire or in an aggressive war fought exclusively for the sake of great power interests. No one wanted to consent to the training of Finns in Russian garrisons outside Finland. A conscription act was not passed with the consent of the Diet until 1878. It provided for a three-year service period and a force of 5,000 men. Nine out of every thousand men were chosen by lottery for military service (in Russia the corresponding figure was thirty-six). Expenditures for defence accounted for about 7 % of the Finnish budget as opposed to nearly 30 % of the imperial budget. The force was based in Finland and was intended solely for national defence although the language of command was Russian.

Russia's position in Europe was strengthened at the end of the 1860s. Prussia – now recognized as a major power – worked with great determination to unify Germany. To achieve this goal it used diplomacy to prevent the interference of other countries in German affairs. Relations with Russia were of particular importance. Otto von Bismarck began to direct Prussian policies in 1862. He had served as his country's ambassador in St. Petersburg and was acquainted with conditions in Russia. Alexander II knew and respected him; this provided Bismarck with the footing he needed when he began to handle relations with Russia. Prussia offered help for the suppression of the Polish struggle for independence and although the request was turned down, a reservoir of good will existed. Russian friendship was crucial when Germany went to war with France in 1870. After the defeat of France, Bismarck's policy of peace in Europe supported Russia's position of strength well into the 1870s.

As Alexander II grew older his enthusiasm for reform waned. He received little support in Russia and encountered the stubborn opposition of the nobility and the bureaucracy. From the beginning of the 1870s onward conditions in Finland reflected the changes in the tsar's attitudes and the stabilization of Russia's foreign relations.

4.

The relentless opposition of the bureaucracy and the intermittent interference of the tsar hindered Finnish national aspirations for more than a half-century. The situation eased considerably in the 1860s and the national movement accomplished a great deal in a relatively short time. Newspapers served as the principal means of struggle. Publication began in the 1770s when the first Swedish and Finnish-language papers appeared. These news sheets – which continued up to the 1850s – were small and often short-lived. Private individuals usually financed them. The same person frequently did the editing, wrote the text or borrowed it from other sources, and arranged for a few advertisements. Circulation was limited. The Swedish-speaking educated class was interested in political and social affairs but small in number; the rest of the Swedish-speaking population was not interested at all. Thanks to the Lutheran church literacy was widespread, although the average Finnish-speaker's interest in public affairs was not particularly great. Here a change occurred in the 1850s. The Finnish-language *Suometar,* founded in 1847, was of special significance. Four students affiliated with the movement to promote the Finnish language founded the paper: Paavo Tikkanen (1823–73), August Ahlqvist (1826–88), D.E.D. Europaeus (1820–84), and Antero Warelius (1821–1904). The *Suometar* became a formidable factor in public opinion under the leadership of Rietrikki Polén at the beginning of the next decade. The paper suffered financial difficulties in the 1860s. It reappeared in 1869 as the *Uusi Suometar* and remained Finland's leading Finnish-language newspaper for over fifty years.

The origins of public opinion in Finland can be traced back to the 1860s. The press shaped it, and thus played a leading role in political development. Many of the most important figures in our political history used the press as a medium of expression. All the important personalities of the 19th century served as journalists at some point, and they maintained close contact with the reading public in conjunction with other activity. A.I. Arwidsson, J.V. Snellman, J.L. Runeberg, and Zachris Topelius all used the press to create public opinion and their articles were important in determining the course of development. They all distinguished themselves in other fields as well. The financial success of newspapers in the 1860s facilitated the employment of professional journalists and journalism ceased to be a part-time vocation.

In 1862 the *Helsingfors Dagblad,* a liberal newspaper, was founded. Robert Lagerborg (1835–1882) served on the editorial staff from the beginning. Lagerborg was a staff officer in the Finnish guard. He had previously been in the Russian service, but left because of his interest in politics. He had shown literary talent as an officer and participated in the patriotic activites of liberal students. Lagerborg became the leading newspaperman of his time – an active politician who kept abreast of intellectual trends abroad. Under his leadership, the *Helsingfors Dagblad* became a model publication; the liberal reform programme took shape on its pages. August Schauman (1826–96) was an experienced polemicist with literary ambitions. In 1864 he founded the *Hufvudstadsbladet,* Finland's first true newspaper. The other publications of the day and those of preceding eras as well were primarily ideological and contained a smattering of belles-lettres. Thanks to its news coverage, the *Hufvudstadsbladet* gradually expanded its circulation. It became the capital's Swedish-language advertising medium. Since news of world events was becoming increasingly available and the *Hufvudstadsbladet* was able to take advantage of these improvements, it succeeded in satisfying the appetite for news of an ever larger readership.

The first truly party newspaper in Finland was the *Helsingin Uutiset.* It was founded in 1863 by Yrjö Koskinen and his "Young Finn" associates who were dissatisfied with the *Suometar*'s moderate stand on the language question. Yrjö Koskinen explained his action in the following manner: "Fortunately for us the time has come for a newspaper to take a stand, for or against ... the principles are now clear and one can discern the differences between them. Each outlook seeks – and we hope it will be permitted to do so – a position of influence from which it can shape public opinion in accordance with its own desires. It is therefore natural for people to form different camps based on these different principles, and for these camps or parties or whatever one wishes to term them, to found their own mouthpiece." A year later the *Suometar* absorbed the *Helsingin Uutiset,* and the two generations were in agreement once more.

Yrjö Koskinen made his greatest contribution to journalism when he founded the *Kirjallinen Kuukauslehti* (the Literary Monthly) which appeared from 1866 to 1880. It was the first significant Finnish-language journal. In addition to events in Finland and social, political, and cultural affairs, the journal also dealt with world politics. It discussed Finland's fate against this background and pointed out how international developments affected Finland.

In 1870 individuals who supported the cause of Swedish nationality founded their own organ, the *Vikingen.* Here the nationality question was discussed in terms of theory, in the spirit of Freudenthal. In a manner similar to that of Snellman's *Saima,* the publication reminded the educated class of its Swedish nationality. It repeated the programme of the Swedish nationalists point by point. The journal never obtained a very wide circulation and ceased publication four years later as more and more Swedish-language papers adopted its programme. The *Nya Pressen* was founded in 1883. Axel Lille (1848–1921) was editor-in-chief of this paper. Under his leadership it soon became the principal spokesman for the language policy of the Swedish party. The *Nya Pressen* distinguished itself by its bold and effective stimulation of public opinion and played an important role in the defence of Finland's rights. In 1900 it was suppressed by the authorities.

The growth of the press has depended on the number of subscribers. Growth increased advertising effectiveness and this in turn meant more income and an opportunity to improve content. Greater variety in content attracted more subscribers, and so the process continued. After the Crimean War had aroused interest in world events and in the wake of the vigorous polemics of the 1860s, public interest grew. The press became a force in politics. Public opinion did exist in Finland and had some influence; it is possible to credit it with the dismissal of Governor-General von Berg in 1861 and the appointment of Snellman to the Senate in 1863. The press had consolidated its position and political influence on the threshold of an era in which Finnish autonomy and national existence were to be in grave danger.

5.

Opposition at various levels of the Russian bureaucracy frustrated the reform policy of Alexander II. Practicality – in addition to compassion – was a major factor in the decision to abolish serfdom. Industrialization similar to that taking place in the West required labour. Here Russia was no different from any other country; agriculture was the only source of the necessary manpower. As long as the peasants were bound to the soil the freedom of movement necessary for industrialization was impossible. Large landholders still opposed the reform, although abolition relieved them of the obligation to maintain the peasants and their families. It went against centuries of tradition and for the most part concerned the advantages of landowners who belonged to the upper ranks of the nobility. Emancipation meant the loss of manpower which had been freely at their disposal. The peasants were also dissatisfied; taxation after emancipation was high and land allotments were too small. The tsar had trouble keeping up with efforts to carry out his will in the vast empire; this was particularly true when progress reports were made by the same bureaucracy that blocked the implementation of the reforms. But promises made by the government did arouse hope for improvement, and when these hopes were not realized, Alexander's well-meaning reform programme succeeded merely in fostering more discontent. In an autocracy all criticism is forbidden – even the constructive variety. Under these conditions the opposition resorted to violence.

Although there was also support in Western Europe for the use of violence against an individual – a tyrant for example – it was restricted to a small group of extremist elements. In Russia public criticism of conditions and the presentation of reforms were prohibited, and a breach of this ban was punished severely. Thus reform was linked with violence from the very beginning. Since the autocrat personified the entire system, there were naturally conspiracies to assassinate him. Some of these were exposed toward the end of his reign, but even so, attempts on his life were made. These threats to his person were not without effect. On March 13, 1881 he signed a rescript aimed at fundamental liberalization. He was assassinated on the same day.

6.

Significant changes occurred in the balance of power in Europe during the reign of Alexander II. Prussia became a great power after the Napoleonic wars and received recognition for this achievement at the Congress of Paris in 1856. A cold calculation of Prussia's interests dictated the policies of Otto von Bismarck, Prussia's minister president and foreign minister. He used both his skill as a statesman and the threat of armed intervention to shift the centre of gravity within Germany from Vienna to Berlin. The military weakness and fumbling foreign policy of Austria and the other states in the German Federation advanced Bismarck's cause. In his efforts to unify Germany under

Prussian leadership Bismarck exploited the German national movement that had gained a firm foothold in all the German states. He drove Austria out of the federation by force of arms. Prussia gained a quick victory over Austria although the largest German states had sided with the latter in an attempt to frustrate the former's ambitions. In making the peace, Bismarck expanded Prussia at the expense of those German states which had opposed him, but was content to see Austria leave the federation. By concluding a moderate peace with his main rival, he preserved the unity of the Danube monarchy and its German leadership and created the foundation for a future alliance between Germany and Austria-Hungary.

Once he had achieved the upper hand in Germany, Bismarck proceeded under the banner of pan-Germanism, making peace and establishing an alliance with his recent enemies. When France fell for Bismarck's ruse and attacked Germany in 1870, all the German states joined forces to repel the enemy. France was defeated and ceded Alsace and part of Lorraine to Germany. Bismarck proclaimed a German empire with great ceremony at Versailles – in the heart of enemy territory – while the fighting still raged. But the empire was not founded on a democratic basis such as the programme of the Frankfurt Assembly of 1849. According to Bismarck's compromise, the individual German states retained their former status. Under the system Bismarck created, the kaiser and his subordinate, the chancellor, governed according to a principle of divide and conquer. National unification remained incomplete, but power was concentrated in Prussia.

Germany's military supremacy was evident in the rapid defeat of France. It was improved systematically after peace was concluded. Since power was concentrated in the new empire, a force emerged in the heart of Europe that was a source of fear and envy in neighbouring countries. The treatment France received at the peace negotiations in 1871 had its effect on future power politics. Humiliation and the loss of provinces on the Rhine – which literally formed a German bridgehead – aroused the desire for revenge and for an alliance against Germany. Bismarck succeeded in maintaining friendly relations with those monarchs who feared revolution and was thereby able to isolate the French republic. In 1879 Germany formed an alliance with Austria-

Hungary for "all time". The result was the formation of a powerful bloc in Central Europe. Its significance was enhanced when Italy joined the alliance in 1882.

Russia did not enter the Franco-Prussian war. Like Britain, she hesitated to support either side openly – there was always the danger that the victor would emerge strong enough to upset the existing balance of power. The struggle was considered an even one; France and Germany were expected to expend all their energy in fighting each other. Germany's quick victory demonstrated the error of this assessment. Thanks to unification, Germany was stronger after the conflict than before. Although Bismarck's skilful diplomacy maintained cooperation between Germany and Russia up to the end of the 1880s, there were doubts in St. Petersburg about Germany's ultimate objectives as early as the Franco-Prussian War in 1870–71. Russia feared that Germany sought the Baltic states – an area that had experienced a long tradition of German rule.

But it was Austria-Hungary that brought about a deterioration in relations between Germany and Russia. Austria-Hungary and Russia were engaged in permanent competition for influence in the Balkans. In its persistent drive to gain control of the Dardanelles, Russia had to achieve hegemony in the Balkans and it was essential for Austria-Hungary to thwart this drive. The realization of Russian goals would have lent strength to Slavic national movements within the Austro-Hungarian Empire and broken up the dual monarchy. Chances for a peaceful settlement were limited indeed. Bismarck did succeed in mediating. He played one side off against the other by offering certain concessions. By the time Kaiser Wilhelm II (1888–1918) dismissed him there were no more concessions to be handed out and the Balkan question rapidly grew critical. Fear of Germany increased constantly and Russia began to seek support from her allies. For the reasons mentioned above, France was ready to enter an alliance against Germany.

Suspicion of differing political systems had impaired relations between Russia and France during the Bismarck era and German diplomacy had exploited these feelings to isolate France. Monarchies were hostile to the republic and the French republicans hated autocracy, especially the variety that existed in Russia. As world politics evolved into nothing more than a struggle for national advantage, differences in political systems were forgotten and the way was open for rapprochement. Beginning at the end of the 1880, France supported Russian armament with loans, and an alliance was formed in 1894. Russia entered the alliance to counterbalance Britain in Asia. Once this situation changed, Britain joined Russia and France in action directed against Germany and her allies.

Relying on Germany's military and economic strength Wilhelm II – who was unskilled in power politics – sought to expand German influence all over the world. On the basis of a mutual understanding with the Turkish government, Germany started to build up the Turkish economy and began work on the Baghdad railway across Asia Minor in 1899. This confirmed British suspicions dating back to the Bismarck era. German economic expansion in this area would threaten Britain's interests in the Mediterranean and India. Britain settled her most serious differences with Russia and France and joined them in opposing Germany.

The new balance of power in Europe outlined above was reflected in relations between Russia and Finland. The Russian national movement – originally known as Panslavism – sought close cooperation among all the Slavic peoples; the tsar would act as their protector. Panslavism was an ideological front for Russian expansionist aspirations in the Balkans and Poland. The Polish struggle for independence in 1863 betrayed the emptiness of Panslavism. Independence was considered more important than Russian "protection" which the Poles sought to end by force of arms. Panslavism subsequently became a chauvinistic movement. Fear of Germany began to affect Russian foreign policy; chauvinism and military considerations began to dictate the attitude of the government toward minority nationalities, including the Baltic states and Finland. Although relations between Sweden and Norway began to deteriorate in the 1880s and the former was more interested in the West than the East, Russia feared Sweden was planning to cooperate with her enemies in the tense international situation of the eighties. Sympathy toward Sweden among Swedish nationalists in Finland also provided cause for concern and Finnish separatism came in for attack from the Russian nationalist movement.

In addition to the Balkans, Russian expansion also sought outlets in Asia. Conquests in Asia proceeded without any great difficulties until

Russia approached the British and Japanese spheres of influence. Central Asia was the scene of competition between Britain and Russia. Afghanistan – bordering on India – felt Russian pressure in the 1880s; Britain interpreted the outbreak of armed conflict as a Russian attempt to conquer the country. Russia could not be persuaded to withdraw by means of diplomacy and in 1885 Britain resorted to a threat of open war.

When a clash appeared imminent, the possible consequences of a war between Russia and Britain were discussed in Finland. Finland feared most for her shipping. A merchant fleet of 250,000 gross tons carried the major portion of Finnish trade. The disruption of Finnish shipping would mean a serious setback in economic development. Russia was aware of the danger; her merchant fleet was young and her navy weak. She considered arming merchant vessels sailing under the imperial flag. Thus the situation became even more acute from the Finnish point of view. Finns returned to a concept of neutrality dating back to the 1860s in seeking a way to minimize losses. Finnish vessels were not to be used for military purposes and were to have their own flag which would insure safe sailing. This proposal was discussed both in private and publicly.

7.

Although the Afghanistan crisis ended in agreement between Britain and Russia, it had far-reaching effects on Finland's relations with Russia. The chauvinist press in Russia attacked the concept of neutrality discussed in Finland and termed it a threat to the empire. In the ensuing polemics statements made by Finns during the Crimean War and the Polish uprising were dug up and given an anti-Russian interpretation; the Finns were accused of having separatist sentiments. Attention was focused once more on anti-Russian sentiment in Sweden and on the sympathies of Swedish nationalists in Finland for the former mother country. Russia grew increasingly uneasy about the loyalty of the grand duchy.

Trust in the sovereign had existed for centuries in Finland. When the behaviour of officials became intolerable, the common people would "go to the king" in Stockholm with their complaints. The tradition continued under Russian rule and in the 19th century Finnish peasants turned to the tsar-grand duke – their appeals frequently in Finnish – to ask for certain changes, particularly in the status of the Finnish language. Measures taken by the government of Alexander I brought about a significant increase in this feeling of security. An attack launched by the Russian press and certain scholars against Finland's special status was considered merely an expression of chauvinism. The tsars pledged to respect Finland's autonomy when they ascended the throne and the Finns considered this pledge irrevocable. Developments in the 1880s and 1890s proved them wrong.

In general, the tsar-grand dukes were favourably disposed toward cultural life in Finland. The university was named after a tsar when it was transferred from Turku to Helsinki and the heir apparent became its chancellor. This turned out to be an important advantage for the university – particularly for research and study concerning Russia. Degrees granted in Helsinki were the only ones valid in Finland and this of course further emphasized the unique status of the institution. Degrees taken in St. Petersburg, Moscow, and other important universities in the empire did not become valid in Finland until 1902. This decision was generally regarded by the Finns as part of Russification. Finnish scholars and artists also received financial support from the Russian state.

The attacks of Russian ultra-nationalists against Finland did have a legal basis. They questioned the existence of Finland's special status and argued that it was separated from Sweden according to the terms of the Peace of Hamina and made a Russian province. The decisions of the Porvoo Diet were studied in the light of history and from the legal point of view. The conclusion was drawn – for example in K. Ord's work on the conquest of Finland published in 1889 – that neither the statements of Alexander I made at the Porvoo Diet, nor the terms of the Peace of Hamina provided any basis for discussion of Finnish statehood. Neither did Finland have any right to be governed according to the laws of the Swedish period. This was the basis for the demand made by the ultra-nationalists – a demand that became increasingly shrill: Russification of the national minorities and an end to Finland's special status.

The Finnish press sensed the danger immediately and began to fight back. As the Finnish defence lacked sufficient scholarly support, Professor J.R. Danielson(-Kalmari) (1853–1933) undertook to provide a historical analysis and Professor Leo Mechelin (1839–1914) dealt with the juridical side. The scholarly debate that followed had no political effect. The Finns were unable to refute the Russian scholars; they had even less success with the press. Nor did the articles in Russian journals reduce Finnish fears. Tension only increased, and the situation became more critical.

The views of Russian scholars and the ultra-nationalistic press in combination with foreign policy considerations changed the attitude of the tsarist government toward Finland. Unlike his father Alexander II, Alexander III (1881–1894) governed as an autocrat and adopted a suspicious attitude toward Finland from the very beginning. Ten years after his coronation the tsar sought to reassure Finland; he publicly reaffirmed his recognition of the rights his predecessors had promised to respect. In 1882 the leader of the Finnish nationalists, Yrjö Koskinen, and the liberal leader Leo Mechelin, were appointed to the Senate. But attacks made thereafter against Finland's special status persuaded the tsar to take steps to limit the Senate's rights. The Finnish postal service was subordinated to the post and telegraph administration of the Russian ministry of internal affairs in 1890. Systematic efforts to reduce Finland's rights did not occur until the reign of Alexander III's successor, Nicholas II (1894–1917). Although years of fierce attacks and attempts to reduce Finnish autonomy preceded it, the "Post Office Manifesto" increased the effects of the blow on Finnish public opinion. Suspicion grew and preparations were made to fight back. Opinion inside Finland was consolidated and appeals were made abroad. When the Russian government was ready to take action at the end of the 1890s, the Finnish public was alert and nationalistic sentiment was aroused – thanks to the increased level of education. Everyone was aware of what Finland's special status meant and there were leaders in the country capable of organizing the defence. The governor-general – the grand duke's representative – had considerable authority. When he enjoyed the complete confidence of the tsar – as we have seen previously – his personal influence on political development in Finland was substantial. As the chairman of the Senate he might exert pressure against individual senators – especially since he had a voice in appointing and dismissing them. In 1899 Nikolai Bobrikov (1839–1904), an infantry general, was named governor-general.

Bobrikov had a fixed conception of Russia's position as a great power and the demands this status imposed; separatist sentiments among the minority nationalities had to be suppressed through Russification of administration and cultural life. Those nationalities which enjoyed a special status were the object of particular concern. They endangered the unity of the realm and threatened to break it up. Bobrikov had the tsar's confidence and had made up his mind to implement the emperor's will without fail, even before he had arrived in Finland. Nicholas II signed Bobrikov's proposal – the so-called February Manifesto – on February 15, 1899. This edict extended Russian autocracy to Finland. In violation of the constitution which he had confirmed, Nicholas himself was to decide which laws concerned the realm as a whole; the Finnish Diet could do no more than express its opinion. Bobrikov subsequently received unlimited authority to destroy Finland's special status.

CHAPTER III

From the February Manifesto to the General Strike

Bobrikov set about his tasks with the enthusiasm of a Russian patriot and began to carry out the major points of the February Manifesto. Officials who remained loyal to Finnish law refused to carry out the instructions they received. They were dismissed and replaced by those with pro-Russian sentiments and in some cases even by Russians. Censorship was tightened; as long as Finland was quiet the system performed without a hitch. Newspapers were suppressed. Those who defended Finland's rights were exiled. A ban on freedom of speech, association, and assembly was imposed. Russian was made the official language of Finland and the most important subject in the schools. The tsarist government reorganized its espionage network. An administrative order disbanded Finland's own military force; henceforth Finns could be sent to serve in Russian units, not only in Finland but throughout the empire as well. All this took place within five years and brought the people of Finland to the brink of despair. Eugen Schauman's assassination of Bobrikov on June 16, 1904 was an expression of the prevailing mood. Schauman, a young civil servant and activist, shot down Bobrikov and then shot himself. The governor-general died on the following day.

1.

During the first period of oppression – the Bobrikov era – the question of relations with Russia dominated Finnish politics. Public opinion in Finland about Russia had been divided ever since the Peace of Hamina, although the uncertainty of the first few decades eventually evolved into trust. The reign of Alexander II in particular had strengthened the belief that union offered advantages to both Russia and Finland. But sentiments changed as Russian attacks against Finland's special status became more severe. Suspicion and even despair existed before the period of oppression began.

After the promulgation of the February Manifesto pessimism about Finland's future appeared wherever the situation was understood and particularly among those Finns who identified themselves with Swedish language and culture. They regarded the Peace of Hamina as a disaster and now their worst fears had become reality. Decades of struggle had made the constitution the touchstone of national existence; Finns had fought for a half-century to regain those rights the constitution guaranteed. Once they had succeeded they had begun to build a state in the hope that political rights could be further expanded. When the February Manifesto wiped out all these achievements, Finns felt they could do no more than stand or fall in defence of the constitution.

In the 1880s the Young Finns formed a "young Finland" group within the Finnish party; this was an expression of their discontent with the "Old Finns," who had adopted a moderate and conciliatory stand on the language question. They were also liberal, and in contrast to the party leadership which they condemned as conservative, they were progressive. Personal quarrels among the leaders deepened the schism between "young" and "old". In 1889 the former founded their own mouthpiece, the Helsinki *Päivälehti* and obtained the support of certain provincial newspapers of the same persuasion. In 1894 they started their own party. They reappraised the situation in drawing up their programme. Official status for the Finnish language was of course included and so were many political and social reforms – more power for the Diet, the expansion of suffrage, improvements in the position of crofters and the landless population, and labour legislation. But in the shadow of the Post Office Manifesto, emphasis remained on the preservation of Finland's special status and on the inviolability of the constitution. Social reform remained in the background; the provisions of the February Manifesto posed a threat to Finland's national existence. The Young Finns and individuals with a Swedish orientation found a basis for cooperation in the struggle for the country's constitutional rights. A constitutional front was formed to combat the flexible policy of the Finnish party.

The leaders of the Finnish party reacted to Russian pressure in the same way the national patriotic movement had at the beginning of the 19th century. They held fast to the belief that the foundations for national development were created at the Porvoo Diet and by the terms of the Peace of Hamina. They still believed they could preserve the constitutional basis for Finland's political existence under the provisions of the February Manifesto as long as relations with Russia were handled realistically. Russia's vital interests had to be taken into consideration and so did her prestige as a great power, a factor that was dependent on fluctuations in European power politics.

When relations between Russia and Finland reached a low point, the most uncompromising constitutionalists either withdrew or were pushed aside. Responsibility for relations with Russia and affairs of state was left to those who supported a flexible policy, primarily to the Finnish party and to officials who had not taken a political stand.

The division of opinion brought about by the February Manifesto was obvious when the Senate dealt with the manifesto. The Senate was unanimous in considering it unconstitutional. But since the tsar's decisions, decrees, and proclamations had to be written into Finland's Code of Laws before they could come into effect, the Senate itself had to decide about promulgation. By refusing to promulgate the manifesto, the Senate could prevent the implementation of the unconstitutional measures. But this was considered a formality. The manifesto had been prepared so secretly that it had caught the Senators by surprise. The Senate also agreed unanimously to present a petition to the tsar pointing out the unconstitutionality of the February Manifesto and requesting assurances that it was not intended as a violation of Finland's rights. At this point there was a sharp division of opinion. Some felt that the manifesto ought to be promulgated immediately and the petition made afterwards. Others demanded immediate delivery of the petition and the postponement of promulgation until an answer had been received. The vote on procedure ended in a tie; ten favoured immediate promulgation and ten supported the immediate dispatch of the petition. Since C. Tudeer (1840–1905), vice-chairman of the financial section of the Senate and a supporter of the former position, had led the discussion, the manifesto was promulgated at once.

The promulgation of the February Manifesto was a shock to the entire country. People could not believe that the tsar had clearly understood the unconstitutionality of the manifesto when he issued it. It was assumed that the manifesto would be withdrawn if a mass deputation could call the tsar's attention to its illegality. More than 520,000 signatures were obtained in two weeks from every municipality in the country. It is noteworthy that towns accounted for only 10 % of the names; the rest came from the countryside. Nearly 500 men were selected to deliver the petition to the tsar. Nicholas II did not, however, receive them although he arrogantly announced that he was not "annoyed with those who had come".

Members of the deputation made the tsar's reaction public and the press conveyed it to the people. The tsar's act was considered a breach of trust, and confidence in the sovereign further declined. In the spring of 1899 there were severe floods in Finland and the record crest left a permanent line on rocks along shores. This high-water mark became known as the "line of perjury" – a reference to the behaviour of Nicholas II. The February Manifesto and the reaction of the tsar to the Finnish appeal indicated that the government had adopted the position of the ultranationalists. The bond between Finland and Russia existing in the person of the tsar was broken.

The legal battle that began when the February Manifesto was issued was of special concern for civil servants. They faced numerous weighty decisions. Should they implement the unconstitutional provisions of the manifesto or should they carry their resistance to the point of their own dismissal? Or would they be choosing the lesser evil if they consented and remained in offices that would otherwise fall into the hands of either pro-Russians or the Russians themselves? Both choices were made. Some refused to carry out any unconstitutional decrees and were dismissed, locked up in prison, or exiled from Finland. Others bent with the wind and held on to their posts, preventing Russification of their own functions.

The conflict in the Senate over procedure in connection with the promulgation of the manifesto spread throughout the civil service. Opinions were sharply divided and split the national forces which were united when signatures for the petition were gathered. The manifesto aroused the entire nation in a few days and made people realize the nature of the struggle; it also fostered opposition to Russification at all levels of society.

The Boer war began in the same year. This conflict had international significance and occupied world public opinion. But neither was Finland alone. People in many countries declared their support. A petition addressed to the tsar from the world's leading scholars demanding the restoration of Finland's right was of particular significance. It had no effect on the tsar's position although it did serve to sharpen opposition in Finland.

The preponderance of Russian strength was apparent during the period of oppression when Bobrikov was governor-general. Opportunities for defensive action were limited. Passive resistance alone had political significance. Here civil servants and teachers were the key to success. Administrative delays could prevent the implementation of undesirable orders. Teachers – with the cooperation of pupils – could frustrate Russian instruction and thwart Bobrikov's plans to Russify the educated class. The provisions of the manifesto concerning compulsory military service were put into effect in 1902; this meant additional opportunities for passive resistance. Members of the clergy, who were supposed to announce the edict in church, and most young men who were to be called up, refused to comply with the illegal decree. Resistance was so stubborn that the Russians eventually came to the conclusion that there was little sense in training Finnish youth in Russian units. A continuation of this policy might even prove a dangerous liability in the future. In this way Finland lost the basis for a national military force provided by the administrative order of 1878. On the other hand, attempts to station Finnish recruits in distant garrisons all over the empire – a policy that had already been applied to the youth of other national minorities – was prevented.

"Kagal", a secret association that took its name from an organization of persecuted Jews in Russia, led the resistance. It included many men and also a number of women who later distinguished themselves in Finland's struggle for independence. The association smuggled illegal literature published abroad into Finland, distributed news sheets that fanned the spirit of opposition, made Russian oppression known abroad, and maintained contact with revolutionaries inside Russia. Plans were also made for armed resistance. But the Russian grip was so firm that opportunities for this kind of action were few. The time for activism was not yet at hand.

Flexibility was required on the part of Finnish officials during the first period of oppression – the most destructive blows had to be warded off. The public had to be constantly on guard and recognize the pernicious nature of Russification. The procedural dispute weakened Finnish unity and it is difficult to judge how long resistance could have gone on. The provisions carried out under the February Manifesto made it clear that Russia was bent on the destruction of Finland's special status. Events on the international scene rather than a lack of Russian willpower prevented a longer test of Finnish endurance. War with Japan meant changes in Russia's attitude and position.

2.

Russian expansion in Siberia began in the 16th century, Russian military scouts reached the shores of the Pacific Ocean on the Kamchatka peninsula in the following century. Peter I began the systematic exploitation of the conquests and initiated colonization. During his reign expansion was also undertaken in the Caucasus and in the region around the Caspian Sea. But a consistent Asian policy did not appear until the reign of Nicholas I and it came into conflict with British interests in the south-east and with those of Japan on the Pacific coast. Japan's population was growing rapidly; it increased from 33 million in 1872 to 46 million in 1903 and it was squeezed into a small area broken up by the sea. In order to offset a loss of population through emigration, Japan began to seek territory for conquest on the eastern coast of Asia in the 1870s. Japan fought a successful war against China and in 1895 concluded a peace that gave her a foothold on the mainland. She was obliged to give up some of the region under pressure from Russia, which had the support of France and Germany. In 1902 – when Russia's hold on the Pacific coast seemed to be growing stronger – Japan formed an alliance with Great Britain. It was in the interests of both powers to prevent Russia from extending her authority into China or Korea. Japan attempted to set up spheres of influence with Russia by means of a treaty. Russia would not agree, and Japan attacked in 1904.

Russia's military weakness was apparent in the Crimean War which was fought a half-century earlier. Although the Turkish War of

1877–78 was a success, this was the result of the opponent's weakness. Efforts to improve training and armaments financed in part by French loans had not led to results. Russian transport was crucial to the war effort since supply lines to the Far East stretched out for 6–7,000 kilometres. Transport was designed to function inside the empire with European conflicts in mind. Roads leading eastward were few in number and in poor condition. The trans-Siberian railroad was completed in 1899 but it was neither intended nor equipped for the strains of military transport. Naval transport also faced serious obstacles; supply lines were long, equipment substandard, and the Japanese fleet harassed vessels in the war zone. Extensive Russian forces stationed in Siberia or sent there after the outbreak of hostilities suffered from a lack of supplies and reinforcements throughout the war.

Preparations for war began once Japan understood Russia's determination in the Far East. The organization of the army, armaments, and training were rapidly modernized. The will to win and a desire to improve Japan's position as a great power – both encouraged during the war with China – inspired the Japanese army and navy. The Japanese regarded the struggle as a national necessity. Japan had to extend her "Lebensraum" and prevent the European powers from establishing themselves on the Pacific coast and thus posing a threat to the islands. For Japan, supply lines meant short ocean crossings. The Russian Far Eastern fleet was bottled up in Port Arthur at the beginning of the war and never succeeded in causing any trouble; Japan destroyed Russia's Baltic fleet, which was sent to Japanese waters during the war. Russia suffered one defeat after another on land and was forced to conclude a disadvantageous peace in 1905. Japan gained a firm foothold on the mainland and drove the Russians out of the naval base at Port Arthur – a base the Japanese had considered dangerous.

War with Japan also revealed Russian shortcomings. In spite of all the warnings it had received, the tsarist government had not made the necessary military and industrial preparation; neither was it capable of fostering the will to victory among the combat troops. Military defeat emboldened numerous revolutionary groups which had previously led an underground existence. These organizations had one goal in common – overthrowing the autocracy. Unrest developed into systematic revolutionary activity and the regime was forced to yield.

On August 19, 1905 the tsar announced the formation of the "Bulygin" Duma, a consultative body, and called for elections. The Duma received the right to take part in the legislative process, although merely in an advisory capacity. The intelligentsia and the workers – the groups behind the revolution – were denied suffrage. Dissatisfied with the regime's response, they continued agitation, concentrating their efforts in the largest cities. General strikes were called in certain vital fields such as the railroads and the postal and telegraph service. But the tsar was again too late. On October 30, 1905, he issued the October Manifesto, which expanded suffrage and the Duma's role in the legislative process. It also provided certain civil rights. If these concessions had come earlier they might at least have satisfied the moderates. Unrest subsequently spread to the peasantry and in December workers in Moscow rose in rebellion. The government crushed this rising. Nicholas II, who had considered abdication in November and issued a new election law that extended suffrage to workers and the intelligentsia, pulled himself together after the suppression of the Moscow rising. The revolutionaries were not united and had been unable to create a programme that satisfied all factions. The moderates strove for a constitutional monarchy; the more radical wanted to overthrow the tsarist regime and establish a republic. Disunity saved the autocracy. Conscious of the extent of his own hereditary power, the tsar issued a new constitution in March 1906. The achievements of the revolution were preserved outwardly, although many of the new provisions reduced their effectiveness, as developments throughout the following year were to show. Reaction had triumphed.

Russian defeats in the war with Japan aroused Finnish hopes; they meant a probable relaxation of the tsarist stranglehold on Finland. Optimism increased greatly once news of the uprisings in Russia arrived. Finns took advantage of the situation and joined in. Russian representatives in Finland were forced to loosen their grip and as a result it was possible to hold demonstrations without interference and exchange views and present programmes for the future without fear of censorship.

For a long time the Finnish nation was of one mind – revolution was out of the question in Finland since it would be directed against the tsar, who was in St. Petersburg. The Old Finns – the supporters of a flexible policy toward Russia who had remained in the Senate after the February Manifesto – believed that Russia's weakness provided a chance to restore constitutional rule. They were inclined to be conciliatory and warned against uncompromising resistance to tsarism; the demise of the old regime was still not certain. The Young Finns and the Swedish-speaking liberals wanted to go further; neither an end to the policies of oppression nor a restoration of autonomy satisfied them. They demanded an extension of the Diet's authority and the implementation of the social reforms they had previously included in their programme. The most radical sought to cooperate with the opposition in Russia.

But a new social class – which up to then lacked political rights – learned the importance of a mass movement in the context of the events of 1905. It was unwilling to go only halfway. The Finnish Social Democratic party was founded in 1899 as the Finnish Labour party. This group was the most enthusiastic about the revolution in Russia and representatives of the working class took the lead in expressing dissatisfaction with the status of labourers in the existing class society. Although discussion of the demand for universal and equal suffrage in Europe had reached Finland, it was not until the Social Democrats took up the cause that all parties were forced to reckon with it.

When the process of industrialization in Finland began, Finnish capitalists had relatively limited resources at their disposal in comparison with those of more advanced countries. Since these individuals were inexperienced, lacked social consciousness, and were mainly Swedish-speaking, little attention was paid to the conditions of the working class. Factory owners concentrated on profitability while they competed with foreign products for domestic markets and export trade. The position of factory workers at the beginning of the 20th century in Finland was as insecure as it was wherever industrialization was just beginning. Workers barely earned a subsistence wage, housing was crowded, and living conditions often endangered health. Working in a harsh climate like that of Finland requires more food, clothes, and heat than in warmer climates. Subsistence calls for a greater income in Finland than in most other countries. Small incomes frustrated efforts to further one's own education or provide for that of one's children.

Crofters and the landless population in the countryside were in the same position. Crofters leased land on the basis of oral agreements and therefore lived at the mercy of estate owners and the land-owning peasantry. Those who owned the land could turn out the tenants whenever they saw fit: often from fields the crofters had cleared themselves. The landless population was – with the exception of those engaged in handicrafts – dependent on seasonal employment. In summer there was work in the fields; forestry was the chief occupation in winter. Since they competed with the crofters and their families for the same work, the landless population had the least security; prospects for a decent existence were not very bright.

In agriculture the person who owned the land had the final say and the hired hand's livelihood and comfort were in his hands. As a result, social problems in Finland were acute. Scholars and politicians alike had taken notice of them, but nothing had been done to relieve the distress of the afflicted.

A demand for reform was an essential element in the programme of the Social Democratic party. In the turmoil created by events in Russia, the party made use of the mass strength of the working class, the crofters, and the landless population in the countryside. But in Finland as elsewhere, agitation was mainly successful in the towns and in other population centres. The sparsely populated countryside was not suited for political activity.

A general strike – termed the "Great Strike" due to its extent and political effect – was organized in Finland to put pressure on the tsar. A united front was effective – facing revolution in Russia the tsar also consented to the Finnish demands and signed the November Manifesto on November 4, 1905. Finns had prepared the draft of this manifesto. The tsar promised to remove most of the illegal decrees issued under the February Manifesto for the time being, although not all of them, as the Finns had demanded. He set the Senate the task of drawing up a bill that would create a parliamentary system based on universal and equal suffrage. Provisions would also be made to guarantee the basic civil rights – freedom of speech, assembly, association, and the press. Limitations on both suffrage and these basic civil rights had clearly hindered development and interfered with life in Finland. Thus in many ways activism was successful. But since the tsar did not repeal the February Manifesto, a threat to political life in Finland still existed.

The Old Finn Senate was incapable of leading the reform effort. Foreign policy considerations no longer lent support to the conciliatory approach of this faction once the Russian government was on the brink of collapse. The public held the Old Finns partially responsible for the unconstitutional acts of the period of oppression – they had of course participated in the Senate throughout that period. In Russia the opposition was victorious. Passive and later open resistance had checked the policy of oppression in Finland. Now the constitutionalists had an opportunity to lead the country. A new Senate was appointed on December 1, 1905. The leading figure was Leo Mechelin – who had a reputation as a champion of Finland's constitutional rights and who had gained experience in government as a Senator from 1882 to 90. Mechelin had returned from exile in the previous year. The Senate was composed of those sharing Mechelin's views – Swedish-speaking liberals and Young Finns. In the beginning it included J.K. Kari (1868–1921), a teacher representing the Social Democratic party. But the party did not approve Kari's participation – he had entered the Senate without its consent – and removed his name from the membership rolls in 1906. Despite this action, Kari served in the Senate until 1907.

Disunity arose in Finland just as it had in the revolution in Russia and differences of opinion about ultimate objectives appeared. The November Manifesto restored Finland's constitutional rights. It satisfied the moderate constitutionalists and the Old Finns. The restoration of autonomy and a trend toward increasing democracy was enough for them. But the leadership of the Social Democratic party was not content. It had encouraged the masses to demand reform only to be denied a role in the establishment of the new order. It had no confidence in the promises of either the tsar or the Senate. Finnish Social Democrats set a more distant goal, following the example set by the Russian working class. Further progress was possible and it was essential to keep up the pressure. Action taken in those days revealed the significance of mass political movements. The "Red Declaration" proclaimed in Tampere during the general strike is an example. Yrjö Mäkelin (1875–1923), the editor-in-chief of the Social Democratic newspaper in Tampere, was the author. The realization of Mäkelin's programme would have meant a revolutionary implementation of the parliamentary reform and the expansion of autonomy almost to the point of separation from Russia. The declaration did in fact urge the citizens of Helsinki to choose a provisional government by secret ballot. Once the worst of the demonstrations were over, the centre of operations shifted to Helsinki. Political decisions were also made in the capital and there the pressure exerted on the established order was more effective. Working class interests no longer coincided with those of the bourgeoisie and the two groups went their separate ways. Workers took up arms and formed an armed red guard. Bourgeois forces responded by creating a national guard made up chiefly of students. Passions flared and armed conflict seemed inevitable. Great efforts were needed to prevent it.

In this tense political atmosphere Mechelin's Senate began work on a new Parliament act and an election law. The Senate committee on reforms wrote the bills and Diet passed them on May 29, 1906.

3.

Parliamentary reform provided Finland with a unicameral legislative body chosen by universal and equal suffrage. Differences of opinion on the structure of the representative institution appeared in the course of discussion of the reform. There was general agreement that suffrage should be universal and equal and there was no opposition to granting women the right to vote. The defects resulting from the absence of universal suffrage in Finland were widely recognized and there was abundant desire to eliminate them. Suffrage had been the privilege of the highest estate in elections to the Diet. The right to vote in elections for representatives of the other Estates – dependent on wealth or land ownership in the two lowest Estates – was exercised by a mere 10 % of those who had reached their majority. In waging what appeared to be a hopeless struggle against autocracy and Russification, the support of all social strata was essential. A sense of responsibility on the part of the entire nation was still regarded as the best guarantee of national existence. The basis for concensus was of minor importance. An appeal to the tradition of equality for all citizens inherited from the French Revolution of 1789, extraparliamentary pressure which the masses were prepared to continue in order to further the revolution, or party tactics could serve as the basis for the necessary unity. Differences of opinion did not coincide with party divisions; support for radical reform and a more cautious conservatism could be found in each group. Although the expansion of suffrage meant a disruption of the balance of power and a particularly severe blow to the influence of the Swedish-speaking population, no party sought to oppose the reform.

There was disagreement over the nature of the legislative body; should it be a unicameral or a bicameral body? Certain Old Finns – Leo Mechelin, for example – feared that a jump from a Diet based on the Estates to a unicameral Parliament would lead to rash decisions and awkward situations. Bicameral systems in other countries had resulted in a serious approach to legislation. The bicameral system also drew support from Swedish-language politicians and those versed in the law; eight representatives of the Noble Estate opposed a unicameral system.

But external pressure and tactical considerations kept the supporters of a bicameral Parliament from pushing their cause; it was feared that the tsar might prevent the reform entirely if the ranks were broken. Unanimity meant the power to resist the sovereign.

Once the direct threat to the existence of the tsarist regime ended, Nicholas began to view Finland as he had previously. The Finns had to make concessions and the tsar put off a final decision for a long time. In the end, fear of renewed revolutionary activity, the promises already made, and the unanimity of the Estates and public opinion led at last to the desired result; the sovereign confirmed the decision of the Diet on July 20, 1906.

In August 1906 an act guaranteeing freedom of speech, assembly, and association was combined with suffrage reform and the new parliamentary order. These acts were great strides towards the realization of democracy in Finland. A contender who lagged behind political development in western Europe and particularly in the Anglo-Saxon countries throughout the 19th century had made a concerted effort, closed the gap, and joined the front runners.

CHAPTER IV

From a Democratic Interlude
to the March Revolution

The first parliamentary elections were set for March 15 and 16, 1907. The campaign was fought under party banners.

1.

The emergence of political parties generally requires that several relatively large groups of citizens have an opportunity to influence the course of public affairs. While competing factions do appear in both autocracies and dictatorships, they represent nothing more than a struggle for power among the country's leaders. Political parties do not appear. A certain amount of political freedom is also essential and there must be a reasonably free exchange of opinion that has some influence on politics. Considerable political activism existed in Britain before democracy in the modern sense of the word was established at the end of the 17th century.

The origins of political parties in Finland date back to the "Age of Freedom" in the 18th century when delegates to the Riksdag worked together. There were two national factions and numerous groupings among the Finnish representatives. These factions did not last long, for the Swedish king introduced changes that did away with them. Genuine political parties did not emerge until the Russian era.

As a result of Finland's unique historical development, and her dependence on conditions in Russia, the parties based on language alone proved vital. Liberalism flourished briefly in the 1860s when there was extensive freedom of the press, although at the beginning of the 1880s nationalist forces had little difficulty in preventing its evolution into a full-fledged political party. Both the Finnish and the

Swedish parties originated in the 1860s. But they were loosely organized and their operations were largely restricted to the Diet and the decision-making that went on there. An ideological structure based on the German concept of state and also on the interrelation of language and nationality was common to both groups. Just as Snellman had challenged the educated class to adopt the language of the majority, the Swedish nationalists emphasized their right and duty to affiliate with their own language group. Both parties sought to advance or preserve the interests of the two linguistic groups and to defend Finland against Russification. Finnish nationalists considered raising the level of education of the Finnish-speaking population the only possible course of action: Swedish nationalists held fast to the traditions of the Swedish period.

The press underwent the development essential for the formation of a party system in the 1860s. There was a considerable degree of political freedom and even though officialdom tightened its hold at the end of the decade, the press remained vigorous. Readers became more sophisticated and took increasingly clear stands on the issues of the day. This in turn forced the press to be consistent. Earlier newspapers presented the views of private entrepreneurs. Due to the developments mentioned above, a paper's editorial policy first became that of a small group of collaborators and later that of an actual party. In Finland most political dailies are owned by stockholders. If a party holds a majority of the shares – which has clearly been the case in the Social Democratic press since independence – the leadership of the party determines the general line of the paper. If the stockholders think alike or a single person holds the majority, ties with a party are not so close. Developments of this kind have occurred in Finland and some papers have stressed the fact that they have no party affiliation. Newspapers are vital elements in the formation of public opinion and an effective party without a mouthpiece is simply unthinkable.

Both political freedom and public opinion are crucial to the formation of parties; the opportunity associations of citizens have to influence political decisions is another. As early as the 1860s Finnish party groupings had a certain direct influence on politics in combination with pressure exerted by public opinion. But as long as everything depended on the tsar-grand dukes, no systematic political activity was possible. Organized parties developed along with the democratization that occurred at the beginning of the 20th century. Efforts to expand suffrage and reforms in the legislative system speeded up the process. The 1907 elections for a unicameral Parliament forced the parties to create permanent organizations. Previously the Social Democrats alone possessed the requisite framework. The rest had to start from scratch. Elections also called for use of the press and public meetings; an election programme that appealed to the voters was absolutely essential. These efforts marked the birth of a party system in Finland. In the 1890s the role of the language conflict in party politics changed. The opposition of Snellman and his followers on the one hand and that of the more extreme Swedish nationalists on the other, frustrated the attempt of Swedish-speaking circles to establish a liberal party that would seek to settle the conflict by means of a compromise. Disunity arose when the more radical supporters of the Finnish language cause broke loose to form the Young Finn faction. When Russian oppression grew stronger in the following decade, liberal elements within both the Young Finn faction and the Finnish party began to cooperate with the Swedish-speakers in order to defend the constitution, thus ignoring linguistic differences. This policy was in sharp contrast to that of the Finnish party led by Yrjö Koskinen, which had partial responsibility for governing the country at the time. The united front against Russia lost its significance once constitutional rule was restored in 1905 and the way was clear for democratic development. Ties between the Swedish-speakers and the Young Finns made during the constitutional struggle did, however, provide the basis for cooperation in the government from 1905 to 1908.

Changes brought about by the expansion of suffrage and the parliamentary reforms reduced the importance of the language conflict. The Swedish People's party (Svenska Folkpartiet) remained the only language faction with a programme based exclusively on nationality. Although an attempt to found this party was made as early as 1896, success was not achieved until 1906. Social problems became increasingly important and the Swedish-speaking upper classes were a powerful economic and political force. As a result the party took a stand on the issues of the day and sought votes by stressing the interests of the Swedish population in rather general terms, defending the use of

Swedish in government offices and schools and advancing Swedish culture. Party programmes drawn up by Finnish-speakers naturally sought to curtail the status of Swedish and the Swedish People's party resisted the encroachments of the Finnish language. Cooperation between the Swedish People's party and the Young Finns in the Senate prevented language from becoming the main issue in elections to the first unicameral Parliament.

A Finnish party came into existence in the 1860s. It concentrated on improving the status of the Finnish language and on training an educated class that spoke Finnish, mainly through the establishment of Finnish-language secondary schools. Supporters of the Finnish language had political influence since the majority of the Clerical and Peasant estates supported their programme. Although Snellman cannot be regarded as a party leader, he was appointed to the Senate in 1863 to meet the demands of the Finnish-speaking faction. This faction became politically significant in 1882 when Yrjö Koskinen, the intellectual leader of the movement, entered the Senate. He was subsequently joined by people of like mind and the role of the Finnish-speaking faction grew.

In 1906 the party drew up a programme of radical social reform with the elections of 1907 in mind. The Finnish faction developed into a real party. In organizing local units it was known as the Finnish Central Society. The party was not involved in the government and its programme had a great deal of appeal. In addition to an extreme stand on the language issue which was also directed against the Young Finns, it made demands for timely social reforms, taking both conditions at home and examples drawn from abroad into account. Improvements in conditions in the countryside were considered to be of particular importance. Although this appeal did represent the social views of the Finnish-speaking educated class that led the party, it was also a tactical device; the aim was to compete with the Socialists for the support of the rural population which also represented a majority of the electorate. The party had a strong press which had won a great deal of prestige among Finnish-speaking readers. The Finnish party succeeded in attracting a considerable following through the medium of the press.

It was the party's position on relations with Russia that caused difficulties in the election. Throughout the era of oppression the party advocated a conciliatory policy based on a realistic appraisal of the facts. Party leaders entered the Senate along with other experts chosen by the tsar and took part in governing the country. In order to avert a disaster they had attempted to react flexibly to the tsarist policy of Russification; the public held them accountable for this action. As long as Russia's leaders were chiefly concerned with great power politics and preserving the autocracy, they expected little more than blind obedience from Finnish politicians, or at least the submission required by the situation. They heeded Finnish advice only when it might in some way benefit their policy for the Empire as a whole. Efforts in Finland to preserve the country's status were doomed to failure and given the attitude of the Russians, did not even constitute an effective defence. The "Old Finns," as people began to refer to those who opposed the Young Finns, were unable to accomplish their aims, and ended up bearing partial responsibility for the era of oppression.

Cooperation between the Young Finns and the Swedish party – the formation of the constitutional front – provided the Old Finns with an issue in the 1907 elections; they appealed to the nationality conflict which had raged in previous decades and made use of the Young Finns' new alliance. The Young Finns got themselves into this awkward position by putting constitutional interests – and those of the entire nation as well – ahead of purely "Finnish" national concerns. Since the leaders of the struggle for constitutional rights were Swedish-speaking, the Young Finns derived no particular tactical advantage from the restoration of constitutional rule. As long as they worked with the Swedish party they had no opportunity to stress the desires of the Finnish-speaking population. Likewise, there was little chance to act as a staunch supporter of radical social reform, although their 1894 programme represented a good point of departure. They were in the government and realism was their watchword.

Even those parties in Finland which appealed to national interests drew their basic ideals from abroad. Purely Finnish ideals were merely grafted on. In comparison with the others, the Agrarian Union, formed as a result of the great upheaval of 1906, was a truly national party. Hannes Gebhard (1864–1933) was one of the party's founders and was himself familiar with agrarian parties in other countries. But foreign models scarcely had any real influence on the Finnish Agrarian Party.

Santeri Alkio (1862–1930), originally a Young Finn and imbued with the patriotism typical of politically active youth in the countryside, became the editor-in-chief of the party's most important organ, *Ilkka,* founded at Vaasa in 1906. Alkio became a major figure in the development of the Agrarian party's ideology. At root he was a Finnish nationalist who idealized rural life and trusted in the essential goodness of man and his capacity for improvement. Alkio believed that a single party could accommodate the entire rural population – despite the conflicts of interests that plagued it – and work on behalf of all those who lived on the land. As a result of the previous affiliation of Alkio and certain other Agrarian party leaders with the Young Finns, the Union adopted a constitutionalist stand on the important political questions of the day.

The Social Democrats were considerably more likely to succeed in the forthcoming elections. They were free of the burden of responsibility for past policies and those of the present as well; indeed, under the existing system, participation in government was hardly more than a dream.

Industrial and political developments in 19th century Finland made the birth of a labour movement inevitable. For years interest in public affairs among the working class was limited, due to a low level of education. But there were educated, idealistic individuals who were willing to lead less fortunate citizens. Their motives were largely humanitarian. Employers were also interested – they were far from indifferent about working class organizations. However, their efforts were not productive.

When the Social Democratic party was founded in 1899 it broke loose from the "bosses'" control and embraced Marxist ideology. At the beginning Social Democrats were hesitant to brandish revolutionary slogans, although the leaders of the working class were even prepared to use violence during the general strike. The brunt of the party's social reform programme was directed at factory workers and at both the landless rural population and the crofters. The objective was radical improvement for all three groups. The party's 1906 platform meant business from beginning to end. It drew more than enough attention to conditions that had to be changed – conditions that affected large segments of the population. Everything between "heaven and earth" was promised as critics argued at the 1909 party convention in Kotka. Marxism was new and difficult to convey to the electorate; it provided speakers with abundant opportunities to explain. The party also played up its role in ending the policies of oppression.

Smaller factions made their appearance in the first parliamentary elections as is usually the case in multiparty systems. They operated under different names and more often than not were offshoots of larger groups; they represent a phenomenon that crops up before every election to some extent. Lacking support, they disappear or return to the mother party. The Finnish Christian Labour party, founded in 1906, was one of these. It rejected Marxism and sought to achieve social reform on the basis of Christianity.

The election campaign was often hard fought. Parties drew up their programmes to attracht voters and thus the tradition of election promises – an essential part of democracy – began with preparations for the first campaign. Promises were made despite the knowledge that progressive measures faced great practical difficulties and that the tsar-grand duke had a legal right to block reform.

The common people, who were exercising their right to vote for the first time, went to the polls to "draw the red line" for the Social Democrats in a festive mood and in many places wore festive attire. The number of voters had increased tenfold thanks to the reforms. Those entitled to vote numbered 1,270,000 and 890,000 went to the polls.

The election results surprised the parties in power. They did not obtain the victory they had anticipated. The Young Finns, the Swedish party, and the Agrarian Union had to be content with the same number of seats the Old Finns obtained; there were 26 Young Finns, 24 from the Swedish party, 9 from the Agrarian Union, and 59 Old Finns. The Christian Labour party won 2 seats. The real victors were the Social Democrats; they won 80 seats in the first Parliament.

The results showed that the constitutionalists enjoyed the support of the majority of the electorate. The burden of compromise was not as important to voters as many had supposed. Internal and social problems proved to be the real issue. The Social Democrats owed their victory to the countryside. Industrial workers were so few in number that it was the support of the discontented landless population, the crofters, and the rural labourers that made the Social Democratic victory possible.

2.

Parliament began work on May 23, 1907 with an enthusiasm comparable to that of the voters at the polls. In addition to representatives of different occupations, Parliament also included the best of the educated class, who considered it an honour to serve the people. The initial years were ones of high hopes; new ground was being broken and morale was high. Legislation to correct many defects was introduced and so many "Western" reforms were introduced that implementation was often delayed until after independence.

Efforts were made from the very beginning to observe a certain regularity and to develop precedents in the sense of those built up by the British Parliament. Although there was yet no fixed relationship between the Senate and Parliament, consistent efforts were made during the first session to establish one.

The Mechelin Senate enjoyed the support of one-fourth of the Parliament. It received support from both the Social Democrats and the Old Finns. The Parliamentary Act included provision for votes of confidence, and the Social Democrats made use of this right in 1908.

The Social Democrats accused the government of neglecting and even blocking reform, oppressing the proletariat, imprisoning and exiling members of the Russian opposition, and giving in to Russian demands. Furthermore, the government had shown itself incapable of halting plans to destroy Finland's autonomy and the freedom of her people. Since the Old Finn party was happy to see the Mechelin government defeated, it abstained from the voting. The motion passed. 71 Social Democrats voted in favour of it and 47 Constitutionalists voted against it. Although the tsar dissolved Parliament because of the outcome of the vote, he did accept the Senate's resignation. From the grand duke's point of view the Senate had been formed under unpleasant circumstances; from Russia's point of view it was simply not trustworthy.

The resignation of the Senate after the vote of no confidence was an indication that a true parliamentary system was in the making. The way was open for the establishment of ministerial responsibility to Parliament. This was the only instance of its kind before Finland gained her independence. Other efforts to stress the responsibility of the government to Parliament were made in the early days of the unicameral legislative body. In 1907 K.J. Ståhlberg (1865–1952) was forced to express his opinion as a Senator before Parliament on a bill for restricting the sale of alcohol. When Parliament expanded the bill to provide for prohibition, which he did not approve, Ståhlberg resigned from the Senate. Ståhlberg was unwilling to present an act passed by Parliament to the tsar which went against his convictions; neither was he willing to present the tsar's denial of confirmation for a measure approved by Parliament. During the second era of oppression it was clear that stands taken by Parliament had no influence at all on the Senate.

Only the first two sessions of Parliament witnessed any great degree of optimism or fruitful work; the reaction in Russia soon began to make itself felt in the Finnish Parliament.

3.

As a result of defeat in the war with Japan and the chaos that followed, Russian prestige was at rock bottom. But the alliance with France did not disintegrate; fear of Germany did not rule out reliance on the weak. Since 1904 France had also cooperated closely with Great Britain, and the Russian debacle in Asia removed all obstacles to a closer relationship between the latter two powers. Russia was no longer a serious rival where Britain's vital interests were at stake. In 1907 the conflict between these two states in Central Asia was ended by a treaty providing for stabilization in the area. Thus diplomacy paved the way for cooperation between three great powers, Britain, France, and Russia. Germany of course had drawn them together. The steady growth of German military power, German involvement all over the world, and the spread of German influence in Africa and Asia – areas of vital interest to Britain – meant increasing fear in Europe. Germany was clearly bent on becoming a world power.

From 1908 onward the danger of war grew, due to the arms race. Russian foreign policy stiffened, and this had an adverse effect on Finland's status. Russian nationalists and those responsible for the Empire's defence turned their attention to Finland. Russia must – at least Russian military leadership so argued – strengthen every area that might possibly become a theatre of war, in accordance with the general plans for defence. Sweden's orientation was once again crucial to Russian military planning. Sweden had preserved her neutrality in all international disputes despite public opinion, which from time to time had demanded a war of revenge against Russia. Both Swedish liberals and the powerful Swedish Social Democratic party were hostile to Russian autocracy; the latter's press was sharply critical of Russia's policy towards Finland. Criticism in Sweden combined with the general state of affairs in Europe kept both the tsarist government and the general staff from trusting Swedish neutrality during the arms race. Despite this distrust, Russia continued to base her policy toward Sweden on defensive considerations, at least up to the beginning of the First World War.

The first era of oppression destroyed Finnish confidence in the tsar. Collaboration between Finns and Russian revolutionaries in 1905 with the aim of achieving Finnish political goals convinced the tsarist government that the grand duchy would not be reliable in the event of war. Finland's own military force – disbanded in 1901 – was not re-established; the country's defence rested with the Russian army and Finland was required to make monetary compensation for her security. Preparations for defence also required the subordination of transport in Finland, particularly the railways, to Russian military needs. The increased Russian military presence in the grand duchy also meant that national forces suspected of separatist sentiment would be forced to toe the line. These points of view began to dominate Russian policy toward Finland as the international situation rapidly deteriorated. As a result, the first democratic era proved little more than a short interlude.

Portents of another era of oppression were discernible as early as 1908. Parliament convened in February and re-elected P.E. Svinhufvud (1861–1944) to the post of speaker. Svinhufvud, a Young Finn active in the battle for Finland's rights, had held the post during the first session of the unicameral legislature. At the opening ceremonies of the new session Svinhufvud warned that demands were again being made in Russia for changes in Finland's status and political system. Svinhufvud's speech irritated the Russians, but Parliament was not dissolved until the Mechelin Senate received a vote of no confidence.

Elsewhere the deterioration of relations was even more apparent. In June 1908 the tsarist government decreed that any Finnish legislation which might affect the entire empire and its interests had to be submitted to the Russian council of ministers before it could be presented to the tsar.

The Parliament that convened after new elections in August 1908 contained four fewer Old Finns, three additional Social Democrats, and an additional Young Finn. Svinhufvud, elected speaker by Parliament, spoke again of the nation's concern about the unconstitutional policies of the tsarist government. Since he had thus acted against the wishes of the tsar as conveyed by the governor-general, Parliament was dissolved immediately. In the elections that followed the Old Finns lost six seats and the Christian Labour party one. The Agrarian Union gained four of these seats, the Young Finns two, and the Social Democrats one.

Relations between the Senate and the Russian government immediately took a turn for the worse. After the resignation of the Mechelin Senate in 1908, a government headed by Professor Edvard Hjelt (1855–1921) representing all the non-socialist parties was formed, but the events of 1909 toppled it. In March the establishment of a joint committee to handle relations between Finland and Russia followed the dissolution of Parliament. In September the governor-general informed the Senate of the tsar's edict; bills brought before Parliament could not deal with administrative matters. The tsar also urged Parliament to prepare changes in the municipal statutes that would grant Russians the same privileges the Finns themselves enjoyed in Finland. In September the Russian minister of transport received the authority to use imperial rolling stock on Finnish railways. In October the tsar signed a manifesto aimed at resolving problems concerning military service for residents of Finland "by means of legislation concerning the entire empire". At the same time Finns were relieved of any personal military obligation for the time being and provisions were made for annual payments to be made for military use. There were also rumours in October that the province of Viipuri was to be separated from the grand duchy and reunited with the empire proper. Parliament was dissolved once more in November when it refused to appropriate funds to pay Russia compensation for performing Finnish military obligations. Later on in the same month Lieutenant General F.A. Seyn, who had served as Bobrikov's assistant, was named governor-general.

As one setback followed another, the Senators took action; in April Hjelt and the rest of the Young Finns resigned, in June the chairman of the judicial section, R.A. Wrede (1851–1938) and the Swedish faction left, and in November Danielson-Kalmari and the other Old Finns followed suit.

These Senators were replaced by officers who had won merit in the service of Russia and by Finns who accepted the system. In November, Major General Vladimir Markov, born the son of Sergeant Ivan Markov in Hamina and a product of the cadet school there, was appointed vice chairman of the financial section. The Senate had come under the authority of the Russian government and the first native Russian senators were named under the Equality Act issued by the tsar in 1912.

Parliament thus became the only political force that could make the voice of the people heard. Parliament denounced all the unconstitutional measures directed against Finland's status, but was powerless to take effective action. The tsar had the right to dissolve it and took advantage of this privilege in November 1909 and October 1910. Russians controlled the Senate and Parliament was paralysed. Although it consistently expressed opposition to the unconstitutional measures when in session, the Parliament chosen at the beginning of 1911 was allowed to remain until 1913. In December 1915 the tsar postponed calling the Parliament elected that year until the state of emergency was past. Regular parliamentary elections were held in July 1916, but the new Parliament did not meet until April 1917 after the overthrow of the tsarist regime. The Social Democrats achieved considerable success in the 1913 elections. Partially due to a lack of interest in the elections on the part of supporters of the non-socialist parties, they increased their share of the seats to 90. A veritable landslide occurred in 1916 when the Social Democrats gained a six-seat majority in Parliament at the expense of both the Young Finns and the Old Finns. Thus a peaceful revolution occurred in the Finnish Parliament before the old regime came to a violent end in March 1917.

As late as the first era of oppression there was a significant political faction in Finland that believed the vital interests of the grand duchy could be protected by a policy of compromise and conciliation that took Russian points of view into account. After the second era of oppression began there was scant sympathy for compromise. From 1909 onward few if any Finnish politicians argued that any kind of understanding could be reached with the existing regime in Russia. Tsarist demands were perfectly clear and the persistence with which St. Petersburg worked to deprive Finland of her rights left no room for doubt. In 1910, when the Russian State Duma approved a bill extending the authority of legislation concerning the entire empire to Finland by a vote of 164–23, the ultra-nationalists concluded that it meant "Finis Finlandiae!". The expression was that of a delegate to the Russian Duma who participated in the decision. Russian military preparations in Finland, made as the international situation deteriorated, only served to emphasize the lack of confidence in Finland. Finns united during the second era of oppression as the threat of a general war increased; separation appeared the only means of preserving Finnish national existence.

4.

Internal developments and changes in Finland's political status that occurred from the 1700s onwards led step by step to a demand for independence. Yrjö Koskinen dreamed of separation from Russia as a young student in the 1850s and in the following decade A.O. Freudenthal expressed similar sentiments. Although they represented two different ideologies, they agreed on what was necessary to achieve the break. Russia must suffer defeat in a major European conflict. Since Finland was part of the Russian empire, any talk of independence was restricted to "whispering" and even then in small groups. The student unions were free, and many a new ideal was brought forth in discussions within these organizations. This was also true of independence. Student leaders discussed independence – even during the darkest days of the era of oppression. Axel Lille, a journalist and a Swedish nationalist leader in the Nyland student union, spoke of independence in 1902. This same ideal was expressed in conjunction with the general strike in 1905 in Yrjö Mäkelin's "Red Declaration". When activists made contact with Russian revolutionaries during the first era of oppression or during the war with Japan from 1904 to 1905, they sought more than the overthrow of the tsarist regime. They sought to pave the way for a more distant goal – that of Finnish independence. The same objective was behind the activities of Kagal and the Gymnasts' Union; they procured arms and learned how to use them. Systematic efforts to achieve independence, however, did not begin until the outbreak of the First World War.

The Russian government ruled out any possibility of compromise once hostilities began. The commander-in-chief of the Russian forces promised that Poland would be re-united and her rights restored. Finland did not receive similar consideration. In September 1914 the tsar confirmed a thorough-going programme of Russification. Initial victories in operations against the Germans made the Russians over-confident. They issued – without demonstrating excessive political acumen – the secret Russification programme to the Finnish press, which published it on November 17, 1914. Although the censor forbade discussion, the appearance of the programme itself was enough to strengthen Finnish determination to use any means necessary to achieve independence. Industrial circles alone remained favourable to cooperation with Russia. War closed off the Baltic Sea and disrupted trade with the two most important purchasers of Finnish exports, Britain and Germany. Russian markets alone could keep factories running and maintain employment. Russian industry was in an early stage of development and faced the severe strain of war; Finnish products were sorely needed. Trade between the two countries increased, and exports continued until autumn 1917, when the chaos in Russia spread to the economy.

Russia's military fortunes were crucial to Finland. Russia's allies included Britain and France – both members of the Triple Entente; Japan – which sought Germany's Asian spheres of influence; Italy – which left the Triple Alliance in 1915; and from 1917 onwards the United States of America. Germany, Austria–Hungary, and Turkey opposed Russia. Russian defeat offered the only possibility for change in Finland's status. But this too had its advantages. Russia was allied with the western powers, and if they emerged victorious they would be obliged to look out for the interests of their defeated ally. But the course of the war boded well – both for the achievement of Finnish independence and for its preservation. Germany crushed Russia and when the revolution elevated the Bolsheviks to power, they made peace with Germany. Vladimir Illich Lenin (1870–1924) adopted the principle of national self-determination for the many nationalities within the Russian empire in devising his doctrines. When Finland declared her independence, the new Russian government recognized it. In order to obtain German aid during the Civil War, Finland was forced to support German policy. Germany's defeat cut off this support. The separate peace treaty concluded with Germany, a violation of the terms of the alliance, released the western powers from any obligation to protect Russian interests. The economic strength of the western powers – and later on the military intervention of the United States of America – made themselves felt on the front. Germany was defeated and Finland was freed from her ties with that power. The right of small countries to national self-determination was one of the principal ideals of the victorious western allies. Here Finland's right was recognized, although she had fought alongside Germany. A reorientation of Finnish foreign policy led to the establishment of diplomatic relations with the victors and persuaded them to recognize Finland's independence.

Efforts to achieve independence were stepped up gradually during the First World War and did not coincide with party lines. It was rather a question of generations; those who had been around for some time were cautious, the young bold. There was virtually no difference of opinion about the overthrow of tsarism and during the second era of oppression only those Finns who had advanced in the Russian bureaucracy or were otherwise of Russian orientation cooperated with the government in St. Petersburg.

The working class supported efforts to overthrow the autocracy and sought both to further democracy and expand Finnish autonomy. Worker participation in the 1905 general strike and the subsequent demonstrations offered ample evidence of the movement's ultimate goals. Contacts were maintained with Russian revolutionary circles with the aim of undermining the tsarist regime. According to the principle of cooperation between the proletariat of all countries, revolution, not national independence, should be of primary importance. The Finnish movement itself became more radical as Russian revolutionaries resorted more and more to violence in the face of the Russian government's efforts to crush them.

The constitutionalists joined the working class in opposing tsarism in Finland; this included the Swedish party, the Young Finns, and the Agrarian Union. It should be remembered that Swedish nationalists in Finland took a clear stand at the very beginning. Finland would leave the Russian empire and restore its former union with Sweden. Once the Finnish national movement became a power to reckon with, Swedish nationalists realized that separation from Russia would by no means lead to reunion with Sweden – in short, a mere exchange of sovereigns. Reunion with Sweden flew in the face of the doctrines of Snellman and his followers. Finnish-speakers were politically mature and their goal was quite naturally independence. Recognition of this basic fact was the point of departure for the ideals advocated by Lille and others of like mind.

The position of the constitutionalists on the question of independence reflected both the personal views of party leaders and party policy as well. Exile had been the fate of a good many leaders of the Young Finns and the Swedish party during the first era of oppression. The new order which the upheaval of 1905 had forced on the tsar meant they could return home; it also permitted the constitutionalists to come to power. The beginning of the new era of oppression and particularly the outbreak of war made it perfectly clear that it was only a question of time before work and even life itself in Finland would become impossible for any patriot who respected the constitution. Determination to work for Finnish independence was most widespread in these circles. Only those who held fast to the letter of the law and condemned the use of violence viewed the efforts of the activists with dismay.

The Agrarian Union – the tradition of peasant freedom was its ideal – joined the constitutionalist front at the very beginning. The party's peasant membership opposed Russian oppression and during the war supported efforts, including activism, to achieve Finnish independence.

The policy of compromise advocated by the Finnish party reached a dead end during the first era of oppression. Attitudes changed in the ranks of this faction, too, and very few continued to cooperate with the Russians. But party leaders remained cautious in their support of efforts to achieve independence. The most important of them were experts on Russian conditions. Even a weak Russia could easily overwhelm Finland and the former also enjoyed the support of powerful allies. This political fact of life had to be understood. Russia had to be prevented from crushing Finland in time of war when there was no hope of obtaining sympathy from abroad as there had been during the first era of oppression. When plans for the Russification of Finland became public, many members of the Finnish party who had hitherto advocated flexibility joined the struggle for independence. The entire party adopted this position after the November revolution in 1917 as did Finnish business circles. The latter held cooperation to the last minute essential in order to maintain production and employment.

Public opinion in Finland became nearly unanimous during the First World War with regard to overthrowing the autocracy and secession from the Russian empire. Wide backing was available for all anti-Russian efforts. Cooperation with Russian revolutionaries while war raged in Europe made little sense. Revolutionary groups fought continually among themselves and had no unified leadership. Disunity made it simply impossible to negotiate with the revolutionaries about Finland's future. The Finns were forced to go their own way.

Efforts were made to train Finnish youth for an armed struggle against Russia during the general strike. Members of the active resistance movement had even procured arms. Sentiment among Young Finns for independence became a political factor after the outbreak of the First World War, and the intellectual leaders of the struggle for independence exploited these feelings. Since Russia maintained an efficient espionage system in Finland and Russian garrisons were located throughout the country, opportunities for military training at home were non-existent. Sweden and Germany offered the only hope. Sweden had not taken sides in the war. If it had been possible to train troops there, there would have been no need to make a choice between the two major European alliances. Language difficulties would also have been minimal if most of the trainees had been either Swedish-speaking Finns or Finnish-speakers who knew Swedish. But Sweden maintained a strict neutrality which also applied to relations with Russia. Permission for Finns to train on Swedish territory would have meant a breach of this neutrality and in the end Germany alone showed any interest.

There was a tradition of German orientation in Finland. German was the first foreign language taught in secondary schools and was thus an important factor in forming cultural ties. But traditions of this kind were of little importance in Finland's struggle for independence during the First World War. In the final analysis opposition to Russia and the possibility of aid in breaking loose from the empire dictated Finland's choice. Germany was the most likely ally. The training of Finnish "Jaegers" began in February 1915 after the completion of negotiations. A couple of hundred Finnish youth made up the first group. On May 1916 the Finns – the 27th Imperial Prussian Jaeger Battalion – were sent to the eastern front for combat experience. By this time the unit was nearly 1,900 strong.

Students – most of whom were Swedish-speaking – formed the backbone of the Jaeger Battalion. All social classes were represented. Young men from farm families accounted for a substantial part, although there were also Jaegers from working class families. But the majority clearly had a so-called "bourgeois" background. In negotiations with the Germans concerning training for the Jaegers and their use in combat, the Finns insisted that the troops be used exclusively on the eastern front – not against the western powers. Finland went her own way during the First World War and events at home were hard to follow even when contacts were maintained. As a rule, those who became Jaegers had not taken an active part in Finnish intellectual life. They had no party affiliations when they left Finland nor did they develop any in Germany while undergoing training for the future independence struggle.

Russian suspicion grew stronger as Finnish sentiment became increasingly anti-Russian and the independence movement gained momentum. The Russian foreign office and general staff had made preparations to meet any threat that might arise as the war progressed. They recognized the possibility of a German landing in Finland combined with an uprising; the objective would be an attack on

Petrograd. Those responsible for Russia's defence also believed Sweden would join the Central powers and thus systematic preparations began in Finland. Work on fortifications began and strong garrisons were established – at maximum strength they included 100,000 infantry and marines. An effective espionage system was built up to keep a check on sentiments in Finland; military and political police forces were organized to crush any opposition ruthlessly.

The political police and the espionage network – in which Finns, too, were involved – concentrated efforts on the activists, particularly the Jaeger movement and those who supported it. Imprisonment, armed clashes, and bloodshed were the result. These developments embittered the populace, and by 1917 the Finns were mentally prepared for a violent break with Russia. But Russia was still strong and a stalemate existed on the fronts. Not until repeated Russian defeats led to revolution in March 1917 was the stalemate broken.

The tsar did not convene Parliament when he proclaimed a state of war in Finland in 1914. Neither were nationalist sentiments permitted any other outlets for expression. All public gatherings such as worker May Day celebrations were banned. Nevertheless the tsar did observe the provisions of the constitution and called for parliamentary elections in 1916. Since Parliament was incapable of action, voting seemed pointless. Participation was still greater than in 1913 when 51 % of the electorate voted, although the percentage climbed to a mere 55.5 %. Social Democratic energy during the election campaign bore fruit; the party took 47.3 % of the votes – enough for a relative increase of 4 % and an election victory. Since the electoral system favoured large alliances and the other parties were divided among themselves, the Social Democrats emerged with a clear majority in Parliament: 103–97.

CHAPTER V

From a Coalition Senate to the Declaration of Independence

Tsarism also lacked defenders in Russia. The revolution that began in Petrograd on March 8, 1917 picked up support from military units four days later. Nicholas II was left without backing and abdicated on March 15 in favour of his brother, Grand Duke Michael. Michael declined the next day, leaving the Provisional Government in charge. The Provisional Government immediately took steps to dismantle the autocracy and restore those rights the latter had taken away. Parliament was convened on April 4. Finland recognized the transfer of power from the tsar-grand duke to the Provisional Government by carrying out the decisions of the latter.

1.

Revolution in Russia encouraged the Finns to seek unity on the basis of nationalism and to investigate opportunities for building Finland's future. Efforts concentrated on finding a modus vivendi between the Social Democratic majority and the non-socialist minority in Parliament. Finnish politicians were put to the test as soon as attempts to form a government began. Bourgeois forces supported the Coalition Senate since it provided them with an opportunity to influence the course of the reforms which were soon to be discussed. Things were not quite so simple for the Social Democrats. They could have exploited their majority in Parliament more effectively if the leadership of the Senate had been Social Democratic. And there were also radical elements in the party; these did not want to join the government as long as there was a chance to further the revolution. After lengthy negotiations a Coalition Senate was formed on March 26 in which the two factions had equal representation. Two Senators each from the Old Finn and the Young Finn groups (33 and 23 seats in Parliament respectively) and one each from the Swedish party and the Agrarian Union (corresponding representations in Parliament, 21 and 19) comprised the new Senate. The position of vice chairman of the Senate financial section subsequently became parliamentary and later corresponded to that of prime minister, although the chairman was still named by the governor-general, who was appointed by the Russian government. In recognition of the balance of power in Parliament, Oskari Tokoi (1873–1963), a Social Democrat, became vice chairman. Tokoi had worked for ten years as a miner in the United States and became interested in socialism there. He returned to Finland as the pace of political life was quickening and was elected to Parliament as a Social Democrat in 1907. He was re-elected to succeeding Parliaments and in 1913 served as speaker. In 1912 he became chairman of the Finnish Federation of Labour Unions. The vote of the vice chairman of the financial section decided in favour of the parliamentary majority in the day to day work of the Senate. But when more important issues were at stake the governor-general took part, joining the ranks of the non-socialist Senators and leaving the Social Democrats in the minority.

The restoration of Finnish autonomy received the consent of the Provisional Government and the unanimous support of the Coalition Senate. Differences of opinion between the Social Democratic majority and the non-socialist minority in Parliament appeared in April. The balance of political power remained outside Parliament and the Social Democratic majority soon grew weary of participation in government. Their parliamentary majority afforded them the opportunity to convert Finland into a socialist state; this state of affairs encouraged them to make more radical demands for reform. The non-socialist parties grew cautious, seeking to block Social Democratic legislation. They had sufficient votes to prevent or postpone those decisions they could not accept. Debate on the so-called "power law"[1] resulted in disunity which shook the very foundations of Finnish politics.

1 The "power law" transferred the authority of the tsar-grand duke to the Finnish Parliament.

The March Revolution and the balance of power in Parliament made the question of Finnish independence more complicated. The Provisional Government restored Finland's rights and gave its consent to increased autonomy. As a result, it seemed likely that Finland would have to deal with the Provisional Government in resolving her status. Many who had followed the balance of power during the war were convinced that Finland could not obtain her independence without aid from the outside. The Russian government was making an effort to continue the war and had a well-armed force at its disposal in Finland.

Immediately after the March Revolution a joint delegation of the non-socialist parties issued a statement announcing their objectives — the restoration of constitutional rule, the convocation of Parliament without delay, and the formation of a government that enjoyed public confidence. The Tokoi Senate, which met the third demand, was content to present the same goals, adding only a rather general statement of the necessity for economic and social reform. But as early as April 4, Yrjö Mäkelin invoked the Tampere "Red Declaration" of 1905 and called for Parliament to demand independence when the time was right. Three days later the Senate submitted a proposal of the constitutional committee to transfer the authority of the grand duke to the financial section of the Senate. The committee had laboured for over a week under the leadership of K.J. Ståhlberg and Oskari Tokoi. It gave cautious support to the ideas presented by Mäkelin in a speech before Parliament on April 20.

The working class celebrated May Day in an enthusiastic mood. Large crowds gathered in honour of the occasion and to take advantage of freedom of assembly. Russian workers were also involved and in Helsinki soldiers took part. It was clear to everyone that the political freedom already won did not go far enough. Life as citizens of a mere Russian borderland no longer satisfied the Finns; they were through with "slavery" and sought the status of a free people.

2.

The rapid growth of sentiment favouring independence aroused the non-socialist parties to action. At a party congress held at the beginning of May, a majority of the Old Finns approved a statement which called for efforts to gain as much independence as possible. Finnish authority over all matters that concerned Finland alone was the immediate goal. Two weeks later the Swedish party was content to demand nothing more than protection for Finnish autonomy and the gradual expansion of it.

Those bourgeois circles which had worked in Finland and abroad for the cause of independence long before the revolution could not accept this approach. They argued that complete independence should be demanded publicly. A few newspapers had opened their columns to articles concerning this demand, but the most important exercised restraint. This led to the establishment of the newspaper *Uusipäivä* as a mouthpiece for those who advocated outright independence. The response from celebrations held in the provinces was unmistakable; the goal must be complete independence.

On June 8 the Provisional Government passed judgment on the Senate's proposal, altering its content. Authority in some areas was transferred to the Senate and the governor-general, although the Provisional Government retained the right to convene, open, close, and dissolve Parliament – essentially the same privileges the grand duke had held. The same held true with regard to legislation that concerned Russia's interests. After discussing the bill, the parliamentary constitutional committee decided at the end of the same month to propose that Parliament take over decision-making that concerned its own functions. By the time the measure had come before Parliament for final discussion, the balance of power was clear; the Social Democrats had won the support of those non-socialists who favoured independence. The "power law" was approved. On the basis of this act, Parliament alone could make decisions. It gained authority to pass laws, confirm them, and provide for their execution. It also gained the authority to decide on other matters that had previously been determined by the grand duke. But the act included an important reservation with regard to complete independence; parliamentary authority did not extend to military and foreign affairs. The decision was made by a vote of 136–55. The vote was 104–86 when the question of submitting the act to the Russian Provisional Government for approval came before the legislators.

The following day Tokoi announced that the Senate was placing itself at the disposal of Parliament; his aim was to emphasize that the law gave Parliament authority to appoint the Senate.

The Provisional Government, however, sought to maintain the unity of the empire and preserve its own authority. The "power law" passed by the Finnish Parliament did not mean separation from Russia and the Provisional Government was unwilling to pave the way for independence. The non-socialist minority in Parliament feared that the legislative body's newly won authority posed a threat to the existing system; they also held that the results of the elections of 1916 did not represent the will of the people. The rift between the majority in Parliament and the Provisional Government offered possibilities; new elections might well correct the balance of power. Carl Enckell (1876–1959), appointed minister state secretary in April, supported this view. Enckell argued that the "power law" should not be confirmed. The Provisional Government followed this advice, and taking advantage of the rights of the grand duke, dissolved Parliament on July 31.

The minority in Parliament, including those non-socialist members who voted with the Social Democrats in favour of the "power law", approved the dissolution. With the support of the governor-general and the non-socialist representatives, the Senate decided to promulgate the order for dissolution against the will of the Social Democrats.

The Social Democratic party took a strong stand against this decision and attempted to keep Parliament in session under the leadership of a Socialist chairman. But the governor-general foiled this attempt; he used soldiers to bar entrance to the legislative chamber. Up to the end of September Social Democratic representatives continued to meet and approve legislation. The Senate, controlled by non-socialist forces after the resignation of Tokoi and most of the other Social Democratic members, refused to enter acts passed by Parliament in the code of law. Thus the legislation remained a dead letter.

The Social Democrats had also been making preparations for parliamentary elections on October 1 and 2. The elections were held in a period of internal conflict and disorder. Alliances between the non-socialist parties and fear that the outcome of the 1916 elections might be repeated brought out more voters and altered the balance of power in Parliament. Nearly 200,000 additional votes were cast in 1917; a mere 70,000 of these voted Socialist. The Social Democrats lost their majority, gaining only 92 seats. The Agrarian Union reaped the biggest victory; it increased its representation by 26 seats.

3.

The elections of 1917 marked a turning point for the Social Democratic party – a turning point that altered the course of political development in Finland.

The following appraisal of the benefits of suffrage was made at the Social Democratic convention at Kotka in 1909: "We were overjoyed when we gained 80 seats in parliament. But what has it really meant? We got the Bakers' Act, but that's as far as it went." The March Revolution opened the way for political activity in Finland and restored Parliament's legislative authority. It looked as though the Social Democratic majority finally had an opportunity to enact its programme and influence the course of future events. But despite a continuing dispute over the legality of the 1917 elections, the non-socialist majority in Parliament was a fact. The labour movement sought to offset this disadvantage with concerted efforts outside Parliament.

Moderate forces in the Social Democratic movement – particularly strong within organized labour in Western and Central Europe – lost popularity during the First World War. This was especially true in Germany, and here the effect on Finland was considerable. Revolutionary elements came to the fore. The Finnish trade union organization was founded in 1907. The membership grew fourfold during the next decade, amounting to 160,000 in 1917. Most new members supported the revolutionary wing. Extra-parliamentary activity in Finland received a powerful impetus on November 6 when a well-led, well-organized, and well-armed group of Bolsheviks seized power. Although small in number, they had the will to win and made effective use of the disunity and incompetence of their rivals. Their success had an immediate effect on the manner in which Finnish Social Democrats in both party and trade union organizations and in the Red Guard reacted toward the legal government. Although the Central Revolutionary Council rejected armed rebellion by a vote of 18–8 as late as November 12, the very fact that such a proposal was considered indicated a decline in Parliament's prestige and more widespread acceptance of violence. The Bolshevik example tended to increase disrespect for election results. The Russian revolutionaries received only one-fourth of the votes cast on December 8 in elections for the Constituent Assembly. But the Bolshevik government remained in power and dissolved this body on January 19 after a brief one-day session.

In Finland, disagreements between the radical and moderate advocates of independence among the non-socialist majority continued. The former had stood side by side with the Social Democrats in drawing up the "power law"; the latter sought to increase Finland's autonomy by working together with the Russian Provisional government. The November Revolution united them. Moderates felt cooperation with the Bolshevik government was simply impossible. Now the roles were reversed. Finnish Social Democrats had previously been unwilling to cooperate with the government in Russia, but now they were ready. The non-socialist parties had been prepared to deal with the Provisional government; they would have used it against the parliamentary majority. Now it was the turn of the non-socialist forces to say no. Those who had formerly supported a policy of compromise also adopted a hard line on cooperation with the new Soviet government.

Efforts were made after the elections to determine who held supreme authority in Finland. Parliament had already decided that this power should be handed over to a 3-member administrative committee. The working class opposed this move and began a general strike. On November 15, before the end of the strike, Parliament decided to assume supreme authority. Some rather feeble attempts were made to form a coalition Senate, but they were unsuccessful. As a result of this failure Parliament stepped in and chose a government. The list headed by P.E. Svinhufvud received the votes of the non-socialist majority; Tokoi's Social Democrats lost. Finland now had a Senate that enjoyed the confidence of Parliament, the supreme authority in Finland. The new Senate was Finland's legal government.

The Svinhufvud Senate comprised advocates of independence from all the non-socialist parties. On December 4 Svinhúfvud presented a proposal to Parliament which provided for the formation of a sovereign republic of Finland and announced that the government intended to seek recognition for Finnish independence abroad. The matter came before Parliament two days later. Parliament was unanimously in favour of declaring independence. The only difference of opinion concerned procedure. The Svinhufvud Senate was prepared to make the declaration without consulting with the new government in Russia, and the majority in Parliament agreed. The Social Democrats favoured prior negotiations with the Bolsheviks.

CHAPTER VI

Civil War and a New Constitution

Svinhufvud's efforts to gain recognition abroad soon revealed that the path chosen by the Senate and the non-socialist majority in Parliament was not leading to results. Germany, which had previously taken a favourable attitude toward Finnish independence, responded with caution, advising Finland to seek Russian recognition first. Other countries took much the same position, thus forcing the Svinhufvud Senate to take the course recommended by the Social Democrats and obtain approval from Lenin and the Soviet government. Since the Bolsheviks had supported the right of national self-determination and even separation from Russia both during the struggle for power and after the November revolution, recognition for Finnish independence came without delay. On December 31 the Soviet government informed the Finnish envoys of its decision to recommend recognition to the central executive committee.

Joseph Stalin, then acting as People's Commissar for Nationalities, was immediately forced to interpret his government's action. As early as November 1917, Stalin, in a greeting sent to Finnish Social Democrats on the occasion of the party's convention, gave his assurance that Finland, like the other national minorities in Russia, was completely free to decide its own future. The Finnish people should join Russia in an honest, voluntary union. This was the only realistic way to unite the peoples of Russia into a single army. Stalin urged the proletariat to seize power and promised to provide aid on request. But in January 1918 Stalin declared that the Council of People's Commissars had been forced against its will to grant Finland independence because the proletariat "had failed to take power due to vacillation and inexplicable timidity".

Russian recognition encouraged other states to take similar diplomatic action. France, Germany, Sweden, and the other Scandinavian countries were the first to do so. Many other governments followed this example after Finnish delegations had called on them. Great Britain and the United States did not follow suit. They felt that conditions in Finland were so unstable that recognition was not yet warranted. Not until the 1919 parliamentary elections, an indication that democracy was firmly established, did these two powers recognize Finnish independence.

1.

The situation in Finland was not nearly so simple. A struggle over the nature of the newly independent state soon began. The revolutionary leaders of the working class were not content with the results of the elections and with the consolidation of power in the hands of the non-socialist Senate that occurred after Finnish independence gained recognition abroad. The shift from the Diet to a unicameral Parliament was rapid. Unrest of a revolutionary nature had accompanied it. A decade of relative instability had prevented the establishment of deep roots and widespread disappointment in Parliament resulted in a lack of confidence in its potential.

Finland's unique rural society with its crofters and cottagers did not produce a coherent political ideology, although it did serve as a source for discontent and even hostility. In his dissertation on Finnish crofters published in 1898, Aksel Warén declared that the law of the land concerning crofters "offered nothing but obligations and not a single right ... any outward display of human dignity has been almost entirely destroyed. The result is a class of slave-like labourers who are humble and obedient but who are also mentally dull and exist on a bare subsistence level. The gulf that has formed between the two classes of citizens is very broad and will not be easy to bridge."

The plight of the landless population in the countryside was even more distressing. Their livelihood depended entirely on vacillations of the business cycle. The war had made the economy sluggish and had reduced employment in rural areas. Even so, the revolutionary movement did not take root in the sparsely settled countryside in 1905 and 1906 and the same was true in 1917 and 1918. Workers in the population centres also suffered from crowded housing and 10–14 hour days. As a rule, living conditions were barely tolerable. The "three eight's" programme, eight hours of work, eight hours of rest and eight of leisure devoted to family and educational pursuits raised unyielding opposition among employers. The working class had to fight for a better life. To make matters worse, war deprived Finland of her overseas partners in trade, cutting off all foreign commerce except that carried on with Russia and to a certain extent with Sweden. Work became increasingly hard to find and hunger grew widespread.

The Baltic Sea became the site of naval operations as soon as war broke out and this hindered the Finnish merchant marine. Trade with Russia picked up, compensating these losses to some extent. Productive capacity in Finland that served the war effort did provide employment. But Finland's isolation proved fateful as the war continued and Russia's military and economic fortunes declined. Grain imports are a good example; in 1917 Finland succeeded in importing a mere 10 % of the 1913 total. The harvest of 1917 was a further setback. Potatoes, an essential element in the Finnish diet, were dear; the crop was 10 % smaller in 1917 than it had been in the previous year.

Consumption had to be reduced to half of that of the first year of the war and although rationing was introduced, distribution was uneven. The agricultural population scarcely suffered at all in this respect and was even able to provide something for relatives who had moved to the towns. The landless rural population felt the pinch severely; they were of course unable to supply food to family members who had left the countryside. The gap between the property-owning class and the proletariat in the countryside, and to an even greater extent in the population centres, became painfully apparent in everyday life. Mass unemployment and hunger came when the Russian markets were lost in the revolutionary upheaval and when the Russians ended work on fortifications in Finland designed to ward off an invasion from either Germany or Sweden. Reduced grain shipments further tightened the squeeze. Wartime inflation had doubled wages, but due to shortages the price of food had increased fourfold. In 1917 misery spread rapidly as winter approached. Its effects were felt by every poor family in Finland.

Paramilitary organizations existed in Finland during the general strike of 1905. Two guards were formed; one bourgeois, the other working-class. Unrest in 1917 also led to the formation of similar groups. Finland's own military force had been disbanded and there was little confidence in the police. Food shortages and undisciplined troops were a source of fear and uncertainty. In the second half of 1917 bourgeois elements organized the so-called "Suojeluskunta" or Defence Corps. This was what the left called the "white guard". Left wing forces responded, creating their own military units. On January 26, 1918, the eve of the coup, they combined to form the Finnish Red Guard. They received some arms from Russian troops.

The executive committee of the Red Guard issued an order for the imprisonment of the Senate on January 27, 1918. On the evening of the same day military operations began. Kullervo Manner (1886–1936?), a former member of Parliament, headed the revolutionary government. This government, the Finnish People's Delegation, took power on January 28 in Helsinki. Tampere became the second centre of operations.

The left prevented Parliament from taking any measures to secure order, forcing the government to turn to the Defence Corps, which had received its training under Jaeger officers. In many parts of Finland stores of arms remained from the era of oppression. These along with numerous hunting weapons and sidearms were transported secretly to centres of operation. In the middle of January the Senate started to build up a force of its own, relying on authority it had received on January 1. It turned over the command of these units to C.G.E. Mannerheim (1867–1951), who had risen to the rank of lieutenant-general in the Russian army. Mannerheim was serving as a corps commander on the western front when the March Revolution broke out and had experience in commanding large military units.

Mannerheim accepted the post with some hesitation. He was by no means certain that Finland could secure its independence in a civil war. He considered the Bolshevik government a temporary phenomenon and viewed counterrevolutionary elements in Russia with favour. He agreed to serve in order to restore order, but left the question of Finland's future status open. Mannerheim was in reality the commander-in-chief appointed by Finland's legal government, although the whites made him their own hero after the war.

Mannerheim journeyed to west-central Finland and on January 28 announced the start of operations; the Russian troops were to be disarmed. Since the rebellion began at the same time as the Russian troops were being disarmed, events in late winter of 1918 have been interpreted differently. Supporters of the legal government argued that the conflict was a struggle for independence. The People's Council of Commissars delayed the departure of Russian troops from Finland at the request of Finnish Social Democratic leaders. These troops had to be forced out of Finland before independence was secured. The coup d'etat in southern Finland forced the government to take military action and Finland found herself involved in a war of liberation and a civil war at the same time. Russian troops provided the insurgents with arms and gave them some military support. The government in turn received arms from Germany and aid from Swedish volunteers. At the end of the war it called on Germany to dispatch an expeditionary force. Thus the conflict developed into a full-scale war with foreign intervention and can be described as a civil war.

Svinhufvud held out to the very end in the belief that civil war could be avoided. After he granted Mannerheim authority as commander-in-chief, he sent a part of the Senate to Vaasa and remained himself in Helsinki. When the rebellion broke out Svinhufvud found himself on the list of those to be imprisoned. He escaped this fate by hiding in the capital.

The information Svinhufvud received from southern Finland in the early weeks of the rebellion was alarming. The insurgents resorted increasingly to terror. Unaware of the course of events in west-central Finland and Mannerheim's plans, Svinhufvud desperately considered requesting intervention, first from Sweden and then from Germany. In private correspondence Svinhufvud apparently suggested that aid might be obtained from Germany.

Since there were no Senators responsible for foreign affairs in the Finnish government and Svinhufvud was isolated from the outside world, Finnish representatives abroad had to make decisions on the basis of their own judgment.

Edvard Hjelt was the Finnish representative in Berlin. Hjelt was well-known and respected and possessed extensive authority. He had served previously as vice chairman of the Senate. On February 21 he requested the dispatch of German troops to Finland; the response was affirmative. Svinhufvud fled Helsinki on a captured icebreaker to Tallinn and arrived in Berlin on March 10. There he was faced with a fait accompli and could only thank the Germans for the aid they had promised.

Mannerheim had not sought German aid. He would have preferred to settle the conflict without foreign intervention. The Jaegers had obtained military training in Germany and combat experience as well. As early as in the autumn of 1917 Defence Corps troops trained under Jaeger leadership were serving as non-commissioned officers. For purposes of training Mannerheim utilized a small group of officers who had served in the Russian army, numerous volunteer officers from Sweden, and the Jaegers, who had both experience and an understanding of the Finnish soldier. Once the main body of the Jaeger force arrived in Finland on February 25, 1918, Mannerheim considered it only a matter of time before his troops could suppress the rebellion.

When the government confronted him with the promise of German aid and when word of the difficult situation in southern Finland reached him, Mannerheim agreed to work with the German expeditionary force. But he hurried to put down the rebellion with his own troops, and concentrated his forces on the revolutionary stronghold of Tampere. The decisive battle for Tampere was already in progress when the German division landed at Hanko on April 3 with naval support.

The revolutionaries were well aware of the significance of the industrial town of Tampere and defended it bravely. The Red Guard had virtually no military training and few commanders suited to their duties. Short of help from the south, the Red Guard's position was hopeless from the very beginning. The Guard had perhaps 25,000 men at its disposal on the Tampere front. Mannerheim sent his best units – some 15,000 strong – to cut off Tampere. Particular emphasis was placed on preventing the arrival of reinforcements. Neither side was equipped with extensive heavy artillery, although government forces were better equipped in this respect. The same applied to munitions. The insurgents surrendered on April 6 to avoid further bloodshed. No help had arrived and by this time the German division had advanced as far as Karjaa. A German brigade which had embarked from Tallinn landed in Loviisa on April 7.

The lost of Tampere was a severe defeat for the Red Guard and meant a serious decline in morale. There were 2,000 dead and 11,000 prisoners. After the fall of Tampere Red Guard resistance broke down in all sectors of the rather loosely formed front. The outcome of Finland's Civil War was decided at the beginning of April. German intervention merely speeded up the process and prevented further destruction.

The People's Delegation had only limited control over the course of the struggle throughout the rebellion. Red Guard units acted to a great extent on their own initiative and there was no overall coordination. Not until defeat was obvious did the People's Delegation take command of action in the field. Manner was named dictator. The rebellion developed rapidly and preparations for it were incomplete. The leaders of the People's Delegation had no experience in government, to say nothing of warfare. Many joined the revolution simply to show their solidarity with the working class and lacked confidence in the ultimate triumph of the uprising. With a very few exceptions, civil servants remained loyal to the legal government, and this prevented the People's Delegation from carrying out its decisions throughout the area under its control.

The Soviet government recognized the People's Delegation as Finland's legal government on March 1, and turned over the Petsamo region to it. The Bolsheviks provided arms and munitions and grain from their own meagre stores to combat famine in Finland. But German pressure forced the Soviet government to limit military assistance when the Finnish revolutionary struggle was in dire need.

Certain members of the People's Delegation believed as late as the beginning of April that the United States and Great Britain were prepared to recognize the revolutionary government. This belief was clearly nothing more than wishful thinking; it is even more remarkable since Lenin predicted the eventual defeat of the revolution in a speech which appeared in *Pravda* in the middle of March. The leaders of the revolution became fully aware of the hopelessness of the situation a month later when Lenin, fearing the German reaction, announced that revolutionary troops in Finland could no longer use Russian territory in military operations.

Nevertheless, foreign powers did play a role in the course of events in

Finland. The Russians armed the Red Guard and provided other kinds of support. The contribution of Jaegers trained in Germany to the cause of the legal government was crucial and the intervention of a German expeditionary force speeded up the defeat of the insurgents. Russian troops were driven out and the rebellion was crushed by the beginning of May 1918. Thus the years of preparation for Finnish independence bore fruit only on conclusion of a civil war. Conditions in Finland precluded the establishment of independence by legal means.

Civil wars are always extremely destructive, and this was certainly true in Finland. Both during the struggle and after the victory of the legal government, the spirit of revenge dictated the use of violence. The insurgents perpetrated violence on the civilian population and vengeance followed the victory of the legal government. Hunger magnified the severity of these measures. There were over 80,000 insurgents and their families in prison camps. Interrogations and release proceeded slowly. Lack of nourishment and summer heat led to disease and the death rate was high. Approximately 10,000 died in the camps. The insurgents killed 1,650 people and the government troops executed 8,500. The combined death toll was 9,000. Deaths on the government side amounted to over 3,600. Those who fell in battle or died of disease caused by war accounted for about 2,500. A total of more than 31,500 people died in the Civil War.

2.

The war rent the fabric of Finnish society severely. Due to the agreements made with Germany and the course of the war in Europe, Finland became dependent on the will of a foreign power. Differences of opinion also arose among those who supported the legal government. Mannerheim wanted to put down the rebellion without foreign help. Arrangements were made for German aid without Svinhufvud's knowledge, although he later approved them. The German troops remained in Finland after the war at the request of the Finnish government. The western allies were attempting to open up a new eastern front extending from the Arctic Sea into East Karelia and maintained a bridgehead for possible intervention in Russia. Svinhufvud granted German officers authority to help organize the Finnish army. Relations between Svinhufvud and Mannerheim deteriorated, culminating in the resignation of the commander-in-chief on May 31, 1918.

The Svinhufvud government believed it could secure independence through friendship with Germany. Commercial relations with Germany were of prime importance. No other trade partners were available – the oceans were in the war zone and Russia faced chaos at home and was in a state of war with Finland.

Finland lacked its own foreign policy during the era of autonomy. Experience was limited to relations with Russia and here the give and take of traditional diplomacy was largely missing. Attitudes toward the Russian empire were generally a matter of principle. Independent Finland did have a corps of trained, skilful civil servants, but none were versed in diplomacy. Svinhufvud spent three years in Siberian exile and isolation during the First World War. He was unfamiliar with the concepts of international politics, lacked knowledge of the existing state of affairs, and was not a diplomat by nature. He had approved the peace treaty signed with Germany on March 7, 1918 – a treaty that stipulated close cooperation – and he had given his word on behalf of Finland. In the early summer of 1918 Finnish foreign policy had two principal goals – the consolidation of independence and the expansion of the Finnish state to include the isthmus of East Karelia formed by Lake Ladoga, Lake Onega and the White Sea, an area inhabited by a kindred minority.

According to the decision made on November 15, 1917, supreme authority in Finland rested with Parliament. The question of restoring monarchy arose as soon as the conflict was over. Talk of a restoration aroused those who supported a republic and a temporary agreement was reached. On May 18 Parliament granted Svinhufvud the right to "exercise supreme authority," i.e. the powers of the tsar-grand duke. In practice the title "regent," used during the Swedish era to indicate a provisional sovereign, was employed. The regent also served as chairman of the Senate, thus enjoying the status of the former governor-generals. J.K. Paasikivi (1870–1956), a bank director and an Old Finn with experience in handling relations with Russia, took up the reins of government. Paasikivi had supported the policies of Yrjö

Koskinen and J.R. Danielson-Kalmari and was of one mind with Svinhufvud concerning Finland's future.

German troops remained in Finland until December 1918 to avert any efforts by the Western allies to join the counter-revolutionary forces and form a second front in northern Russia. Germany sought Finnish aid in repelling any threat in this quarter by encouraging expansion in East Karelia. This was part of Germany's military strategy. Germany concluded the treaty of Brest-Litovsk with the Soviet government on March 3, 1918 and considered the fulfilment of this accord vital to its efforts on the western front. The task of German military leaders in Finland then became one of preventing a Finnish attack on Russia. Finland was to follow Germany's lead in foreign affairs.

Adherents of the Finnish national idea began to take notice of the Finnish minorities beyond the eastern border in the 19th century. Collectors of folk poetry had made many valuable finds in this area; Elias Lönnrot discovered the basic material for the Kalevala in East Karelia. Numerous native customs and techniques, in addition to folklore, had been preserved in East Karelia. The East Karelians were Finland's neighbours; other Finno-Ugric peoples were scattered over the vast plains of Russia. In the middle of the 19th century Finnish scholars began research which eventually included all these minority peoples.

Chaos in Russia and the Finnish struggle for independence fostered the belief that Finland must take advantage of the historical situation and create a state which could defend itself against Russia on "three isthmuses". Mannerheim issued an order of the day concerning this strategy during the war. His aim was chiefly to arouse enthusiasm in his peasant army but he also wanted to show counter-revolutionary forces in Russia that he intended to drive the Bolsheviks out of those areas just beyond Finland's eastern border. Although Mannerheim withdrew from politics in Finland and could not even attempt to carry out his programme, Svinhufvud included the same goal in his foreign policy.

The Svinhufvud Senate presented before Parliament a bill providing for a sovereign republic at the same time as it issued the declaration of independence. Under the circumstances this was regarded as the only possibility; Social Democrats who were threatening to make a revolution would never have participated in establishing a monarchy. In late 1917 Svinhufvud himself supported a republican form of government. But the events of late winter 1918 had such a strong effect on him that he began to doubt Finland's readiness for the democratic processes essential in a republic. Foreign policy considerations also seemed to recommend the selection of a German prince and Svinhufvud thus decided to lead the Senate in efforts to establish a monarchy.

Svinhufvud's views enjoyed considerable support among the educated classes; a strong state would spare the country a recurrence of the disaster that had recently befallen it. A hereditary monarchy free of the crises that so often plague a republic would provide the necessary stability. Those that took part in the rebellion had to be denied access to power. The necessity of maintaining a consistent foreign policy also recommended a monarchy; the monarch would assure continuity despite a shifting balance of power in Parliament. Germany offered the only hope of withstanding a strong Russia. Since Finland was in an exposed position on Russia's doorstep, German support was essential. The selection of a German prince as Finland's monarch was the solution.

After the declaration of independence, many politicians considered the establishment of a republic the natural step – K.J. Ståhlberg was one of these. He pondered Finland's future while he hid in Helsinki during the rebellion. Immediately after German troops took the city he proclaimed his plans for a republic, but at this time there was no chance to realize them.

All the Social Democrats with the exception of two who had not been involved in the rebellion remained outside Parliament. The result was a new balance of power that favoured monarchy. In June the Senate introduced two bills in favour of monarchy. Kyösti Kallio (1873–1940) and E.Y. Pehkonen (1882–1949), both members of the Agrarian Union, resigned in protest when the Senate passed these two measures. The bills did not, however, receive a sufficiently large majority to be declared urgent. Those supporting monarchy then appealed to the constitution of 1772. In the event that there was no heir to the throne, the Estates were to meet and elect a king. In August Parliament decided by a vote of 58 to 44 to advise the Senate to prepare for an election.

Although the German foreign minister informed the Reichstag as early as mid-summer 1918 that Germany could not win the war, Finland's political leaders remained unconvinced. Neither did the failure of the great summer offensive in France – a clear indication of impending German defeat – convince them. Finland continued policies based on confidence in German victory. Svinhufvud was not the kind who would desert a friend in distress.

Svinhufvud and the Senate he led held fast to their plans for monarchy and on October 9 Friedrich Karl (1868–1940), Prince of Hesse, was chosen King of Finland. The Western allies interpreted this as a sign that Finland was binding herself to Germany and thereby heading for destruction. Finland was warned. The Senate discussed advising Friedrich Karl not to come and considered holding a plebiscite before the coronation. Both Svinhufvud and Paasikivi supported the latter. Other Senators were cautious and they too failed to press their own views. As a result acceptance of the crown was left up to the discretion of Prince Friedrich Karl. He announced he would not accept in December 1918, after the defeat of Germany. Thus Finland's German orientation came to an end. The resignation of first Paasikivi and then Svinhufvud meant an abrupt about-face in Finnish foreign policy.

General Mannerheim was chosen regent on December 12 to succeed Svinhufvud. He had travelled abroad after his own resignation in the early summer. As a former Russian army officer, a military commander loyal to the western allies, and an opponent of alignment with Germany – this of course was the reason he resigned – Mannerheim could succeed where his predecessors had failed. He was well suited for the task of establishing good relations with the victorious powers. He was intelligent, he was familiar with court circles, and he was skilled in languages. His reputation for repelling Bolshevism was widespread. The monarchical faction in Finland saw him as the "white" general responsible for the country's liberation and were prepared to approve his election even if they did maintain their friendship with Germany.

Mannerheim had the backing of the republican minority in the "rump" Parliament in his efforts to consolidate Finland's status abroad and gain recognition for her independence. Leaders of the republican faction had maintained contacts with western diplomats in

Petrograd during the war, seeking to strengthen Finland's position in the event that the western powers – as they hoped – should win the war. K.J. Ståhlberg, who became a university professor in 1908 and Rudolf Holsti (1881–1945), a doctor of philosophy, are two examples. They worked on the basis of a mutual understanding and the latter had ties with western diplomats. During the festivities held on May 16 in conjunction with the army's triumphant arrival in Helsinki, Mannerheim demanded a strong form of government. Since the monarchical faction appealed to Mannerheim's remarks in arguing their case and Mannerheim was an aristocrat – both by nature and conduct – the republican forces were not enthusiastic about his selection. But despite their differences, both sides recognized that isolation had to end. Finland had to cooperate with those powers who would control the future of Europe. Since Mannerheim enjoyed the confidence of ruling circles in both Britain and France, the republican faction in Parliament accepted him.

Upon his return, Mannerheim's first action was to dissolve Parliament and call for new elections to be held on March 1 and 3, 1919. Widespread dissatisfaction with the "rump" Parliament existed in Finland and both the United States and Great Britain demanded the restoration of democracy before they would recognize Finland's independence.

3.

The suspension of constitutional rule during the First World War ruled out any effective political life in Finland. Numerous clubs – some of them secret – took the place of normal political activity. Individual members of the Finnish party took part. A clear split appeared in the ranks as soon as independence appeared possible. There were those who advocated a cautious policy toward Russia for the sake of continuity and who would have been content with a restoration of autonomy. Others sought to break away from Russia – either by parliamentary means or force of arms. These differences were particularly clear in the summer of 1917 during the conflict over transfer of the supreme authority to the elected representatives of the people of

Finland. Advocates of independence affiliated with different parties joined the Social Democratic majority even though the more active elements in the Finnish party had long since rejected the parliamentary approach and concentrated their efforts on preparations for an armed rising. The party's basic policy – compromise with Russia – proved unrealistic. The decline in electoral support was unmistakable; its representation in Parliament dropped from 58 in 1907 to 32.

The November Revolution in Russia changed party attitudes. Non-socialist advocates of independence could continue the course they had chosen earlier. They also picked up abundant support from previously hesitant non-socialists in Parliament. After the October elections Svinhufvud was supported by a parliamentary majority which included the Old Finns. On the other hand, the sympathy of the most radical leaders for the new rulers in Russia reduced Social Democratic activism.

The Finnish party came to power at the end of the Civil War in spring 1918 along with other advocates of monarchy. The rebellion forced Finland's political leaders to reassess their attitude toward the establishment of a republic. Finland's leaders felt Germany was strong as late as the summer of 1918 and assumed that German support for a policy of expansion would be available once Finland was ruled by a German king. Many Old Finns believed that monarchy would become even more widespread in the postwar period; republics had proved ineffective in marshalling national forces for the war effort. The fierce struggle over Finland's form of government that raged throughout the summer and autumn of 1918 – up to the German collapse – created the foundation for a new party system.

The anti-Russian stand of the Swedish People's party and its ideological precedessors was based on a close relationship with Sweden; separation from Russia and restoration of the union with Sweden were the basic goals of A.O. Freudenthal, the founder of this school of thought. The Finnish national movement made reunion with Sweden unrealistic. Finns did not consider it a worthy objective. Independence was the only unifying goal.

The Swedish People's party viewed efforts to achieve independence with some hesitation. But its membership did work actively to separate Finland from Russia and party leaders participated in the non-socialist resistance movement. Efforts of the working classes were led almost exclusively by Finnish-speakers. The balance of power shifted to Parliament when conditions returned to normal in 1917. The significance of Swedish-speakers decreased and at the beginning the leadership of the official independence movement shifted to the Social Democratic majority in Parliament.

After the elections in October 1917 the responsibility fell to the advocates of independence in the non-socialist majority in Parliament and they too were mainly Finnish-speakers. The participation of Swedish-speakers on the side of the legal government in the Civil War exceeded their relative proportion of the population. This in turn tended to limit support for the rebellion among the entire Swedish-speaking population. The Swedish People's party joined the monarchical faction after the war and worked actively on its behalf. Georg Schauman (1870–1930), a member of Parliament, was the only representative of the Swedish People's party to support the republicans. He served the cause as a tactician and publicist.

The outcome of the 1919 election showed that the party had acted in the interests of the Swedish-speaking electorate and enjoyed their confidence. The concept of monarchy disappeared from Finnish political life once the act establishing a republic was approved in 1919. But a group of individuals – mainly Swedish-speakers – continued to consider monarchy the ideal order of state.

The effects of the independence struggle and the constitutional conflict were most apparent among the Old and Young Finns. Conflicts of principle grew more severe during this period and personal relationships suffered. Both had to be taken into account in competing for positions of party leadership at different levels. But the new alignments did have roots in past developments. The reform programmes that each party approved for elections to the unicameral parliament contained a good many similarities. Young and Old Finns alike adopted progressive stands which included mush of the western democratic tradition. Social and political programmes had much in common. More differences disappeared after the declaration of independence. The non-socialist factions joined in the struggle for the legal order. Certain Young Finns did attempt to arrange a compromise at the end of the rebellion, but they were few in number. The battle had to be fought to the bitter end. There were shades of difference with regard to the treatment of the insurgents, but these cut across party lines. It was largely a question of principle and personal convictions. The desire for revenge was stronger among those from areas that had been under insurgent control than among those who lived elsewhere in Finland.

Conflicts arose concerning German aid during the final phase of the war and they grew more severe during the postwar period of German orientation. The struggle between monarchists and republicans soon became more important. The monarchists appealed so strongly to Germany that the republicans grew cautious. The liberals were sympathetic toward the West and hoped Finland could remain neutral and thereby avoid losing the support of the western allies. On the other hand the monarchists were convinced of the advantages of cooperation with Germany. Other points of view would simply have to give way. Thus the stands taken by Old and Young Finns on the form of government represented a watershed. Individuals in both parties were rapidly becoming estranged from one another.

Ståhlberg kindled the conflict with a letter published after the liberation of Helsinki in which he outlined the future of the independent republic. The monarchists replied at the beginning of May with a public statement signed by the most important figures in both the Swedish People's party and the Finnish party and the leaders of the Young Finn party. The conflict flared up in Parliament during the summer and autumn when the form of government was deliberated and the king chosen. The situation became so acute that anyone taking part in political life was forced to take a stand. Although the question of monarchy did not come up for final discussion before the defeat of Germany, personal relations had already deteriorated beyond repair. Representatives of both factions met to form two new parties. The lines were drawn between monarchists and republicans. The former became the National Coalition party,[1] the latter the National Progressive party. The proportion of the Young Finn leadership joining the Conservative party exceeded that of Old Finn leaders joining the Progressive party. The outcome of the 1919 elections revealed a decline in support for the coalition since both parties gained approximately one-eighth of the

[1] Hereafter called the Conservative party.

seats. Even more significant was the fact that new parties lost votes to the Agrarian Union, whose support increased by over 50 % on the 1917 elections.

The Agrarian Union owed its success in the 1919 elections to the straightforward stand it had taken on independence. Members of the Union joined the independence movement at an early stage. They worked with the advocates of independence and the Social Democrats in the summer of 1917 to pass the "power law". The Union's position as a mediator between the bourgeois and Social Democratic factions of the movement was shaky after the elections of the same year, but gained strength after the Bolshevik revolution. At that point the Union sided with the rest of the non-socialists. Two Agrarian Union representatives, Kyösti Kallio and E.Y. Pehkonen, were members of the Senate that declared Finland's independence and they enjoyed the unanimous support of the party. The Agrarian Senators resigned in the summer of 1918 when Paasikivi adopted a monarchist line. The party itself unwaveringly fought for the republican cause. In addition to the reason mentioned above, the Agrarian Union's success was also very likely due to a defection from the Social Democratic fold on the part of poor people in the countryside that had opposed the rebellion.

Despite its size the party was still somewhat politically immature. The party's representatives in Parliament, including some of the leaders, were self-taught farmers with neither sufficient experience nor sufficient prestige to carry much weight in politics. Farmers did not consider themselves the equals of the cultural elite making up the leadership of the other non-socialist parties. Alkio, the party leader, was an exception but even he seemed more like a popular leader than a member of the government.

The Social Democrats continued to press for reforms during the period of rather complex politics that preceded the outbreak of the First World War. Despite their activism, they were steadfast in their refusal to take part in government. Autocracy and repression directed against labour organizations determined their attitudes toward Russia. Consequently the Social Democratic party was the most anti-Russian faction and Russian revolutionaries received shelter and support from Finnish Social Democrats. Opposition to Russia continued throughout the First World War – there was even some cooperation with those who advocated independence, e.g. in the Jaeger movement. The Social Democratic party had a majority in Parliament when the pace of political life in Finland quickened after the March Revolution in Russia. Social Democrats had primary responsibility for political decisions. The coalition Senate made up of representatives of all parties and headed by the Social Democrat Oskari Tokoi was prepared to introduce radical reforms including universal suffrage in municipal elections and the eight-hour day. Revolutionary stirrings in the summer and the ascendancy of extremist elements within the ranks of the Social Democratic party broke down the basis for cooperation. Although the Social Democrats did not approve the dissolution of Parliament by the Russian Provisional government they did take part in the elections of October 1917 and were defeated.

As long as they had a majority in Parliament, the Social Democrats believed that both far-reaching reform and independence – perhaps even the establishment of a socialist state – could be achieved by parliamentary means. This opportunity was lost in the October elections. In the new revolution that broke out a little more than a month after the elections and brought the Bolsheviks to power, extremist elements in the Social Democratic party found an example to follow. Moderate leaders had either been pushed aside during preparation for the elections or had decided against running. After the elections power shifted rapidly to radical elements that were ready to take action. The party machinery thus formed the organization for the uprising that began in January 1918. Local party leaders either joined the Red Guards as a matter of principle or out of a sense of solidarity with fallen comrades. Although the party did not officially take responsibility for the events of the Civil War – the supreme authority had rested with the People's Delegation – party leaders did participate and as a result the organization was a shambles at the end of the war. The party simply ceased to exist. Its representatives in Parliament were either imprisoned or hesitant to make an appearance, fearing arrest.

Moderate Social Democrats, who had remained aloof during the rebellion, condemned violence. Under the leadership of Väinö Tanner (1881–1966) they outlined a new programme for the party, relying heavily on the Swedish model. They stressed parliamentary means and peaceful progress. This alone would guarantee the working class lasting prosperity. Both humanitarian and tactical considerations led them to act forcefully on behalf of the imprisoned insurgents. They demanded rapid consideration of the insurgents' case, release of the vast majority of prisoners who had merely followed along, and an end to the prison camps. Later on they also called for pardons. In autumn 1918 they succeeded – despite interference by officials – in reviving the party press so necessary for political action. The party was re-established in December of the same year. The Social Democrats made far-reaching conclusions about the split in Finnish society in 1918. Alongside the party organization they formed their own educational, athletic, youth, and women's organizations and founded a cooperative movement.

The Social Democratic party consolidated its position rapidly and gained strength to fight off both pressure from the right and the infiltration tactics of the Communists, who concentrated on taking over the labour movement's press. After the dissolution of Parliament at the end of 1918 the Social Democrats had an opportunity to test their popularity with the electorate. The March elections showed a considerable decline in support for the party. The differences of opinion concerning the use of violence mentioned above, a lack of organization, and fear of pressure from the winning party all contributed. Despite the odds, the Social Democrats took 40 %, or 80 seats, the same number they obtained in elections for the first unicameral Parliament held 12 years previously.

The most important task before Parliament – ever since the March Revolution – was to determine the new form of government. The problem was a constitutional one, and a five-sixths majority in Parliament was necessary for rapid passage. The former supporters of monarchy controlled one-fourth of the seats and were strong enough to block rapid passage of these constitutional changes. Since the necessary constitutional changes had to be made immediately, and the dissolution of Parliament and new elections seemed expedient, the minority had to be permitted its say.

There was general agreement on the basic course to be taken. The nation clearly wanted a republican form of government. The principal source of discord concerned the division of power, in particular the authority to be granted to the president. The goal of the right-wing minority in Parliament was a strong state and restrictions on the role those responsible for the rebellion of 1918 could play in politics. Democratic elections tend to emphasize Parliament's authority and the Parliament elected in 1916 had done much to frighten the right. The answer was a strong president to counterbalance the power of the legislative branch.

The left favoured Parliament as a matter of principle. The people must be able to exert a direct influence on politics. Tactics were also involved. There was general suspicion that the representatives of that segment of the population which had recently taken part in the rebellion would not be allowed to serve in the government. Parliament provided an opportunity to work free of pressure. Therefore the authority of the legislative body should be expanded; Parliament should elect the president, for example. Only part of the centre joined the left in support of these views.

In order to ensure rapid passage of the constitutional changes, the republican majority was forced to compromise with the right. Further deliberations on the division of power were the result. Agreement was reached on a process whereby three hundred electors woud be chosen in separate elections. These electors would then choose the president. Thus the authority of the head of state came directly from the people, bypassing Parliament. The compromise proved flexible. In times of crisis when affairs of state have called for decisive action on the part of the president and cabinet, the balance of power has shifted in favour of the government without violating either the spirit or the letter of the constitution. During periods of peaceful development when social, educational, and economic reform have had priority, power has shifted back to Parliament. The people have remained throughout the basic source of authority. Parliament is the most important organ of state and the people surrender their authority to it for a specified period of time by means of elections. Then come the president of the republic and the government. The president, by virtue of the authority he receives from the electors, shares the executive power with the government, which in turn enjoys the confidence of Parliament.

Using the extensive authority afforded by the constitution when he served as regent, Mannerheim might simply have left unconfirmed the constitutional changes passed by Parliament. Relying on the prestige that was his as commander of the government forces he would have had the authority needed to ignore the will of Parliament in internal affairs. His opposition to the German orientation afforded him the strength needed in foreign affairs. At the urging of his advisers Mannerheim actually considered this course of action. In the end he declined and confirmed the new form of government on July 17, 1919. The vast majority of the nation had cast its vote for a republic and the leaders of the Conservative party refused to cooperate in a coup d'etat.

Authority rests with the people under the republican form of government established in 1919. While in session, Parliament exercises this authority and the government is in turn responsible to Parliament. Finland became a republic with a democratically elected Parliament. The head of state, the president of the republic, holds the supreme executive authority and is chosen by the people through a system of indirect elections.

A presidential election with considerable importance for future political development followed the passage of the new constitution. Since the nation had already gone to the polls to elect a new Parliament in the same year, the legislative body chose the president in accordance with the constitution. There were two candidates: General Mannerheim and Ståhlberg, the leader of the republican front and the president of the Supreme Administrative Court, which was established in 1918. Ståhlberg participated in the heated controversy over the form of government and consequently enjoyed considerable prestige. But his supporters included some whose politics differed from his own. They were unwilling to see Mannerheim remain as head of state and accepted Ståhlberg as the lesser of two evils.

Sharp differences of opinion came out in Parliament, although there was no election campaign. Mannerheim had the unanimous support of the right. Rightist members of Parliament considered him the only person capable of guiding the republic along the course they favoured. Ståhlberg had the support of the Social Democrats, whose chief objective was to get Mannerheim out of the way. The Agrarian Union also sided with Ståhlberg as did the Progressive party which Ståhlberg himself had led. Ståhlberg won by a vote of 143 to 50.

Thus constitutional reform paved the way for further political development. As president, Ståhlberg used his theoretical knowledge of jurisprudence and his political experience to increase the prestige of the newly founded republic.

CHAPTER VII

From the Founding of the Republic to the Crisis of Democracy

Finland now had a new Constitution and began to develop her political system on the basis of it. Numerous conflicts still divided the country. Part of the nation had fought against the legal government and gone down in defeat. The consequences of the struggle – the trials and sentences – widened the split between victor and vanquished and encouraged suspicion and bitterness toward the state. The dispute between monarchists and republicans also split Finnish society. Personal relationships – particularly between politicians – became so strained during the constitutional struggle that even those who had fought for the legal government during the Civil War found it difficult to work together and of course these individuals bore primary responsibility for leading the country. Those who were defeated in the constitutional struggle felt that credit was due to them for winning the Civil War. They were embittered when this achievement provided no political influence. They doubted that independence could be preserved under the new system once Mannerheim had been pushed aside.

1.

Language was another source of conflict. Competition between the two language parties declined when national existence itself was threatened during the first era of oppression. The conflict remained in the background throughout the First World War and the Civil War when attention was focused on basic political rights. Neither did language have a decisive effect on the Jaeger movement even though most of the insurgents were Finnish-speaking. New legislation on Finland's two official languages became essential once the country gained independence and established its own legislative body. The Swedish-speaking minority enjoyed privileges inherited from the Swedish period. The majority had fought these privileges in the name of equality for the Finnish language. The adoption of a unicameral system weakened the position of the linguistic minority; now representation in Parliament corresponded to the actual size of the Swedish-speaking population. Swedish-speaking politicians reacted in 1919, founding a council of their own. Later in the same year they proposed a union of the four Swedish-speaking regions to be headed by a governor. These efforts to safeguard Swedish culture did not bear fruit and were actually unnecessary; new laws on language would merely ensure fair treatment for Finnish-speakers. In any event, the final solution depended on the Finnish-language majority in Parliament.

The Social Democrats viewed the Swedish-speaking minority with considerable favour, due both to basic principles and the bilingual nature of the party. After independence, public opinion in Sweden also exerted considerable influence. Sweden followed the language controversy closely and defended the status of the Swedish language. As a result of its stand in the controversy, the Finnish Social Democratic party received considerable support from Sweden in the struggle for its rights that took place after the Civil War. Sharp criticism of the actions of Finnish officials was voiced in Sweden. But the leading politicians of the Finnish-language parties were moderate. A nation in Finland's position could not afford permanent political tension arising from linguistic differences. The bitterness caused by the conflict had to be forgotten; a just solution to Finland's language controversy was in order. This was also the position of Professor E.N. Setälä (1864–1935). Appointed professor of Finnish language and literature in 1893, Setälä fought for improvement in the status of Finnish in the university. But despite his role in the struggle, Setälä was basically a liberal and took a favourable attitude toward the Swedish-speaking minority. Thus the final solution protected the rights of the Swedish language.

According to the 1919 Constitution, Finnish and Swedish were the official languages of the republic. Every Finnish citizen was to have the right to use his mother tongue in courts of law and in dealings with public officials. Provisions for supplying public documents in the language of each citizen's choice were also made. Swedish had been the language of state – for example in government offices – and the new legislation quite naturally reduced its importance. This irritated Swedish-speaking citizens. On the other hand, implementation of the reform proceeded slowly and Finnish-speakers – students in particular – worked to accelerate the process. The conflicts that arose in drafting the language act led to a renewal of the language conflict in the 1920s.

2.

Finland's foreign policy remained a major source of discord. Attitudes based on emotion often determined the views of the uninitiated on foreign policy; the same failing was frequently apparent in the positions taken by politicians. Finnish foreign policy had a distinctly ideological basis; the nature of the political system or the ruling party in a particular country often determined attitudes toward it. The memory of past events also played an important role; this was especially true in relations with Russia and Germany. In anti-Communist circles the new Russia bore the burden of guilt for the sins of the old. Bourgeois circles in Helsinki were ever willing to express their gratitude for German aid received during the Civil War but they gave little thought to the ends Germany sought or the means she employed. Neither did they think what the consequences were for Finland. The same aid was a considerable inconvenience when the left had responsibility for foreign policy; Germany's role in the white victory was not forgotten.

Normal relations were established with all the victorious powers after the 1919 elections. Great Britain and the United States of America recognized Finnish independence in May 1919. Work on a new world order was under way and there was general interest in the course of events inside Russia. The victors condemned the Russian revolution and made plans to overthrow the Bolshevik regime. Finland took part in the planning.

Western efforts to intervene in Russia were based on the following factors: 1. the Russian counter-revolutionary forces backed up by former Czech prisoners of war, 2. the bridgehead held by the western allies in northern Russia, 3. military intervention launched from Poland and the Baltic countries, and 4. Finland, which had blocked the spread of Bolshevism and whose head of state was a general with considerable knowledge of Russia.

In 1919 the Russian counter-revolutionary forces and the officers that led them were still a source of hope in the West. The newly independent countries which had previously made up the Russian empire's western borderlands sought support from the western powers and were prepared to join the struggle against the Soviet government. The troops that landed in northern Russia in 1918 formed a bridgehead and the counter-revolutionary forces planned to make use of it. Revolutionary Russia was surrounded by hostile armies and Finland's position was important.

Although both France and Britain had important commercial interests in Russia and sought to secure repayment of substantial war loans, the prospect of a new war was not very attractive. The trials both nations had experienced in the World War increased the desire for peace. The ministries of war in Britain and France were much more determined to encourage Finland to participate in the struggle against Bolshevism. There were, of course, influential people in Finland who felt independence was in danger as long as the Bolsheviks were in power. Despite the belief held in these circles that the regime would eventually fall victim to its own violence, many saw advantages in intervention. Finnish participation might even pave the way for territorial expansion. Plans were made to take Petrograd. Mannerheim, then serving as regent, backed this approach. The general sought western aid in order to continue what he considered his task in world history: to defeat Communism in cooperation with the leaders of the Russian counter-revolutionary forces.

Mannerheim's defeat in the presidential elections undermined these plans. He remained in constant touch with interventionist circles in the West after his resignation. The general presented them with his programme; he called for a military campaign which would remove all the dangers threatening Finland from the east. Finland was to remain at war until Russia had a government which the rest of Europe could accept. In a letter he delivered to President Ståhlberg, which he subsequently made public, Mannerheim urged the Finnish government to initiate an attack on Petrograd. The appeal had no effect; the chances for success were considered minimal. The western powers were losing interest and the counter-revolutionary leaders were fighting among themselves to determine who was to save Holy Russia. The latter were unable to agree on a common strategy and the Red Army won victory after victory. Western troops stationed in Murmansk started to withdraw at the end of 1919 and the former western borderlands began to sue for peace. Germany had mediated peace feelers between Finland and Russia in the summer of 1918. At that time, however, Finland made substantial territorial demands. Partly due to these demands and partly due to the growing strength of the Soviet government, these negotiations were broken off. Finland was forced to reassess the situation and come to terms with totally different conditions.

3.

The Soviet government offered to make peace with the western borderlands in 1919 with the aim of reducing some of the pressure. An offer was also made to Finland in September of the same year. The Finnish government and a parliamentary majority, however, argued that negotiations could not begin without the cooperation of the other states that were in a similar position. The Soviet government renewed its offer at the beginning of 1920, and the Baltic countries responded favourably. Estonia concluded a treaty in February, Lithuania in July, and Latvia in August. In each case the terms of peace were generous.

The Social Democrats were prepared to normalize relations once the chances for peace looked promising. Uprisings occurred in East Karelia in conjunction with counter-revolutionary operations there. Volunteers from Finland participated, equipped with arms obtained from the Finnish army. Social Democrats opposed these efforts and called for votes of no confidence to prevent the dispatch of aid. They used similar means to pressure the government into peace negotiations. These developments – the conclusion of peace between the Soviet government and Estonia and the opening of talks with the other Baltic States – led the Finnish government to appoint a peace delegation in May 1920. The right still hoped for a white victory in Russia and kept a close watch on efforts to crush Bolshevism abroad, particularly the Polish offensive then in progress. They argued that concluding a treaty under these circumstances was like buying a sinking ship.

Rafael Erich (1879–1946) was prime minister when the government began peace negotiations. Erich, a professor of jurisprudence and international law, had switched his affiliation from Ståhlberg's Progressives to the Conservatives. He had previously been an advocate of passive resistance and joined the independence movement during the World War. Erich was the movement's legal expert; in 1917 he argued that the authority of the grand duke actually belonged to the Finnish Parliament and succeeded in winning over most of his faction. President Ståhlberg had sought the participation of all political parties in the cabinet in view of the disagreements that existed. Failing to accomplish this, he aimed to establish the broadest front possible. Erich, however, succeeded in forming a government composed exclusively of representatives of the non-socialist parties. Unity was nonetheless achieved since the Social Democrats favoured negotiations and the Erich government accepted the Soviet offer. As a result, members of all parties served as negotiators.

Paasikivi was named chairman of the delegation. He had both experience in Russian affairs and the confidence of the Social Democrats. Although he had joined Svinhufvud in support of a German orientation two years before, his past did not prove a liability, as relations between Germany and Russia were improving at this time. The government appointed him head of the delegation since the most strident opponents of talks were on the right. Paasikivi's affiliation with the Conservatives was to help soothe that segment of the population which was wary of any attempts to make peace with Russia. Aided by Paasikivi and Väinö Tanner, the Social Democratic representative, the delegation brought its work to a conclusion by the end of September.

Peace talks began on June 10, 1920 in the university town of Tartu in neutral Estonia. Both groups opened by demanding more than they could ever expect to receive. The Finns sought territorial expansion. The Russians resisted and demanded economic concessions. After considerable bargaining, Petsamo remained a bone of contention. In the 1860's Finland had agreed to Russian annexations on the Karelian isthmus in return for Petsamo. The tsarist government had simply "forgotten" its promise. In the agreement concluded with the People's Delegation this matter was corrected and at Tartu the Russians agreed to grant Finland an outlet on the Arctic Ocean. They did, however, retain a base on the shore of the Gulf of Petsamo.

Finland made concessions with regard to East Karelia, the other major source of disagreement. The municipalities of Repola and Porajärvi – formerly on the Russian side of the border – remained under Finnish jurisdiction after the suppression of the uprisings among the Finnish-speaking population of East Karelia. The people in these two districts were accustomed to Finnish administration and expected to remain part of Finland. The Finnish peace delegation favoured striking a bargain. But a majority in Parliament with the support of the President tried to persuade the Russians to give up these areas. The Russians refused, threatening to break off negotiations. Russian persistence and fear of a general strike at home led the government to retract its demands. The treaty was signed on October 14, 1920. Finland received the Petsamo district. Otherwise the border was that of autonomous Finland in 1812. Finland agreed to withdraw her troops from Repola and Porajärvi and these municipalities became part of the East Karelian autonomous area which in turn was granted a certain degree of national self-determination.

The wisdom of the government's tactics in forming the delegation were apparent when the treaty came before Parliament; only the most extreme nationalists and opponents of Bolshevism spoke against it. Mannerheim was one of the latter and bitterly reproached his own confidant in the negotiations, Rudolf Walden (1878–1946). The Peace of Tartu became the rallying cry of the extreme right-wing opposition to Communism and Russia as political tension increased at the beginning of the 1930s. These elements denounced it as a disgrace; it was a treaty that revealed the rottenness of parliamentary government. Combined with increased tension all over the world, these attitudes strengthened suspicion of Finland in the Soviet Union.

4.

Åland islands hindered the development of better relations with Sweden after Finland obtained her independence. Russian sovereignty in Åland was limited and fortifications in the archipelago were prohibited according to the terms set by the Congress of Paris in 1856, at the end of the Crimean War. At the outbreak of the World War all the powers that played a major role in the Congress – with the exception of Prussia – were allied with Russia. An end to the restrictions was in the interests of the anti-German coalition. While Russia was in the throes of revolution, Åland had no master. It became Finnish territory after the declaration of independence. Finland was unable to establish its own sovereignty or guarantee the archipelago from attack and the war threatened to spill over into the northern Baltic. At this point Sweden began to feel that its own security was endangered, and occupied the islands. The archipelago became militarily significant when Germany sent troops to Finland. The Germans needed Åland in order to secure passage for their own troops to Finland and keep the lines of supply open. They occupied the islands following the Swedish withdrawal.

After Germany's defeat Sweden demanded Åland – an indication that her occupation was more than a mere defensive operation. A popular movement developed in Åland at the end of 1917 in support of Sweden's foreign policy. National ties and uncertainty about Finland's future were the basis for the movement. Trade relations with Sweden had been close in the Russian period and the people of Åland feared they would suffer discrimination at the hands of the Finnish majority.

Finland used all the diplomatic means at her disposal to frustrate the separatist movement. Ståhlberg discouraged any bargaining that would weaken Finnish sovereignty in the area and forbade Finnish diplomats to consent to a settlement arranged by the great powers. In the summer of 1920 the leaders of the separatist movement were arrested and sentenced to jail. At the same time Finland passed legislation granting Åland autonomy and guaranteeing the preservation of Swedish nationality. The Swedish-speaking population elsewhere in Finland was prepared to use the Åland issue to secure its own national interests. But Swedish-speakers also supported Finnish sovereignty in the area and their contribution in keeping Åland part of Finland was significant.

The Åland question came before the newly established League of Nations. The League investigated the matter and decided in favour of Finland on the condition that Åland's autonomy be expanded. Finland agreed, and also consented to the re-establishment of the ban on fortification stipulated by the Congress of Paris. Thus Åland became neutral territory. Despite the efforts of the League in settling the dispute, Åland was a sore point until the 1930s; the Ålanders themselves were dissatisfied as were those in Sweden who had backed unification. Public opinion in Finland condemned the Ålanders' "treason" and there was sharp criticism of Sweden's attempt to expand while Finland was fighting for her very existence. For many years Finland maintained an attitude of watch and wait toward her western neighbour.

Bitterness towards Sweden went even further; many resented Sweden's refusal – in accordance with her neutral foreign policy – to offer Finnish youth an opportunity for military training during the World War and the sympathy Sweden's influential Social Democratic Labour party had shown toward the insurgents in the Finnish Civil War. Public opinion in Sweden also supported the struggle of Finnish Social Democrats for their rights in the aftermath of the Civil War. Those Finns who had fought to put down the rebellion considered this unwarranted interference in Finland's internal affairs and remained somewhat cool toward Sweden. Sentiment of this kind gradually faded away as conditions changed.

Finland's linguistic conflict proved more durable; it flared up again in the 1920s and continued into the following decade. Swedish public opinion once again supported the demands of Swedish speakers as it had in the 19th century. Right-wing Finnish-speakers also regarded this action as interference in Finland's internal affairs. These differences dampened enthusiasm among educated Finns for cooperation among the Scandinavian countries, a policy recommended by both common sense and historical development.

5.

The security and national integrity of small countries, whether their independence was of long standing or a recent achievement, kept those responsible for foreign policy busy. The great powers had shown abundant disregard for the rights of small independent states, particularly when the interests of the former were at stake. Regaining lost territory and the expansion of existing borders were the main objectives. Intricate diplomatic manœuvring was employed and when diplomatic means were exhausted force was applied.

Estonia, Lithuania, Latvia, Finland, and Poland broke away from Russia in the aftermath of the World War. Poland aspired to great power status and had been more persistent than the others in trying to wring concessions from Russia. She waged war with varying success against Russia in 1920 and received French aid in her efforts to expand eastward.

All these border states sought primarily to preserve their independence. It was generally believed in diplomatic circles both on the Continent and in Scandinavia that Russia considered the annexation of these states a strategic necessity. If Russia should become a great power once again, their sovereignty would be in danger. The future was not promising. If Soviet power in Russia remained, which the governments of the border states considered unlikely, the Moscow-based Comintern's programme of world revolution would pose an even greater threat. On the other hand, if the white forces won, they would demand a restoration of the pre-1914 borders of "Holy Russia".

Plans for an alliance of these countries were made in 1922. All of them feared Russia, regardless of the type of government in power there. A border dispute prevented friendly relations between Poland and Lithuania, and the latter was excluded from the plans. The concept of an alliance was advanced by Poland. Polish ambitions made the smaller states wary. Poland wanted diplomatic influence in both eastern and central Europe; the rest of the states were uninterested in the latter. A defensive agreement was signed. The alliance was not directed against any state. Its aim was merely to guarantee mutual aid in the event that the Soviet Union should attack one of the members of the alliance. Foreign Minister Rudolf Holsti signed the treaty in Warsaw on behalf of President Ståhlberg.

When the treaty came before Parliament it was immediately apparent that a substantial majority of the representatives opposed it, mainly the Social Democrats and the right. Both groups had doubts about Poland. Its foreign policy was uncertain and belligerent; unresolved conflicts remained in the east and in the west where areas ceded by Germany at Versailles, such as the Polish corridor, contained the seeds of future strife. Finland had no business becoming involved in the uncertainties of Polish foreign policy. The left felt the treaty was directed against the

Soviet Union and was a breach of Finland's neutral foreign policy. Sympathy for Germany left its mark on the discussion; the right was well disposed to Germany because of the aid given in 1918 and the Social Democrats because of the role then played by Social Democrats in the German government.

References to cooperation between the borderlands with the aim of increasing security were made again, at the end of the 1920s. Students also advocated cooperation of this kind and maintained ties with student organizations in Estonia, Latvia, and Lithuania. But despite these sentiments, the position taken by Parliament continued to set the course of Finnish foreign policy. This stand took on even more significance as the strength of the Soviet Union grew. Finland sought increasingly to avoid any action that might appear to be directed against her eastern neighbour.

Finnish diplomacy groped at the same time for a new foreign policy. Switzerland's internationally recognized neutrality offered possibilities. Finland should proclaim her permanent neutrality and obtain guarantees from the great powers. But this did not suit Finland's geographical position and was simply unrealistic. Finland did not benefit from a balance of power among the larger states surrounding it as did Switzerland. Proposals for the neutralization of the Baltic Sea suffered from the same weakness; they simply did not suit a world dominated by the great powers. Russia had been pushed back to the far end of the Gulf of Finland and Germany was weak. Poland, the "breastpocket" power, had only the most tenuous link to the sea – the corridor obtained from Germany at Versailles. The other Baltic states were small. Peace and neutralization were in their interest; at least this was the general view.

The establishment of the League of Nations in 1920 evoked a favourable response in Finland. Finland considered the existence of an organization pledged to settle international conflicts by peaceful means extremely important. But doubts also arose. The League had no military force at its disposal to enforce its decisions and unanimity was required before action could be taken. Unanimity on international conflicts was impossible. Doubts increased when it became evident that the victorious powers sought to use the League to maintain supremacy over the defeated. This caused bitterness in Germany and the Soviet

Union which suffered as a result of this exploitation. The suspicions of the neutral countries were aroused and the prestige of the League began to decline. But the League still appeared to be the only organization that might provide some guarantee of security for the smaller countries. A measure of security and the international recognition of Finland's independence that membership brought with it assured widespread support for the League. Finland joined the same year the organization was founded. The benefits of membership became immediately apparent when the League resolved the first issue before it, deciding the Åland question in Finland's favour.

Finland took part regularly in the work of the League of Nations and was even a member of the League's council from 1927 to 1930. But the League accomplished nothing significant in the 1920s. A modicum of hope in the League was maintained artificially until the first few years of the following decade. Dictatorships indifferent to international agreements were on the rise in those countries which were dissatisfied with the Treaty of Versailles.

In searching for an appropriate foreign policy in the early 1920s, Finland did not seek support for territorial aggrandizement. Her main objective was the peace necessary for development at home. She inherited no machinery from the Russian era with which to handle foreign affairs. Requests for the establishment of a Finnish consular network in the 19th century were turned down and autonomy sufficient for an independent foreign policy remained a dream. The Senate in power when independence was achieved maintained a rather simple foreign policy. It sought recognition from foreign powers and filled posts in the newly formed diplomatic corps with individuals who were skilled in foreign languages and who could conduct themselves in public. Svinhufvud made the most important foreign policy decisions or they were made with authority he had granted. Heikki Renvall (1872–1955), one of the Senators who went to Vaasa, took over immediately before the outbreak of the Civil War. Foreign policy assumed much greater importance in the summer of 1918. Otto Stenroth (1861–1939), a bank director, was appointed Finland's first foreign minister, serving in the Paasikivi Senate. Scholars were chosen for the most important diplomatic posts. They found adaptation to their new duties demanding but they did benefit from their prestige as academics. Since the international situation remained stable until the beginning of the 1930s, there were no crises in which Finnish diplomats would have betrayed their inexperience. Conflicts involved in internal reform occupied Finnish politicians in those years.

6.

Relations with the left were a particularly delicate matter. An attempt by left-wing insurgents to overthrow the legal government had recently been put down and a coup planned by extreme leftists who had fled to Russia was discovered during the presidential elections. As long as the powers capable of affecting Finland's status – primarily the Soviet Union and Germany – lacked international influence, unity at home seemed of minor importance. Those politicians whose vision was limited to concern for the problems of today and tomorrow could plan Finland's future although the nation was divided, composed of the rulers and the ruled. There were leaders who had more foresight. They anticipated a world where conflicts of interest between the great powers would again decide the fate of small nations. The experience of past decades boded ill in this respect; the more thoughtful wondered how Finland would survive. Many of Finland's more responsible politicians were on their guard and advocated a policy of conciliation. The right weighed the advantages of conciliation against those of releasing the insurgents from prison. The wisdom of releasing the prisoners immediately was questionable; it might encourage them to start another rebellion. Mannerheim had warned against increasing the forces of disorder in the country, as had many others. Strict adherence to the law in all its severity would undoubtedly increase respect for legality and the existing political system.

Everyone agreed that all those who had merely been drawn into the rebellion should be pardoned. They could not be held responsible for the rebellion. The rank-and-file insurgents who fled to Russia were pardoned according to the terms of the Treaty of Tartu. Similar treatment for those who remained at home was regarded reasonable; even the most extreme forces on the right merely wished to prevent the former insurgents from participating in politics until conditions were stable. Differences of opinion did arise concerning treatment of insurgent leaders and those who had committed criminal acts. Court martials held by government troops during the war pronounced irrevocable sentences just as the insurgents had carried out executions. Courts dealing with treason had sentenced insurgent leaders and those guilty of crimes against the state to death, penal servitude, and prison. Amnesty was the only means of revoking these sentences or reducing them. Should amnesty be granted, and if so, how rapidly? This was the root of the question. The right opposed an immediate amnesty while both the Social Democrats and the Communists – who participated in the 1922 elections as the Socialist Labour party – called for a final settlement at once. President Ståhlberg moved cautiously, stressing the inviolability of law and order, which the insurgent leaders had ignored. As a result the left accused the president and the government of delay; the right censured the former for acting with excessive haste in consenting to the demands of the left. These conflicts might have been resolved during Ståhlberg's term of office without becoming an even more serious burden on Finnish political life if the Communist party, which advocated the same revolutionary programme backed by the insurgents in 1918, had not caused new friction. This friction led to the formation of a right-wing radical movement which shook the foundations of democracy during the term of Lauri Kr. Relander (1883–1942), Ståhlberg's successor.

7.

A nation's economy is the basis for social development. A higher standard of living, increased social welfare, the foundation of educational institutions, and provisions for health care and old-age pensions all depend on the nation's productive capacities. The World War cut off outlets for Finland's foreign trade and led to reliance on Russian markets. These were lost in chaos and revolution and trade did not pick up even after the Soviet government consolidated its power. The reasons were partly economic; recovery in Russia was slow. Political factors also played a role. Dislike for the Soviet government was felt and it in turn showed little interest in foreign markets, except those of

Germany. On the other hand, Finland was successful in winning back the export markets lost during the World War. Industries in the belligerent countries concentrated on the production of arms and other military supplies and the conversion to peacetime production took time. Finland's productive facilities survived the war intact and products of the wood processing, dairy, and meat industries found buyers, primarily in Great Britain and Germany. Economic growth could begin once the period of inflation had passed.

The state's role in business was discussed in the early years of Finnish independence. The resources available and the distances involved necessitated state ownership of both railways and canals. The private sector was simply incapable of undertaking projects of this scale. Forests were Finland's only natural resource, or so people believed in those days and the state owned 40 % of them. Domestic control of forestry throughout Finland was essential. Thus the state sought to buy out foreign-owned wood processing installations and create legislative obstacles to foreign investment. Power was of extreme importance and its production had to remain in Finnish hands. Since the state alone had the resources needed to harness rapids, it sought control over them. The ministry of finance, led by members of the Finnish party, proposed a project of this type while the independence Senate was still in office. A similar trend in favour of the public sector appeared in the crucial field of mining. There was general agreement that public ownership of mineral resources was essential; the state alone seemed capable of exploiting this wealth rationally.

8.

The execution of the 1878 act on military conscription in Finland was interrupted during the first era of oppression. The unconstitutional decrees regarding conscription issued thereafter met with stubborn resistance. Russia became suspicious and eventually disbanded the Finnish forces. The Voluntary Defence Corps formed the backbone of Mannerheim's army, although draftees were also trained on the basis of a conscription act. Officers trained in Russia, non-commissioned officers from Finland's own military forces, and most important of all,

Jaegers who had returned from Germany, commanded both the Defence Corps and the conscripts. Although there was some aversion felt toward the Jaegers and Svinhufvud permitted German officers to help organize the army in 1918, the former took command of the regular defence forces established by the conscription act of 1922. Former Russian army officers served in upper echelon duties for only a few years. The act of 1922 provided for a "cadre" system. This meant compulsory military service for all male citizens. Differences of opinion arose while the act was being discussed in Parliament. The Communists felt that the army was intended for use against the Soviet Union. The Social Democrats favoured disarmament, but since this was obviously impossible, they announced their support for a popular force similar to the Swiss militia.

The Defence Corps was the source of the sharpest conflict. It remained a voluntary national defence force after the war and was joined by a women's auxiliary, the Lotta-Svärd organization. The victors argued that the Defence Corps was an essential safeguard for national security and the existing political system. President Ståhlberg did not agree; he feared that the Defence Corps might become involved in politics and threaten democracy. The President did not confirm the selection of Mannerheim as commander-in-chief during the crisis involving the Corps in the summer of 1918. He was unwilling to give Mannerheim a "private army". Ståhlberg restricted the independence of the Defence Corps and sought legislation that would guarantee their political neutrality and ensure their subordination to the legal government. Both participants in the rebellion and the Social Democratic party continued their opposition. They considered the Defence Corps a "class" army designed to maintain the authority of the bourgeoisie. The attitudes of Social Democrats did not change until the Defence Corps became a permanent army reserve after the Winter War.

9.

Parliament functioned after the Civil War at considerably less than full strength. Although there was no definite quorum, its acts were considered legal in view of the existing circumstances. This was an exceptional state of affairs. Ståhlberg approved it in 1918, but adopted another position as president. Parliament once again lacked a quorum when the Kallio government imprisoned 200 leading Communists, among them all 27 Socialist Labour party M.P.'s. Although a majority in Parliament and half the members of the cabinet argued that Parliament should remain in session, Ståhlberg disagreed. The president, whom the Social Democrats supported by calling for a vote of no confidence, considered dissolution necessary. If Parliament remained in session a dangerous precedent would be set; the government might obtain parliamentary compliance merely by imprisoning a sufficient number of M.P.'s. The Kallio government resigned in January 1924. The ministers were unwilling to involve themselves in conflict with the representatives of their parties in Parliament and aid in its dissolution. Ståhlberg named a caretaker government and called for new elections.

Stable domestic politics required the participation of Social Democrats who adhered to the principles of western democracy. The fact that this group played a significant role between 1919 and 1922 is of considerable significance. Work on a variety of reforms aimed at correcting the defects that had led to the rebellion was begun. Since the Social Democrats were in the minority, the necessary legislation could not have been passed without the support of the non-socialist parties. In accordance with their programmes, and sensing the necessity for national unity, non-socialist governments sought to improve conditions. Since there were no reactionary parties in Finland, work on social, educational, and economic development got off to a good start in the newly independent state. This trend was important for the Social Democrats. When the Communist party began to compete for the support of workers and smallholders, the Social Democrats were able to argue that the parliamentary system could protect the interests of these groups even in the difficult circumstances caused by the events of 1918. Although support for the Social Democrats declined by one-third in the 1922 elections due to Communist competition and remained the same in the next elections, they persisted in their support of Parliament and even participated in government.

Those forces who supported the legal government during the Civil War were far from united. The constitutional struggle, relations with the left, and independent Finland's first presidential elections split their ranks to the extent that cooperation based on a parliamentary majority was difficult to achieve. The government that concluded the Treaty of Tartu was a non-socialist coalition headed by Rafael Erich and remained in power for a year. Conflicts between parties led to a series of minority and caretaker governments until Lauri Ingman (1868–1934), a professor of practical theology, succeeded in uniting the non-socialist forces. Ingman took up the reins of government when Paasikivi resigned and arranged for the elections of 1919 while Mannerheim was serving as regent. This politically skilful theologian enjoyed respect in all circles. He formed a non-socialist majority government in May 1924 that remained in power for ten months. This success was then followed by a series of six minority governments.

The Social Democratic role in government in 1926–27 was a significant step forward. The basis for a non-socialist majority government was lacking. Kyösti Kallio's coalition of Agrarians and Conservatives had foundered by 1926. Fearing what it considered a further deterioration in the status of the Swedish-speaking minority, the Swedish People's party was prepared to work with the Social Democrats to overturn the government but was unwilling to join in forming a new one. Since no other non-socialist party felt it could cooperate with the Social Democrats, Väinö Tanner formed a minority government with members of his own party in December 1926. For the first time the cabinet included a woman. Miina Sillanpää (1866–1952), who had accomplished much in improving the status of working-class women, became the second minister for social affairs.

The significance of the Tanner government lies neither in legislation – in making initiatives it had first to be sure of support in Parliament – nor in its successful efforts to restore the civil rights of the insurgents, both those on probation and those who had served their sentences. The party's role in government demonstrated that the burden of the past was decreasing and that at least when internal circumstances required it, Social Democrats were eligible to take part in the nation's government. This was a victory for those Social Democrats who advocated western democracy. But a role in government also included certain national obligations such as maintenance of the country's defence forces. Responsibilities of this kind provided grist for the mill of radical Social Democrats and the extreme left as well. Tanner was criticized personally for reviewing a parade composed of regular army troops and Defence Corps on May 16, the anniversary of the end of the Civil War. The prime minister was forced to stand in for President Ståhlberg, who was ill at the time. As a result, Tanner found himself excluded from the leadership of the Social Democratic party for four years. The labour movement had come a long way since the Civil War. By consenting to form a government the Social Democrats had exchanged their revolutionary banners for the national colours. Great strides had been taken on the road to national unity, although the gap between Social Democrats and Communists had widened in the process.

The first decade of Finnish independence witnessed a considerable departure from the policies of both extremes, the right and the Communists. The growth in the influence of the centre and left that began with the first parliamentary and presidential elections weakened the right, and consequently those who had played a decisive role in winning independence. Rapid economic, social, and educational development did not lend support to Communist assertions that conditions were steadily deteriorating. Unemployment and the stimulus it provided in all political camps led to a crisis that threatened democracy itself when Relander, a weak-willed individual without a political programme, was elected president in 1925. The centre was solidly behind Ståhlberg, and when the Social Democrats offered their support a second term was a virtual certainty. But Ståhlberg declined to run. In 1919 Ståhlberg felt that he had no legal basis for refusing to run and was elected against his will. Despite the fact that he had frequently stressed the role of the office of president in maintaining continuity, and did not want to set a precedent that might prevent future presidents from serving more than one term, Ståhlberg sought to increase support for the republican system among its opponents by declining to stand for re-election.

10.

The insurgent leaders fled to Russia once defeat for their cause was apparent. They began the rebellion as radical Social Democrats. When they sought to exert influence on events in Finland while remaining in exile, the nature of the Soviet regime prevented them from organizing under the banner of Social Democracy. Competition between Social Democrats and Bolsheviks during the years that led up to the revolution had turned into hostility. After the Bolshevik victory those who refused to conform were denied access to power. Finnish Social Democrats in Russia founded a Communist party in August 1918. In joining the struggle for world revolution the party made its goal the destruction of the existing system in Finland by all the means provided in Marxist–Leninist doctrine, including violence. Since O.W. Kuusinen (1881–1964), the leader of the party, became secretary of the executive committee of the Comintern in 1921, the party's basic policies were formed in Moscow. These policies did not take into account changes in Finnish conditions and Communists operating in Finland used their own judgment in the beginning. Once the party leadership received precise information it adapted its programme accordingly and took control of operations in Finland.

Public opinion in Finland considered Finnish Communists the hirelings of Moscow. An unceasing series of trials in which Communists were accused and sentenced for espionage lent support to this belief. The interests of the Finnish Communist party and the Soviet Union were regarded as identical: the overthrow of the existing system by force of arms and the destruction of the country's independence. This was the source of opposition to the party. The party was permitted to take part in the elections of 1922 as the Finnish Socialist Labour party. It was banned under this name, but participated in the elections of 1924, 1927, and 1929 as the Workers' and Smallholders' party. These events led to the organization of opposition to Communism that had existed since Finland obtained her independence. The result was the Lapua movement.

The ideological cornerstone of the anti-Communist movement was the preservation of the gains made during the Civil War. Force was the only answer to revolution and threats to Finnish independence. From the very beginning the movement also meant a struggle for the Christian faith. Right-wing elements that had suffered neglect, peasants who had taken part in the Civil War on the side of the government, and workers who had served in the Defence Corps only to experience

Communist harassment on the job made up the hard core of the movement. Discontent and unemployment caused by the world-wide depression that began in 1929 were also exploited. The methods used were familiar. They were all part and parcel of previous mass unrest in Finland and included terror directed against both individuals and large groups of opponents, demonstrations, pressure on the government and Parliament, and rebellion.

The Lapua movement began in November 1928 when a group of local citizens stripped the red shirts off Communists in the small town of Lapua in west-central Finland. People who believed they could put an end to Communist activity by means of a legal mass movement signed on in the beginning. They soon found themselves in a minority. Resort to violence was made again when extremists took control. The Communist press in Vaasa was destroyed in March 1930. Communists were also beaten up and later on some were murdered. In July 1930 the personal inviolability of members of Parliament was broken when two Communist members of the constitutional committee were kidnapped at the house of Parliament. In the same month the deputy speaker of the house, Väinö Hakkila (1882–1958), a Social Democrat, was kidnapped and subjected to abusive treatment. On the 10th anniversary of the signing of the Treaty of Tartu the former President Ståhlberg and his wife were kidnapped.

Pressure was exerted on the government and Parliament at mass meetings. These meetings drew up sharply worded statements demanding an end to Communist activity which were then delivered to the government. Large demonstrations were also part of the campaign; the most important of these was the march on Helsinki by 12,000 farmers in July 1930. The right-wing press and to some extent that of the Agrarian Union supported these efforts.

The movement brought results. The president was favourably inclinded, considering it a healthy expression of the nation's instinct for survival. Beginning in August 1929, the third Kallio government took action to restrict freedom of the press and association for Communists. Parliament passed legislation to prevent Communist organizations once banned from reorganizing under another name. Parliament convened on July 1, 1930 and gave the government a vote of confidence on the following day, although the government immediately requested permission to resign. Due to pressure from the Lapua movement and the acquiescence of the President, permission was granted.

Svinhufvud had come to an understanding with the anti-Communist movement and President Relander assisted in drawing up the list of ministers. A new government was named on July 4. This government responded on the following day to the kidnapping of the Communist members of the constitutional committee by imprisoning the entire Communist parliamentary group. When the government did not obtain the broad powers it requested for suppressing Communism, only the minority prevented the matter from being declared urgent, and Parliament was dissolved. The authorities kept Communists from standing for election. Opposition to Communism and cooperation between the non-socialist parties was the keynote of the campaign. The left went down to defeat, Social Democratic representation declining from 82 to 66. As a result, the Social Democrats could not even muster the one-third majority needed for blocking constitutional change. With this balance of power, Parliament approved the government's anti-Communist legislation without amendment and the Communist party ceased to function openly. The movement had achieved its original goal. Even Ståhlberg contributed to this end, making good his promise to his electors.

The anti-Communists still wished to consolidate their gains. Prime Minister Svinhufvud won the approval of Parliament for the anti-Communist laws and was the movement's choice for president. He backed the movement and was the only candidate who could beat Ståhlberg. The latter had the support of the Progressives, the liberal Swedish-speakers, and the Social Democrats. Since the campaign was a contest between Svinhufvud and Ståhlberg, neither the Agrarian Union nor the Social Democrats were able to arouse their voters. The turnout for previous presidential elections had been lighter than that for parliamentary elections. Voters in the first presidential elections numbered some 250,000 less than those in the parliamentary elections held the previous year. This time 836,000 voters took part as opposed to 1,130,000 in the 1930 parliamentary elections.

Svinhufvud won by a vote of 151 to 149 as the Lapua movement and the Defence Corps exerted a certain degree of pressure on the electors.

11

The anti-Communists misinterpreted the situation and overestimated their own strength. Reliance on increasingly unrestrained violence, assassination, and kidnapping turned many of the original supporters against the movement. As it felt its strength, the movement sought to deny political influence to all those with a Marxist orientation, including the Social Democrats. The latter fought back hard. When the extra-parliamentary pressure exerted by the anti-Communist movement appeared to be sweeping all the powers of the state before it – the president, the government, and even Parliament, supporters of democracy and parliamentarianism in all parties rose to the challenge. The radical leadership of the movement was not even content with Svinhufvud's performance as president, keeping up the pressure and ignoring the law. It soon aroused the opposition of that hoary veteran of the constitutional struggle, the man the movement itself had elected and whose hostility was the most dangerous of all. The leadership of the movement took up arms against the legal government; this marked the end of its road.

The physical scope of the rebellion was modest. The Social Democratic Labour Association in Mäntsälä planned to hold a meeting on February 27, 1932. Mikko Erich (1888–1948), a doctor of philosophy and candidate of jurisprudence, was to serve as chairman. Erich was a Social Democratic M.P. who had previously represented the Conservative party in Parliament. He was an energetic opponent of the anti-Communist movement. A group of approximately 400 armed men gathered at Mäntsälä to prevent Erich from speaking. They demanded that the sheriff prohibit the meeting. Shooting started when the latter refused. Since shots were also fired at the labour hall, the sheriff broke the meeting up. But the mob did not disperse. Contact was made with the leaders of the Lapua movement who had gathered in Hämeenlinna to follow the events in Mäntsälä. A telegram was sent from Hämeenlinna to the president and the government in which the leaders of the Lapua movement announced that they were unable to "maintain order in the country unless the present government resigns at once and the country's political orientation changes." An additional two hundred men joined the crowd in Mäntsälä and reports about groups of armed men including members of the Defence Corp filtered in from other parts of the country.

The government took action aimed primarily at preventing this force from marching on the capital. An order was made for the immediate arrest of the leadership of the Lapua movement, whereupon the leaders went to Mäntsälä. Dissent appeared within the government. Two Conservative ministers resigned, arguing that there was no cause for the arrests. Svinhufvud replaced them. The president issued a proclamation to the Defence Corps in which he ordered them to "obey the law and their oath" and return home immediately. The commander-in-chief of the Defence Corps refused to read the proclamation over the radio. The minister of defence then made the announcement. Although the government had decided to put down the rebellion, it wanted to avoid bloodshed. Svinhufvud took on the task of restoring order and made a speech on the radio the same day in which he again ordered the insurgents to return home and made the following appeal: "I have fought to maintain law and order all my long life. I will not permit anyone to trample the law under foot and pit one group of citizens against another in armed conflict."

The president's speech dampened the rebels' enthusiasm and the rebellion quickly lost momentum. On March 6 the leaders gave in as the rank and file received permission to return home in accordance with the promise granted. The leaders were sentenced in court and the rank and file was pardoned under the terms of a special act. The Lapua movement was banned. The Patriotic People's Movement (IKL) founded in 1932 carried on the struggle against Marxism and democracy but never obtained any substantial support as a party. In 1933 they won 14 seats at the expense of the Conservatives who retained only 18 of the 42 seats they had won three years earlier. Thus the anti-Communist movement decimated the Finnish-speaking right.

The crisis had reached its climax, but was not yet over. The struggle had been so fierce and the wounds so deep that the restoration of democracy took time. The right was still up in arms and the depression went on. Even with the threat recently posed by the Lapua movement fresh in mind, the defenders of democracy were unwilling to cooperate with each other. The Social Democrats remained isolated. But the prestige gained by Svinhufvud in putting down the rebellion did enhance the powers of the presidency, and this had a decisive effect on government policy.

12.

T.M. Kivimäki (1886–1968), a professor of civil law, won Svinhufvud's confidence. Kivimäki had experience as a civil servant, businessman, M.P., and as minister of internal affairs from 1928 to 1929. His efforts during the Mäntsälä uprising as minister of justice in the government headed by J.E. Sunila from 1931 to 1932 were of particular significance. When the Sunila government resigned due to a disagreement with Svinhufvud concerning measures for easing the effects of the depression, Svinhufvud called on Kivimäki to form a government. In a week's time he appointed the cabinet proposed by Kivimäki – a cabinet that had the narrowest parliamentary support conceivable. Kivimäki enjoyed the support of only 11 Conservative M.P.'s; the rest of the party's contingent declined to take responsibility. Kivimäki used his personal contacts to attract a group of experienced, non-socialist politicians who enjoyed widespread respect. With their help the new prime minister proceeded to reduce tensions and stabilize the economy. He was careful to avoid conflict with the Social Democrats and kept his government in power for nearly four years.

Attempts were made to keep the anti-Communist movement alive after the Mäntsälä rebellion was put down. The Social Democrats held a party convention in Tampere in May 1933. The red banners of the party lined the main street, the site of the convention, and the sports field. Supporters of the Patriotic People's Movement threatened to tear down the flags, and actually did so at the sports field. Members of the Defence Corps who had been called in to maintain order removed the banners from the main street. Social Democrats were assaulted in the riots that followed. Thereafter paramilitary political organizations and the use of party symbols at mass meetings were banned. Legislation to prevent agitation that might prove dangerous to the state and society was passed. Provisions were made to disqualify those guilty of treason from public office for six years and to prohibit school children from participating in political activity.

Improvements in social legislation were also made. Accident insurance for employees, municipal welfare programmes, care for alcoholics and migrants, and child welfare were included in the government's programme. A filibuster frustrated the government's attempt to pass a university act which it had approved in a special session of Parliament. The bill was opposed by Finnish-speaking university students. Demands for a restoration of parliamentary rule grew stronger with time. But Kivimäki's government had the confidence of the president and drew support from either the left or the right, depending on the issue at stake. It was spared a vote of no confidence until 1936. The Kivimäki cabinet resigned after Parliament rejected its bill providing for more stringent punishment of treason by a one-vote margin.

The Social Democrats should have been given a chance to form a government. But Svinhufvud's position was clear. As long as he held office, there would be no Social Democractic ministers. He had not forgotten the events of 1918 and did not let the political development of the Social Democratic party influence his stand. Since Communists and Social Democrats were constantly lumped together by the right, Svinhufvud feared that passions might be aroused once more. Kyösti Kallio formed his fourth government on October 7, 1936. In addition to representatives of the Agrarian Union it included two Progressives and two Conservatives. Rudolf Holsti, recommended by Ståhlberg and supported by the Agrarian Union in the disputes of the 1920s, was named foreign minister.

The new government took office in the middle of the presidential election campaign. Although the Social Democrats backed Väinö Tanner and the Agrarian Union Kyösti Kallio, the contest was actually between Svinhufvud, the incumbent, and Ståhlberg, who was seeking a second term. The situation was similar to that in 1931, although there was an essential difference. Now the Social Democrats considered Svinhufvud's defeat absolutely necessary; the other parties had to take this into account in planning their strategy. The Social Democrats offered to vote for Ståhlberg in the first round. If Ståhlberg was not elected, they would then offer their unanimous support to Kallio. Ståhlberg fell one short of a majority. In the second round the Social Democratic electors voted for Kallio, who obtained 177 votes to Svinhufvud's 104. The Social Democrats had accomplished what they set out to do, as had the right wing of the Swedish People's party, which had sought the defeat of Ståhlberg.

The basis for large-scale cooperation between the Social Democrats and the Agrarian Union was created in negotiations that preceded the presidential election. Social Democratic support grew steadily after the decline brought about by the Lapua movement. Representation in Parliament rose from 66 in 1930 to 78 in 1933 and up to 83 in the 1936 elections. The Agrarian Union lost a mere three seats in the same period, winning 53 in 1936. Thus the "red-green" coalition enjoyed a two-thirds majority in Parliament. Two Progressives joined the coalition; A.K. Cajander (1879–1943), a well-known scientist in the field of forestry, director of the board of forests, and M.P. became Prime Minister and Holsti, who had previously served in the Kallio government, became foreign minister.

Great strides had been made. Instead of a government based on extremely narrow support in Parliament and backed by the president, Finland had a broad-based cabinet with two-thirds of the M.P.'s behind it. This was the widest support any government had enjoyed in the course of Finnish independence. The crisis ended in a period when international tensions were increasing alarmingly and all nations were forced to prepare for the worst.

CHAPTER VIII

The Maelstrom of Great Power Politics

Germany, the Soviet Union and Italy – the powers that either suffered defeat or were denied the fruits of victory in the World War – became important factors on the international scene in the 1920s. All three were dictatorships in the following crucial decade. Japan continued to strive for a larger sphere of influence as she had at the beginning of the 20th century and also grew in international stature. Under the leadership of Benito Mussolini (1883–1945), Italy sought hegemony in the Mediterranean and Near East, and territorial expansion in north-eastern Africa. Mussolini was a Socialist at the beginning of the World War. As soon as war broke out he joined those who demanded intervention on the side of the western allies, against Germany and Austria–Hungary. He fought on the front and then founded the Fascist party which exploited Italian frustration at being denied a share of the spoils. He faced no resistance. Mussolini marched on Rome in 1922, took power, and ruled thereafter as a dictator. The crises Mussolini caused had no more effect on Finland than a distant storm and required nothing more than a stand in the League of Nations and participation in the economic sanctions it passed. Japan's policy on the Asian mainland posed a direct threat to the Soviet Union as it had to Russia during the tsarist era. It also affected Finland's position, albeit indirectly. In contrast, manœuvring on the part of the Soviet Union and Germany always involved Finland's vital interests.

America's withdrawal from European affairs immediately after the First World War meant a shift of responsibility to the leaders of Great Britain and France. It was in their interests to keep Germany and Russia weak. They failed even though they manipulated the League of Nations to serve their ends. This failure led to the creation of a network of alliances aimed at isolating the so-called "have-nots," the powers which were dissatisfied with the Treaty of Versailles. Smaller countries soon found themselves caught in the web, involved in great power conflicts. Two important milestones marked the demise of this policy. Cooperation between Germany and the Soviet Union began in 1922. The first six years of Nazi rule, 1933–1939, destroyed this accord. The economic and military build-up in both Germany and the Soviet Union was the second. Neither large war reparations, the occupation of important industrial areas, nor the fear of armed intervention deterred German recovery. In the case of the Soviet Union, economic development proceeded apace despite the threat of outside intervention and economic isolation. By the mid-thirties both states possessed considerable influence on international affairs. In the 1920s the major political event in the Soviet Union was the rise of Joseph Stalin. Stalin served as a people's commissar from 1917 to 23 and in 1922 became first secretary of the central committee of the Communist party, thereby gaining the key position in the party hierarchy. Stalin made his move after the death of Lenin in 1924. In the ruthless power struggle that followed, Stalin strengthened his hold by defeating one opponent after another: Leo Trotski (1877–1940), the leader of the left opposition, in 1927, and Nikolai Bukharin (1888–1938), the leader of the right opposition, in 1928. Stalin ruled by terror and suspicion reigned at every level. By the middle of the 1930s purges which extended as far as the army were in progress. International developments in the thirties, particular in Germany after 1933, impressed upon Stalin the importance of time for stabilizing conditions at home and for industrialization. Time was needed to build up a heavy industrial base and reorganize the army after the purges; Stalin believed that time was on the side of the Soviet Union.

Adolf Hitler (1889–1945) served at the front line in the First World War, as did Mussolini. Hitler also exploited sentiment against the Treaty of Versailles. The belief that the treaty represented a "stab in the back" was widely held, and Hitler did his best to exploit it. Empire builders have always needed a sense of spiritual superiority and a nation striving for greatness. Austria, Hitler's native country, was too small. He moved to Germany, founded the National Socialist party in 1921, and in 1923 led the unsuccessful putsch in Munich. Hitler was sent to prison and there formulated his political programme in *Mein Kampf*. He continued his work after his release and attracted an increasingly large following with both his programme and his oratory, playing upon the widespread discontent and fear of Communism that existed in Germany. In 1930 the National Socialists won 107 seats in the Reichstag and 230 (out of approximately 600) two years later. In the presidential elections of 1932 Hitler received 12 million votes to Marshal Paul von Hindenburg's 19 million; Hindenburg had served as president since 1925. Hitler became Reichskanzler in January 1933 and head of state in 1934 after von Hindenburg's death. Hitler thereby gained dictatorial power and proceeded to carry out his programme with ruthless efficiency.

Hitler knew the odds. He had no serious opposition at home or abroad, at least until the end of the decade. Once the modernization of the army began, Hitler initiated an unabashed programme of territorial expansion. He achieved immediate success at home, strengthening his domestic appeal as the one leader who could restore Germany to greatness. Elsewhere he aroused fear and brought his enemies together.

1938 was a turning point for the Soviet Union. When Hitler threatened to carve up Czechoslovakia, Stalin offered the aid stipulated in the terms of the alliance between the Soviet Union and France, but Britain and France succeeded in forcing Czechoslovakia to turn over the Sudetenland to Germany. For Stalin the partition of Czechoslovakia was proof that Hitler had begun to carry out the historical task described in *Mein Kampf*, the defeat of Communism and the conversion of southern Russia into a German colony. Soviet diplomacy went to work in those countries within the German sphere of influence which exerted some influence on the course of events in central Europe. These advances were made regardless of social systems or previous attitudes toward Bolshevism. Without really trusting the government of a single state, Stalin employed all the means at his disposal to frustrate any attempt to form an anti-Soviet alliance. In the west the desire to isolate Germany led to increased interest in the growing strength of the Soviet Union. After a period in which the Soviet Union and the western powers cautiously explored each other's intentions, negotiations aimed at blocking German expansion began in the early winter of 1939. Assured of her own bargaining power and convinced of the seriousness of the threat posed by Germany, the Soviet Union felt justified in demanding guarantees throughout the former Russian territories from the Black Sea to the Arctic Ocean. The terms of the alliance would grant the right to march unhindered through all those countries located between the Soviet Union and Germany and the right to occupy them should their governments collaborate with Germany.

The western powers felt that consent would mean the loss of independence for Romania, Poland, Lithuania, Latvia, Estonia, and Finland and the sacrifice of the principle of national self-determination that had meant so much during the First World War. Efforts on the part of the western powers to assess what effect concessions might have on the future and to gain time by prolonging the negotiations proved a mistake; Nazi Germany and the Soviet Union concluded a treaty on August 23, 1939.

For Finland the situation was similar to that after the Tilsit agreement in 1807 when Napoleon I placed Finland in the Russian sphere of influence in return for certain concessions from Alexander I. Hitler made the same concession to the Soviet Union on the eve of the Second World War.

1.

Although the terms of the decision made in Moscow concerning Finland were secret and were part of a deal made by two great powers, they were an outgrowth of relations between the Soviet Union and Finland.

Although documentation of the views of Soviet leaders on foreign affairs from the end of the First World War up to the beginning of the Second is not available, Soviet historians have written about the factors affecting relations with Finland. Despite the lack of access to both Soviet and Finnish archives, the analysis presented here seems conclusive. Decisions in any given period affecting relations between states are most frequently made on the basis of facts that are inadequately understood and on what political leaders term national interest. When opinions about national interest and the validity of the information available differ, serious conflicts of interpretation arise. Different points of departure – the Marxist approach in the Soviet Union and the traditional western approach to history in Finland – also make consensus difficult.

Relations between the Soviet Union and Finland were heading for disaster from the very beginning. The views of the two parties at the Tartu negotiations differed greatly. Agreement was not reached until the talks seemed likely to break up and both parties backed down from their extreme demands. Peace was concluded, but mutual suspicions kept tensions alive. Finland feared the loss of her independence. The Soviet Union feared that Finnish territory might some time serve as the base for an invasion. The German presence in 1918 and plans made by the western allies for cooperation with counter-revolutionary forces as late as 1919 gave credence to this belief. This interpretation was mentioned frequently in the Soviet press and in discussions among diplomats.

Finnish intentions with regard to East Karelia were another source of distrust. "Greater Finland" was not realized between 1918 and 1920 and the Treaty of Tartu confirmed Finland's historical borders. Narrow ultra-nationalist circles branded this a shameful peace. Considerable attention was paid in the Soviet Union to university youth who supported the Greater Finland cause. When it suited the purposes of Soviet diplomacy in the 1930s, Finland's official policy of neutrality and non-involvement in great power conflicts was also termed chauvinistic.

Neither did the Soviet Union forget Finnish participation in plans to overthrow the Bolshevik regime in the aftermath of the First World War. This memory remained fresh throughout the 1920s and 1930s. In the opinion of the Soviet leadership the non-aggression pact signed in 1932 offered very meagre assurance at best. Soviet distrust of Finland increased as the international situation deteriorated.

From 1918 onward, anti-Communist measures taken in Finland were interpreted as a sign of hostility to the Soviet Union. When this attitude became generally known in Finland, hostility toward Communism and fear of the Soviet Union grew. Means were sought to defend Finland, both ideologically and militarily. The Soviet Union interpreted these moves as proof of Finland's aggressive designs. It accused Finland – with a new world war already looming on the horizon – of unwillingness to defend her own neutrality and of a desire to attack the Soviet Union. Soviet leaders did not believe that Finland would undertake an attack alone, although they did fear she would permit the use of her own territory as the base for an invasion by any European ally supported by the United States. Fortifications built in 1939 on the Karelian isthmus were viewed exclusively in this light, although by this time territorial expansion was no longer a motive. Even the Academic Karelian Society, a large student organization which had previously backed the Greater Finland cause, was simply reacting to international tensions and the existing balance of power when it proposed to send volunteers to work on the fortifications. Finland had no designs on Soviet territory; she merely feared the loss of her independence. Soviet historians have argued that work on these fortifications was supported by France, Sweden, Germany, and the United States. In addition, military leaders in Great Britain were also interested in using the Karelian isthmus for an attack on the Soviet Union, particularly against Leningrad, which was situated a mere 32 kilometres from the border.

Both the Soviet press in the autumn of 1939 and later historians have described the mobilization carried out in the middle of October as an indication of aggressive intentions. This mobilization, referred to as "extraordinary manœuvres," could be justified only in the event that outside aid was forthcoming. The balance of power was satisfactory and the actions of the Finnish government would otherwise have been unwarranted.

Relations between Finland and the Soviet Union were put to the test as the international situation became more acute. In the end the two countries reaped the harvest of several centuries of tradition and the diplomatic errors of the preceding two decades.

In the beginning, the western section of the Soviet foreign ministry handled relations with Finland. Later on, in 1921–23, responsibility was shifted to the Scandinavian section. Finland's "borderland" policy led to another shift in 1923; Finnish affairs were then grouped with those of the Baltic countries and Poland. Soviet diplomats took several initiatives with the object of starting a dialogue. In Finland these moves were regarded as an attempt to cut the country off from its natural ties and defensive allies. Failing to understand or perhaps avoiding recognition of its own special status among the countries that broke away from Russia, Finland continued its search for protection from the threat posed by the Soviet Union. Moscow considered all these phenomena part of allied preparation for aggression.

Hostile articles in the Finnish press also lent support to this view. Freedom of the press permitted a constant flow of criticism; impassioned attacks were made against every move made by the Soviet Union from the crushing of the Georgian independence movement at the beginning of the 1920s to the power struggle after the death of Lenin and the purges carried out by Stalin in the 1930s. At one point the Soviet ambassador to Finland claimed that the Finnish press was the most hostile in the world toward his country. The Swedish government maintained a realistic policy toward both Germany and the Soviet Union, although Swedish public opinion swung violently from one extreme to the other. This was not the case in Finland. Articles in the press played a very great role in the decisions and choices made. The press even dictated attitudes toward official Soviet representatives stationed in Helsinki. They were simply isolated.

Finland also shunned the Soviet Union commercially. Finnish exports found a relatively responsive market in the West immediately after the end of the First World War. As a result, the barter agreements offered by the Soviet Union and the difficult negotiations they involved did not appear vital. Nevertheless, Estonia's trade with the Soviet Union was five times greater than that of Finland and Sweden's seven times greater in the interwar period. Moscow could interpret these figures unfavourably; Finland's unwillingness to trade was merely another example of her hostile foreign policy.

Personality also played an important role in foreign policy during the Stalin era. Stalin's personal suspicions and sympathies set the course of Soviet foreign policy. This was particularly true of relations with a small state like Finland, whose strategic significance – except in certain key areas – was minimal.

Viewed from Moscow, Finland appeared to emphasize her anti-Soviet orientation in choosing her leaders. In reality, the most extreme period ended when Svinhufvud was defeated in the 1937 elections. But neither Svinhufvud's successor, Kallio, nor Prime Minister Cajander, moved to repeal the anti-Communist legislation. Likewise, efforts to improve relations with the Soviet Union did not materialize. Holsti, the new foreign minister, did reassess the situation, making a trip to Moscow in 1937. This initiative did not lead any further and Holsti resigned the following year. This appeared to mark the end of the thaw. The immediate cause of Holsti's resignation was an after-dinner speech in which he expressed his hostility to National Socialism. Moscow regarded Holsti's departure as a harbinger of closer relations with Germany, the power that had supported Finland two decades earlier.

Although Holsti's successor, Eljas Erkko (1895–1965), was equally critical of Hitler and his system, as were all Finland's leaders with the exception of the right-wing extremists, Soviet diplomats merely noted that the newspaper *Helsingin Sanomat,* which Erkko owned and edited, had advocated a western orientation since Finland gained independence. In the Soviet Union pro-western sentiment meant anti-Soviet sentiment. Since Erkko's paper, the largest in Finland, was always one of the first to expose the shortcomings of the Soviet system and the consequences of Stalin's dictatorship, the significance of the appointment was clear. Finland was uninterested in building better relations and merely sought to isolate herself further from Moscow.

General Mannerheim was named chairman of the Finnish defence council in 1931. Mannerheim was promoted to the rank of marshal the following year and would probably serve as commander-in-chief in the event of war. He attempted to use his prestige to improve military preparedness for the troubled times he foresaw. Mannerheim's appointment to a position of such importance meant a further strain on relations between the Soviet Union and Finland. In the Soviet Union Mannerheim was regarded as an implacable enemy of Communism and the Soviet state.

On the basis of obvious German intentions, suspicion towards Finland, and the threat confronting Leningrad, the Soviet government privately proposed consultations on the international situation as early as 1938. The Soviet government then demanded permission to fortify Suursaari island. In March 1939 it widened the scope of its demands, requesting a thirty-year lease on Suursaari and Lavansaari islands and of Seiskari and the Tytärsaari islands, all in the Gulf of Finland.

The Finnish government was unaware of disagreements within the Soviet government or of the fall of Foreign Minister Litvinov, the advocate of a staunch anti-German policy, into disfavour. Since the initiative was not made through official diplomatic channels, the Finnish government was wary. There was some suspicion that negotiations on territorial concessions might tip the scales in favour of the right wing Patriotic People's Movement in the 1939 parliamentary elections. Since a balance had not yet been struck between the demands of foreign policy and those of defence, and precise assessments of the international situation had not been made, the government's reply was somewhat inflexible. It took the position that Finland's neutral foreign policy provided sufficient guarantee that an attack on Leningrad would not be launched through Finnish territory. The arms build-up was purely defensive; Finland had no intention of attacking anyone. Thus the Finnish government turned down the private offer of negotiations.

On September 1, 1939, after the signing of the Molotov-Ribbentrop Pact and the outbreak of the Second World War, Finland declared complete neutrality in the state of war existing between Germany and Poland and maintained this stand when France and Great Britain declared war on Germany two days later. Finland now had to face the hard facts and the prospects were none too bright. International support for Finnish independence and the durability of Scandinavian neutrality maintained in the First World War were soon to be put to the test.

The search for a foreign policy that would secure Finnish independence failed in the 1920s and the League of Nations proved ineffectual in the following decade. Finland then turned to economic cooperation with other small, neutral states. Sweden, Norway, Denmark, the Netherlands, Belgium, and Luxemburg agreed to work towards a joint policy on customs duties in 1930. Finland joined them in 1933. These states attempted without success to agree on methods for applying the economic sanctions against Italy called for by the League of Nations after the outbreak of war in Ethiopia. A Scandinavian orientation appeared to offer greater hope for success.

Circles close to Marshal Mannerheim were the source of this initiative. In order to lay the foundations for cooperation with other Scandinavian countries they appealed to the university students to stop the linguistic conflict. The Kivimäki government adopted this line and in 1935 Parliament gave its unanimous support to a policy of Scandinavian neutrality. Appeals were made to the successful neutrality

of Sweden, Norway, and Denmark during the First World War. It was
considered obvious that cooperation among the Scandinavian countries
could not be directed against any state or groups of states. In this way
efforts were made to win general recognition for neutrality, establish a
consistent foreign policy, and secure neutrality through military
preparedness. Both the fortification of the Åland islands and a mutual
defence pact were discussed.

This approach turned out to be excessively simple. Denmark had no
particular interest in Finland's eastern border nor had Finland any
interest in defending Denmark's border with Germany. In Norway faith
in the miracle-working properties of neutrality was strong. Separate
treaties guaranteeing the independence of each neighbour would have
been in Sweden's interests. But this would also have meant a very
serious responsibility. Both the Soviet Union and Germany were
suspicious of a Scandinavian defence alliance. The fortification of
Åland was another bone of contention. Finland and Sweden signed an
agreement in January 1939, providing for the fortification of the
islands. The issue was brought before the League of Nations. The
Soviet government complained that the agreement would not prevent
an aggressor from using the fortifications against the Soviet Union. The
League of Nations was unable to arrive at a decision.

Finland's position was extremely precarious. The German invasion
of Poland meant penetration of the security zone which had been the
subject of talks between the Soviet Union and the western powers. The
terms of the pact between Hitler and Stalin provided both for the
invasion of Poland and the transfer of certain territories to the Soviet
Union once the Polish defence was crushed. The course of events in
September 1939 corresponded closely with predictions made previously by the Soviet leadership.

Stalin worked fast to avert any surprises the Germans might have in
store. The Soviet government summoned representatives of Estonia,
Latvia, and Lithuania to Moscow, one after the other. Between
September 26 and October 10 the Baltic states signed treaties granting
the Soviet Union the right to establish military bases on their territory.
On October 5 Foreign Minister Molotov asked the Finnish diplomatic
representative in Moscow to request that a Finnish delegation be sent
to the Soviet capital for negotiations.

Sweden, Norway, and Denmark expressed hope that the Soviet Union would not make any demands that might endanger Finland's independence and neutrality in the forthcoming talks. The United States did likewise. A meeting of the prime ministers and foreign ministers of the Scandinavian countries had been held on September 18 and 19 in Copenhagen. This conference – like the meeting of heads of state in Stockholm that took place a month later – did not lead to any results. The Scandinavian countries were unable to agree on a common approach. Each country was forced to deal with the situation as it saw fit.

The Finnish government was aware of the talks between the Soviet Union and the western powers and of the demands made by the former. She knew nothing of the terms of the Ribbentrop pact. On the other hand, the Finnish delegation did know of the demands made on the Baltic countries and of the outcome of the negotiations before it left for Moscow. All three countries had given in and agreed to the establishment of Soviet bases. Finland was deeply suspicious of Soviet intentions and chose not to follow the example set by Estonia, Latvia, and Lithuania. She did not want to be caught unawares. Reserves were called up for extraordinary manœuvres which looked like mobilization. Other precautionary measures were taken, including the evacuation of the largest population centres. The Swedish People's party entered the cabinet.

Each one of the Baltic states had sent a delegation with plenary powers to Moscow. Finland wanted to be more careful and above all, to gain time. Paasikivi, the Finnish ambassador to Sweden, was chosen to lead the delegation. He set out for Moscow four days after Molotov's request. The Soviet Union was in a hurry and demanded that the Finnish delegation be given sufficient authority. The Finnish government met this demand and sent the Finance Minister, Väinö Tanner, to join the delegation. The instructions issued by the government were extremely inflexible. Relying on diplomatic support promised by Britain, the United States, and Sweden, Foreign Minister Erkko informed the parliamentary committee on foreign relations during the talks that no concessions would be made. All available means would be used to resist Soviet demands. Participation in the delegation by the leader of the Social Democrats was logical, at least from the Finnish point of view. Unfortunately the Soviet Union regarded Tanner as a major factor in the conflict between Social Democrats and Communists in Finland and interpreted his actions as anti-Soviet.

Paasikivi learned of the minimal demands on October 14. Finland was to lease the town of Hanko and its environs for a naval base, permit the use of the harbour at Lappohja for anchorage, surrender the outer islands in the Gulf of Finland, cede Koivisto on the Karelian isthmus and the area south of a line running between Liipola and Koivisto, and the western part of the Rybachi peninsula, in the Petsamo region. Fortifications in the border zone were to be destroyed. If these concessions and a clarification of the non-aggression pact were made, the Soviet Union was prepared to permit the construction of fortifications in Åland as long as Finland performed the work alone.

Finland would have agreed to cede the small outer islands in the Gulf of Finland in exchange for territorial concessions on the part of the Soviet Union on the Karelian isthmus. Removal of the so-called Kuokkala salient – which would have shifted the border some 23 kilometres further away from Leningrad – would also have been acceptable. The Finnish government rejected the demand concerning Hanko outright; ceding this territory would violate Finnish neutrality and threaten her security. In further negotiations the Soviet Union agreed to some minor modifications; the size of the Hanko garrison would be reduced from five to four thousand men. Both parties clung to the positions they had taken when the talks began. Finland made some concessions when the Soviet Union proved adamant.

Events took a turn for the worse on the evening of October 31. Foreign Minister Molotov made the Soviet terms public and the dispute became a question of prestige. At various stages of the talks foreign powers had sought to support Finland diplomatically, although the Soviet Union had rejected all attempts to intervene. In sessions held on November 2 and 4 it became clear that the concessions Finland was ready to make did not satisfy the Soviet Union. Stalin, who participated personally in the negotiations, was in fact prepared to trade Hanko for the islands located south of the town. The Finnish government again made some minor concessions in the new instructions, but these did not concern military bases. Finland was unwilling to negotiate on this point and the delegation was given the authority to break off the talks. The new contacts were not productive and the Finnish spokesmen returned on November 13 to receive new instructions.

There were legal grounds for Finland's intransigence. Finland did not represent a threat to any foreign power. No power had requested permission to use Finnish territory for an attack against the Soviet Union, nor would Finland have permitted such an attack. Finland had made assurances on numerous occasions that she would defend her territory against foreign invasion, regardless of the aggressor. The inviolability of Finnish territory was the basic principle involved; President Ståhlberg had appealed to this principle during the talks leading up to the Treaty of Tartu. Finland would not surrender a single square inch of ground. Even this did not satisfy certain groups during the negotiations in autumn 1939 and the principle was applied to underwater rocks as well. Finland's territorial integrity was at stake. The smallest concession would mean the abandonment of this principle and it would no longer be of any consequence how much territory was actually ceded. The nation firmly believed that it could stay out of the war and safeguard its independence by remaining neutral and by pledging to defend this policy by force of arms, if necessary.

Finland received no encouragement to defy the Soviet Union during the course of the negotiations from any foreign power. Neither the western allies nor Germany offered her aid. There were also parties in the Finnish government which openly opposed National Socialism. The only sympathy held in government circles was for the western powers, although no genuine pro-western orientation existed. Whatever sympathy did exist played no role in determining Finnish foreign policy, although due to the country's intransigence, the Soviet government believed otherwise.

Like the arguments used during the struggle against tsarist oppression, Finland's bargaining position in the 1939 negotiations was intellectually sound. Unfortunately no effort was made to consider the international situation or the demands of selfdefence of the great powers in a world governed by force. Finland's stubbornness had little relation to the resources at her disposal. The Soviet Union had repeatedly asserted its desire for peace. Finland accepted these assertions and this in turn encouraged the country's leaders, convincing them that the Soviet Union would not attack. They faced nothing worse than a war of nerves. Foreign Minister Erkko urged Paasikivi in effect to ignore the great power status of the Soviet Union in the instructions he issued on the delegation's departure for Moscow. Official optimism spread throughout Finland; convinced that there would be no war, the government terminated the precautionary measures taken at the end of November and the population that had been evacuated returned to the towns.

The Finnish nation received a serious warning when the Soviet Union made its demands public. The danger was not clear until Molotov delivered a note to the Finnish ambassador in Moscow on November 26. The note accused Finland of firing on the Soviet village of Mainila, killing and wounding some of the troops stationed there. In order to avoid incidents of this type Finland was to withdraw her troops a distance of 20–25 kilometres from the border. Finnish authorities investigated the matter and decided that fire from the Finnish batteries could not have reached Mainila. There was shooting, but it had come from the Soviet side of the border. The Finnish government was willing to have the incident investigated and to agree on mutual troop withdrawals from the border area. This did not satisfy the Soviet government; the Finnish proposal would have meant the withdrawal of Soviet troops to the gates of Leningrad.

Soviet historians support Molotov's claims. Reactionary forces in Finland exploited national feeling and incited the population to the point of hysteria; this led to the provocation at Mainila. Finnish historians have rejected this interpretation, pointing out that the Finnish artillery simply did not have the range to reach Mainila. In view of the international situation at the time, a provocation by Finland would have been competely senseless.

No previous preparations or phase of the Winter War provided any substance for claims that several powers planned to launch an attack on the Soviet Union from Finland. Plans to aid Finland militarily were not made until after the outbreak of war and no aid was actually sent until the western powers were convinced that Finnish defences would not collapse immediately, as almost everyone believed at the outset. A few thousand foreign volunteers were trained at the end of the Winter War, although none of them were sent to the Karelian isthmus, where the heaviest fighting took place. The French made plans to bomb Soviet oil production facilities in Baku during the Winter War. Here the most rudimentary strategy called for coordination of military efforts in the north and south. Finland was guilty of intransigence based on a misunderstanding of the international situation, but not of provocations like the firing at Mainila.

On the other hand, there is justification for assuming that once the Soviet Union made the conflict into a question of prestige it was necessary to provide a good reason for initiating hostilities, especially in view of previous declarations of peaceful intent on the part of the Soviet leadership. The Mainila incident and other alleged border violations appeared sufficient to justify an attack by troops of the Leningrad military district. World public opinion was not convinced by Molotov's claim.

The action taken after the Mainila incident was followed by more drastic measures and Finland was accused of posing a threat to Leningrad. The Soviet Union then gave notice that the non-aggression pact concluded in 1932, which had been extended in 1934 to remain in effect until 1945, was no longer valid. Diplomatic relations were broken off, and on November 30 the Red Army invaded Finland at several points. Air raids on population centres such as Helsinki were made simultaneously.

Whether or not Finnish concessions might have prevented the Winter War cannot be determined until the Soviet archives are opened and the nature of the Soviet government's intentions with regard to Finland are clear. Everything that the Soviet Union undertook after hostilities began was interpreted in Finland as proof that the aim was to deny Finland her independence. On the other hand, the statements of certain Soviet leaders, including Stalin, and arguments made by historians, indicate that greater flexibility on the part of Finland might have averted war.

But the Soviet Union and the demands it made represent only one side of the story. Fear and traditions of both constitutionality and neutrality were deep-rooted. It is a matter for conjecture whether or not the Finnish nation would have consented to territorial concessions and whether or not Parliament would have agreed to pass the necessary legislation. Warnings conveyed by the Soviet Union through private channels in 1938 did not result in the slightest increase in flexibility. Mannerheim, Paasikivi, and Tanner, who were all to a certain extent in favour of concessions in autumn 1939, made no effort to work together and exert pressure on the government. In view of these facts it is difficult to understand how the government could have convinced the nation in the course of a few weeks that concessions were essential. Any government consenting to more extensive territorial concessions would have received a vote of no confidence and unity at home would have been lost. Unanimous support in Parliament for a policy of no concessions – which led to war – and the small number of individuals who refused to take up arms indicate how just Finland regarded her cause.

The Soviet Union wanted nothing to do with the new cabinet which enjoyed unanimous support in Parliament and which announced that its chief goal was the restoration of peace between the Soviet Union and Finland. In the Soviet Union plans to create a friendly government had already been under way for a couple of weeks. As soon as war broke out the Soviet Union announced that it recognized only the Terijoki government, established by Stalin and headed by O.W. Kuusinen. The presidium of the supreme soviet decided to "recognize the democratic government of Finland and establish diplomatic relations between the Soviet Union and the Democratic Republic of Finland." Kuusinen, who in 1921 had written that "Finland itself is of course an insignificant and passing phenomenon," concluded a treaty of friendship and mutual aid with the Soviet government on the following day. The treaty went into effect immediately and "the documents of ratification were to be exchanged as soon as possible in Helsinki, the capital of Finland," as the final article of the treaty stipulated.

According to the treaty, the Soviet Union received most of the Karelian isthmus, although in order to fulfil the "age-old wishes of the Finnish nation" it agreed to surrender the purely Karelian parts of East Karelia to the Terijoki government. Red Army propaganda made the attack into a triumphant march on the capital of Finland, which would precede the liberation of the people from the white terror and the formation of a democratic republic. According to the order issued by the commander of the Leningrad military district on November 30, the Soviet army was to cross the border, destroy Finnish military units and guarantee the security of the northwestern border of the Soviet Union for ever.

The failure of collective security during the first two decades of independence meant that Finland was isolated at the outbreak of the Winter War. World public opinion supported the weaker party, the victim of unjust treatment. The League of Nations branded the Soviet Union the aggressor and expelled it in what proved to be the final act of the international organization. Seven out of fifteen of the powers represented took part in the voting held on December 14. The League also urged its members to send aid to the victim of aggression in accordance with the League charter. This remained a mere expression of intent. Very little aid was provided and the attempts of foreign powers to arrange a peaceful settlement failed. The Soviet Union rejected all offers of mediation. It contended that the conflict concerned only the two powers involved in the fighting and sought to settle the dispute alone.

Finland's armed forces, mobilized for extraordinary manœuvres since October, were not caught off guard. Although the attack was not anticipated and the nation suffered a considerable shock, recovery took only a few days. The information that the Soviet Union received about morale and the feelings of the Finnish nation was either faulty or distorted. Opportunities for domestic reform which began in the mid 1930s and the economic upswing in western Europe caused by the arms race benefited worker and small farmer alike. Educational opportunities were improved systematically and the well-organized work of voluntary educational organizations was successful. A sense of nationhood developed and the people learned to value independence.

Social Democratic participation in government had a twofold effect. The working class knew that its leaders were involved in formulating foreign policy and trusted them. The right wing, which had been uncertain of Social Democratic support for independence, was forced to make a reappraisal. The language conflict had lost much of its sharpness since the mid 1930s. Distrust between the two language groups diminished as danger increased. Dissension of this type was practically non-existent by the outbreak of the Winter War.

A new government was formed immediately after war began. Parliament gave the foreign policy of the Cajander government a unanimous vote of confidence in an evening session on November 11. But Soviet mass media had voiced increasingly sharp criticism of the cabinet throughout the autumn. Now criticism had given way to outright hostility. Cajander offered his resignation so that a government capable of dealing with the Soviet Union could be formed. A new government headed by Risto Ryti (1889–1956), chairman of the board of the Bank of Finland, was formed. Väinö Tanner became foreign minister. The new prime minister had served as a Progressive party M.P. from 1919 to 24 and from 1927 to 29 and as minister of finance on two occasions between 1921 and 1924. Ryti concentrated on financial affairs after his appointment to the Bank of Finland. Although he had no real experience in politics, he had kept abreast of international affairs and agreed to the president's request, assuming office at a time when Finland's position appeared hopeless.

Both sides took the offensive in the early phases of the fighting, although Russian superiority was nonetheless clear all along the front. Finnish resistance under the leadership of Marshal Mannerheim was consolidated in two weeks. After the Russian attack was turned back a few times, the Soviet Union realized that the Finnish nation was solidly behind the war effort and would put up a tough fight. The advance of motorized units across the border along narrow, backwoods tracks ground to a halt; a number of large Red Army units were surrounded and destroyed. The Karelian isthmus was the only part of the front where Soviet superiority in men and material could be used effectively. Underestimating Finland's capacity and will to resist, the Red Army leadership mistakenly believed that units of the Leningrad military district alone would be nearly sufficient to bring the war to a successful conclusion. Once they understood this mistake they concentrated their efforts on the isthmus and broke the Finnish defence on the narrow Summa sector of the front in February 1940. Finland barely succeeded in stemming the tide.

At the end of January it was obvious that the Soviet Union no longer supported the Kuusinen government, which present-day Soviet historians do not mention. In an official note sent to the Swedish foreign minister, the Soviet Union announced that in principle it had nothing against concluding a peace treaty with the government of Ryti and Tanner. It was prepared to consider Finnish initiatives aimed at negotiations.

The primary reason for the Soviet leadership's change of heart may have been the serious deficiencies in training and arms that appeared in the course of the fighting. The lessons obtained in the war did not recommend additional risks. Although the Soviet Union must have been aware of the insufficiency of British and French preparations to aid Finland, fear of bombing raids on unprotected production centres in the south, such as Baku, had to be taken into account. In the atmosphere caused by the Soviet attack on Finland, Stalin's fear of a sudden alliance of imperialist powers also played a role.

Stalin was ready to make contact with the Ryti government once Leningrad was secure and negotiations between France and Great Britain regarding the creation of an expeditionary force to aid Finland, opened in February 1940, began to complicate the situation. The initial contact was made through private channels using the mediation of Alexandra Mikhailovna Kollontai (1872–1952), the Soviet ambassador in Stockholm.

The Finnish delegation, consisting of Ryti, Paasikivi, R. Walden, and Väinö Voionmaa, flew to Moscow on March 7. The negotiators did not learn the peace terms until they arrived in the Soviet capital. The option of accepting aid from the western powers was kept open due to the severity of the terms.

The governments of Norway, Sweden, and Denmark declared their neutrality when war between Poland and Germany broke out. Finland did likewise. Denmark had neglected to make her own defensive preparations. In contrast, both Norway and Sweden were prepared to defend their territorial integrity by force of arms. Both were heavily dependent on trade with Germany and the areas under German control once the oceans became zones of war. This was especially true in the case of Sweden, whose iron ore deposits were also essential to the German war effort. Plans to aid Finland made by the British and French were followed closely in both Oslo and Stockholm. Neither favoured granting Britain and France permission to cross their territory in transporting men and material to Finland. Sweden declared she would do everything in her power to prevent it.

The Finnish government was aware that control of iron ore transport in Sweden was the primary goal of the aid offered by Britain and France. Daladier, the French prime minister, stated on February 21 that the "main goal must not be forgotten." The expeditionary force would be too small and would arrive too late to accomplish anything. Thus Finland decided to accept the Soviet terms. On the evening of March 12 Parliament instructed the negotiators to sign the agreement.

According to the terms of the treaty, Finland surrendered the south-eastern part of the country up to what was approximately the border established by the Treaty of Uusikaupunki, Suursaari island and the islands to the east of it in the Gulf of Finland, the Salla area, and part of the Rybachi peninsula. The Soviet Union obtained a 30-year lease of Hanko and the surrounding sea area for the establishment of a military base. Finland was obliged – if possible before the end of the year – to build a railway east from Kemijärvi to link up with the Soviet line coming from Kandalakshka. Both countries agreed to refrain from attacking the other or from joining any alliances directed against each other. Parliament passed the treaty on March 15. The vote was 145 in favour and 3 against. There were 9 abstentions and a total of 42 M.P.'s were absent.

Finland lost 25,000 men in the Winter War and 10,000 were permanently disabled.

2.

The Treaty of Moscow did not stabilize relations between the two countries. The struggle merely shifted to the field of diplomacy and domestic politics. The views of the weaker party were not taken into account in the negotiations and Finland's interests suffered whenever the treaty was interpreted. Representatives of the Soviet Union in Finland supported domestic Communists openly and powerful Red Army units were stationed near the border, prepared to intervene should the need arise. These facts of life were fully comprehended in Helsinki. The commander-in-chief was ready to carry out a mobilization on two separate occasions during this war of nerves; each time the president refused to give his assent. Everything indicated that the Soviet Union still maintained the goal she had declared at the beginning of the Winter War; the overthrow of the existing political system in Finland. The occupation of the Baltic states and the conversion of these countries into Soviet republics in the summer of 1940 was another link in the chain of evidence. The Soviet Union gained the territory she needed to guarantee her security in the west and northwest as the war spread. Stalin remained convinced that sooner or later Hitler would seek to realize the plans set out in *Mein Kampf* and launch an attack. No responsible Finnish politician was convinced that Stalin would be satisfied with the border provided for in the Treaty of Uusikaupunki or the base at Hanko; after all Alexander I had conquered all of Finland. Neither could anybody convince the Finnish public that the Soviet Union's aims were so restricted.

In the atmosphere of mutual suspicion prevailing in the months after the Winter War, German preparations for an attack on the Soviet Union were followed with unflagging concentration in both Helsinki and Moscow. Hitler demanded that Norway accept German "protection" on April 8, 1940 after Britain had mined Norwegian coastal waters in order to hinder ore shipments from Narvik. When Norway did not consent, Germany occupied Denmark and attacked the former. By the beginning of summer the Germans were on the coast of the Arctic Ocean, face to face with Soviet troops.

Peace between Finland and the Soviet Union was restored. The Ryti government considered its task completed and resigned at the end of March. Ryti then went on to form another government and Väinö Tanner's term as foreign minister came to an end. Although it was well known that Stalin disliked him, it was essential to have a representative of the working class in the government. Tanner remained in the cabinet administering supplies for the civilian population. The post was a difficult one. Professor Rolf Witting (1879–1944), a bank director, became foreign minister. Witting had previously been engaged in marine research and therefore had personal contacts in both the West and in Germany. The new foreign minister's sentiments were largely unknown in the Soviet Union and he could not immediately be branded as anti-Soviet. Ryti felt he could supervise the actions of his foreign minister, who was unfamiliar with the intricacies of diplomacy.

Finland announced the return to a policy of Scandinavian neutrality and non-belligerence as soon as the Winter War ended. In order to calm a population which had received a severe shock as a result of the hard terms dictated by the Soviet Union, Tanner immediately made public information regarding discussions of a Scandinavian defence pact. The idea was even more unrealistic in 1940 than it had been in the 1930s. Certain Scandinavian politicians made statements which confirmed the Soviet government's belief that the pact was intended to right the wrongs of the Treaty of Moscow. Molotov quickly denounced the plans and public discussion was broken off at once.

Close cooperation between Finland and Sweden continued after the German occupation of Denmark and Norway. Sweden provided financial support for reconstruction and improvements in Finland's defences. When it became obvious that the war begun in 1941 would end in defeat, the concept of a federal state under a single head of state was put forward as a means of saving Finland from occupation. A similar scheme had been under discussion in the autumn of 1940.

Division within the Finnish government prevented the formulation of any precise policy of security. According to plans made in the 1930s, the commander-in-chief of the armed forces was to receive extensive authority. Mannerheim was to assume this post. This was of course what happened during the Winter War. The Marshal grew accustomed to considerable independence since President Kallio often took little part in making decisions. As Mannerheim's prestige increased – also among those who were involved in the 1918 rebellion – his ambitions grew. The Marshal was not one to let an opportunity of this kind slip by, and sought an even greater role. Since the Treaty of Moscow did not bring any security it was expedient to retain Mannerheim as commander-in-chief. No changes occurred in this respect when Ryti became president in 1940.

The double standard maintained by Finland's leadership was obvious in relations with the two great powers that controlled the country's destiny. Relations with the Soviet Union remained on the diplomatic level. Those with Germany were more complicated. Here normal diplomatic channels were supplemented with consultations between military commanders; this was also true when extremely delicate questions and far-reaching decisions were involved.

The peace that ended the Winter War and the tensions that followed broke the poor health of President Kallio. He resigned on December 19, 1940, dying on the day his successor was chosen. On the basis of emergency legislation passed by Parliament, the electors chosen in 1937 selected a new president. The interests of foreign powers, including those of the Soviet Union and Germany, were expressed by diplomats. Satisfaction with some candidates was expressed and warnings were made that the election of certain others would be considered unfriendly. Such interference irritated the Finnish people, but had no effect on the decision made by the electors. Prime Minister Ryti, whose name was not on either list, had won the nation's confidence in the preceding months of war and peace. He was chosen by an almost unanimous vote to complete President Kallio's term of office.

J.W. Rangell (born in 1894), a bank director, was requested to form a government. Rangell had a legal education and had worked in financial institutions, most recently as a close associate of Ryti in the Bank of Finland. He had no political experience, although the president's confidence in him and his own skill in personal relations largely made up for this deficiency. The composition of Rangell's government, appointed on January 3, 1941, differed little from that of its predecessor, although the Patriotic People's League joined the cabinet. Witting remained foreign minister.

Finland's official policy of neutrality was impossible to maintain after the Winter War, the Treaty of Moscow, and the occupation of Norway. The Soviet Union had little faith in Finnish intentions and Germany did not favour a neutral Finland. Germany took the conflict between Finland and the Soviet Union into account from the very beginning in making plans to march eastward. She also exploited the pressure exerted by the Soviet Union on Finland, which included the threat of a new war, and Finland's dependence on foreign trade.

Commercial cooperation between Finland and Germany was traditional and the Baltic Sea offered a safe route for transporting Finnish goods. Trade with the Soviet Union had not increased appreciably in the interwar period and there was no indication that it would grow rapidly with a new war in progress. The outbreak of war further reduced this potential, for the Soviet Union was soon hard-pressed to provide for its own population. Nor had the normally secure commercial channels between Finland and the Soviet Union developed. Germany's leaders knew that Finland had no choice when it came to picking trade partners. There was only Germany and the area under her control.

The Treaty of Moscow deprived Finland of 12 % of her most fertile land and although these areas were retaken in 1941, Finland still relied on imported food products. The shortage of bread grain was nearly 100 kilos per inhabitant during the worst winter, that of 1941–1942. Finland had no domestic supplies of coal, oil, and the raw materials for many branches of industry. All replacements for machinery also had to be obtained abroad.

In order to maintain production and the employment that depended on it, Finland had to secure a market for her products. Since the oceans were no longer open to shipping, the range of opportunities became limited to the Baltic Sea. Germany needed the products of the Finnish wood processing industry and copper and nickel shipped from Finland were also essential. Although attempts were made to increase trade between Finland and the Soviet Union in 1940 and 1941, little success was achieved, except for some deliveries of grain. Closer relations with Germany, to some extent on German terms, were an economic necessity for Finland.

Finland's defensive position suffered considerably in the Treaty of Moscow. The new south-eastern border was four times as long as the old frontier on the Karelian isthmus. It cut across the natural line of defence and was entirely unfortified. Along with the loss of men in the Winter War, much equipment was destroyed and what remained was either obsolete or worn out. Since the Soviet Union continued to threaten, the military leadership had to prepare for a new attack.

On September 8, 1940, the Finnish government concluded an agreement with the Soviet Union permitting military shipments to be sent through Finland to the area leased at Hanko. The agreement was very precise with regard to the number of troops and the quantities of supplies. Other matters were also stipulated in very exact terms. Negotiations between certain Finnish officers and German military leaders, which Mannerheim was aware of, led on September 22 to an agreement permitting the transport of German soldiers on leave through northern Finland to Norway. Sweden had previously found it necessary to make a similar agreement. In the agreement between Sweden and Germany, as in that between Finland and Russia, the numbers of troops to be transferred at a given time were stipulated precisely. Even though approximately 1 million German soldiers passed through Swedish territory during the Second World War, Sweden succeeded in preserving her neutrality. In contrast, Finland did not restrict the number of German troops to be transported through Finland, the number stationed in Finland at one time, nor the extent of German armaments.

Thus two powers, who were on the verge of war, transported large military units through Finland. The risk was great. Some feared that when war broke out between the Soviet Union and Germany, the former would try to cut the latter's supply lines in Lapland. Such action would involve use of the Salla railway, a route provided for in the Treaty of Moscow which the Soviet Union had worked hard to complete. On the other hand, the Soviet base at Hanko represented an obstacle to German operations in the Baltic. The fact that German troops in Norway already faced the Red Army and that the vital nickel deposits at Petsamo were in the same area, also had to be taken into account. The preservation of neutrality under these circumstances would have required a high degree of military preparedness; it would have meant maintaining the forces then mobilized with all the financial and social strain that such efforts involve.

The government of Finland repeatedly stated its intention to remain neutral and to normalize relations with the Soviet Union. But the threat of a new attack continued, especially after Molotov's visit to Berlin in November 1940. Neither was the government able to prevent Finnish military leaders from carrying on further negotiations with the Germans in order to prepare for the possibility of a renewed Soviet attack against Finland.

By spring 1941 Finland's neutrality was clearly biased in favour of Germany. Cautious hostility characterized policy toward the Soviet Union. Economic dependence on the former encouraged this trend. Negotiations between military leaders went even further; the aim was cooperation with Germany in an attack on the Soviet Union in accordance with the plans for operation Barbarossa.

There were rumours in May and June 1941 about a new treaty between Germany and the Soviet Union that would again relegate Finland to the latter's sphere of influence. These rumours were actually German propaganda designed to increase Finland's involvement in the plans for an invasion of the Soviet Union.

There was widespread feeling in Finland that the nation was entitled to regain the territories lost in the Winter War without further military efforts and sacrifice. The Winter War and the peace that followed were regarded as a violation of the basic rights of nations. The country also had considerable difficulty providing for the Karelian refugees, who made up one-tenth of the total population. The evacuees nurtured the hope of eventually returning to their homes and rumours of impending conflict between the Soviet Union and Germany encouraged them. Despite the government's efforts to check demands for revenge, the desire to regain the ceded territories grew stronger.

Väinö Tanner resigned from the government in August 1940 in order to reduce tension between the two countries and the government consented to new Soviet demands, many of which were not based on the peace treaty. The government abandoned whatever hopes it had of improving relations with the Soviet Union in late winter 1940 when it became evident that a favourable change had occurred in Germany's attitude. Finland called up her troops for extraordinary manœuvres on June 17, 1941, immediately after reliable information on the schedule for the German invasion of the Soviet Union became available.

Looking at it from Moscow, Finland's policy appeared quite consistent. Finland was bound to fight alongside Germany against the Soviet Union. Military consultations with Germany which could not be kept secret, the movement of German troops through northern Finland, the stationing of German units in Lapland, and the action mentioned above convinced the Russians that Finland was preparing for an aggressive war.

Finnish participation in the attack coincided with Germany's interests. Although Finland alone could never have launched an attack along the entire length of its border, military preparedness was essential. Finnish troops could tie down a substantial number of Red Army units. In order to ensure Finnish involvement, Hitler announced on June 22, at the outbreak of war, that Germany's Finnish "comrades in arms" were taking part in the attack. Hitler's statement was worded to convince the Soviet Union that Finland and Germany were acting as allies. Although Finland immediately rejected this claim and declared that she intended to preserve her neutrality, the Soviet Union paid no heed. German bombers attacked Leningrad from airfields on the south coast of the Baltic, flying over the south coast of Finland en route. The Soviet Union responded by initiating military operations against Finland. This action provided the Finnish government with an opportunity to claim that the Soviet Union was again the aggressor. Thus the continuation of the Winter War has been described as a defensive operation. But the military preparations and the deployment of troops performed in conjunction with mobilization were clearly designed for an offensive war. There was also considerable sentiment in government circles to seek compensation for losses sustained in the Winter War and to regain the ceded territories.

The purpose of the statement made by the government to Parliament on June 25 was to obtain approval for mobilization. Continued Russian attacks forced Prime Minister Rangell to reword his statement at the last minute, declaring that a state of war existed between Finland and the Soviet Union and that Finland had responded to the attack. Parliament supported Rangell unanimously.

Disagreement about the ultimate ends of the war arose. The government would have been content to redress the wrongs of the Treaty of Moscow. Both the commander-in-chief and the president had larger objectives. Ryti announced privately that both secure borders and the creation of a "Greater Finland" were the ultimate goals. Mannerheim did likewise in his order of the day issued on July 10, 1941. The action of the commander-in-chief came as a surprise to the government and evoked sharp criticism. Mannerheim clearly did not accept the concept of a defensive war. Mannerheim's action created confusion among the country's political leaders and disagreement about the war aims. This state of affairs persisted for a long time; plans for large-scale settlement of the conquered areas in East Karelia under the jurisdiction of the general staff were made with permanent annexation in mind.

The advance across Finland's historical border also evoked criticism from Social Democrats in the government. The government accepted the move simply because it was a military necessity. The general staff's plan to push the enemy as far back as possible, denying him the advantages obtained during the Winter War, was approved. The advance to the Svir river and Lake Onega was also justified: the conquered territories would serve to increase Finland's bargaining power at the peace table.

The government was somewhat wary of these war aims. Although it was generally believed – until the summer of 1942 – that Germany would defeat the Soviet Union, most people felt that Germany would eventually lose the war, just as she had in 1918. On November 29, 1941 Parliament passed a bill declaring that Finland sought only the restoration of those territories lost according to the terms of the Treaty of Moscow. Parliament supported the measure unanimously.

The attack begun after Mannerheim issued his order of the day achieved almost immediate success. Red Army defences along the north-western border proved weak. Either the Soviet Union did not really consider a Finnish attack likely or regarded the threat posed by Germany so great that she concentrated her best units to meet it. The Soviet Union was fighting for her very existence on the western front; under these circumstances war with Finland was of little importance. The Finns sometimes achieved a 4–1 superiority in man and fire power in massing to break through the meagre Soviet defences.

Optimism in Finland caused by the lightning advance of the German army in 1941 began to fade during the first winter. Trusting in the success of his "blitzkrieg," Hitler spread his forces too thin and was unable to take either Moscow or Leningrad before the arrival of an early winter. Nor was he able to engage the Red Army in any decisive battles. The German war machine ground to a halt in the severe cold of the Russian winter and the armies began to retreat. The Red Army proved tough and its leaders exploited the huge front as their predecessors had done in turning back Napoleon. The Soviet Union's western allies were also able to organize largescale shipments of supplies in a relatively short period of time.

The renewed offensive of summer 1942 was stopped on the banks of the Volga. The German 6th Army was surrounded and forced to surrender on February 1, 1943. Two days later the military and political leaders of Finland agreed to seek a way to disengage from the fighting. Finland of course maintained that she was fighting her own struggle, and this facilitated plans to make a separate peace. Prospects for peace did not arise until some 18 months later. A stalemate existed on the Finnish front from December 6, 1941 until the great Russian offensive in June 1944.

Ryti's term of office ended on March 1, 1943. He had been branded a "war president" and his chances to lead the country to peace seemed scant. In addition to Ryti, Mannerheim alone enjoyed the prestige necessary to serve as head of state, and the latter's name was mentioned during preparations for the elections. In the end it seemed probable that the war would continue for some time. Finnish plans to disengage began to drag out, and it seemed advisable to save Mannerheim until the likelihood of peace was greater.

The electors previously chosen by means of emergency legislation carried out the election. Ryti was re-elected, this time for two years, since it was anticipated that the war would last that long. Alignments of electors were not the same as they had been in 1940. Mannerheim would have had considerable support. Since he declined to run against Ryti, the latter obtained the votes of 269 electors.

In accordance with the accepted parliamentary procedure, Rangell turned in his resignation at the end of the presidential term. Both his prospects and those of Foreign Minister Witting were not good. Criticism was especially strong in Parliament. Many M.P.'s maintained that Rangell had neglected to keep them abreast of the increasingly alarming course of events. Both the prime minister and the foreign minister had been labelled "war ministers" and the latter was known as a leader of those who favoured uncompromising support of Germany. Neither minister could possibly lead the nation to peace.

Professor Edwin Linkomies (1894–1963), a Conservative M.P. and deputy speaker of Parliament, formed a new government. Henrik Ramsay (1886–1951), a shipowner, became foreign minister. Without gaining a reputation as a foe of the Soviet Union, Ramsay had maintained contacts with the West and had built up some influence in Germany. The restoration of peace was the new government's primary goal. In order to facilitate this policy, the extremely pro-German Patriotic People's League was not included in the government.

The Linkomies cabinet found the realization of its goal more difficult than it anticipated. Despite numerous defeats, Germany remained strong in 1943, particularly in northern Europe. Germany sought to keep Finland at war. In Finland it was generally believed that any attempt to disengage would result in a German occupation or at least an attempt at it. In either event, Russian occupation at the end of the war would be a foregone conclusion. Breaking relations with Germany would obviously put an end to shipments of raw materials, manufactured goods, and food supplies. A break of this kind would also wreck Finland's export trade. The combination of the demand for unconditional surrender made by Britain, the Soviet Union, and the United States and Finland's distrust of traditional Soviet objectives also hindered efforts to get out of the war. The Finnish lines remained firm in late winter 1944. Both civilian and military morale was high.

The first peace feelers were made in February 1944. Prime Minister Linkomies explained the government's view of the situation in a statement made at a secret session of Parliament held on February 29. Linkomies announced his decision to seek peace. He also explained the probable nature of the Soviet terms on the basis of what scanty information the government had received. They did not include demands for unconditional surrender, the occupation of the country, or for military bases; Linkomies considered these significant concessions. But there were certain provisions in the terms which the government considered "dangerous to accept in advance". The prime minister stated that the government considered it advisable to seek the most advantageous peace possible.

The Social Democrats, the Swedish People's party, and the Progressive party agreed. A motion made by representatives of the Agrarian Union and supported by a majority of the party's representation in Parliament rejected the terms set out in the government's report. But should "terms exist which would permit us to withdraw from the war, and guarantee our right to self-determination, freedom, and security, then the government should investigate them and inform Parliament of its findings."

The government had the support of 105 M.P.'s. The Conservatives and the Patriotic People's League joined in support of the motion introduced by the Agrarian group. The motion received 78 votes. One M.P. abstained and 15 were absent.

A new report was presented on March 15. The government had studied the terms and requested authority to turn them down. Members of the peace opposition criticized the government's passiveness severely, but did not propose a motion of their own.

The Soviet Union then agreed to receive Paasikivi in Moscow and provide him with the precise terms for peace. The government informed Parliament of the terms it had received on March 27 and 29, again in a closed session. Prime Minister Linkomies announced that the government expected Parliament to reject the terms unanimously. Insufficient time was allotted for ousting or interning German troops in Finland and the demand for 600 million dollars in war reparations was excessive. Only a few M.P.s spoke, and all of them agreed with the government's stand. Even professor Furuhjelm (1879–1944), a member of the Swedish People's party and a leader of the peace opposition, approved the government's action. Speaking on behalf of his parliamentary group, Furuhjelm backed the government to the hilt. Parliament thus gave the government a solid vote of confidence.

Events on the principal fronts and the disengagement of Germany's allies from the war made a decision urgent. The rapid success of the great Soviet offensive on the Karelian isthmus at the beginning of June 1944 revealed the true balance of power and convinced the nation that the conditions for peace would be harsh. German Foreign Minister Ribbentrop arrived in Helsinki on June 25. Exploiting the seriousness of the situation on the front, he forced the president to sign an agreement at the end of June stipulating that Finland would not conclude a separate peace. President Ryti signed the agreement in his own name in order to avoid binding Parliament to it. On the basis of this agreement Germany provided effective military aid, mainly in the form of anti-tank weapons and air support. When the Soviet Union had apparently achieved its objectives on the Karelian isthmus, it transferred its best troops to fight against the Germans. This permitted stabilization along a line north of Viipuri.

President Ryti resigned on August 1, 1944, and Mannerheim was elected president three days later. Finland's war effort was thus unified in the hands of one man. Antti Hackzell (1881–1946), a Conservative M.P. with a background in law and economics, was called upon to form a government. He had served in various functions in St. Petersburg from 1911 to 18, as the Finnish envoy in Moscow from 1922 to 1927, and as foreign minister in the Kivimäki government from 1932 to 36. Thus the prime minister had considerable knowledge of Russia. He was joined by another expert. Carl Enckell (1876–1959), Mannerheim's trusted friend, became foreign minister. Enckell, like

Mannerheim, was a graduate of the cadet school in Hamina. He resigned from the Russian army during the era of oppression, became an engineer, and then worked in industry until 1917. Due to his exceptional skill as a negotiator, he was appointed to the Finnish diplomatic corps. He was foreign minister from 1918 to 19 and in 1922 and 1924, the chief Finnish delegate at Versailles in 1919, and ambassador in Paris from 1919 to 1927. Enckell had consistently advocated a policy that took the Soviet Union's interests as a great power into account and had demanded diplomatic efforts to improve relations between the two countries. The Hackzell government expressed the same intentions as its precedessor: the restoration of peace between the Soviet Union and Finland.

Mannerheim informed Hitler's representative, then in Finland, that he did not consider the agreement made by Ryti binding. Relying on his personal prestige, Mannerheim could make peace knowing that the nation was behind him. The new government undertook to arrange talks at once. At the end of August it became clear that the Soviet Union did not intend to occupy Finland or terminate its independence. The Soviet Union did insist that Finland publicly break off relations with Germany and drive out the remaining German troops by September 15. Only then could negotiations begin.

Parliament dealt with these initial terms on September 4 and 9 on the basis of the government's report. Prime Minister Hackzell announced that in contrast to the demands made in June, the Soviet Union no longer required unconditional surrender. He also informed Parliament of the views of the country's military leaders: "Finland is on the way to ultimate defeat, which would be a disaster for the nation." He expressed the cabinet's hope that Parliament would approve its efforts to achieve peace. The session was convened so quickly that nearly one-fourth of the members were unable to attend. Parliament supported the cabinet by a vote of 108 to 45.

The government moved rapidly once it had received the necessary authority. On September 4 Hackzell reported to Parliament that Mannerheim had appointed a delegation headed by the prime minister and that the Soviet Union had agreed to a cease-fire, to begin the next morning. The government had nothing further to report with regard to the peace terms.

Peace talks began in Moscow on September 8. Prime Minister Hackzell suffered a severe stroke in Moscow and Foreign Minister Enckell took his place. By September 18 the negotiations had progressed so far that Parliament was summoned to meet at 6 o'clock on the following morning. Again, the necessity for immediate action prevented a large number of M.P.'s from attending. Many simply did not receive word or were unable to reach Helsinki in time. One-third of the representatives were absent.

Ernst von Born (1885–1956), minister of internal affairs and the senior member of the cabinet, presented the government's report. The terms for peace had been distributed to the M.P.'s in advance. Von Born made reference to these terms; in order to underscore the seriousness of the situation he read a telegram from Enckell, head of the Finnish delegation in Moscow. Enckell conveyed Molotov's sharply-worded demand that Finland agree to the territorial concessions or face Soviet occupation. With a few words intended to instil faith in the future, the minister of internal affairs made his case. He also declared that the government expected support from Parliament and requested authority to sign the truce. Parliament backed up the cabinet unanimously; not onecounter-proposal was made.

The truce required Finland to recognize the treaty of 1940, withdraw her troops behind the border established therein, and disarm German military forces remaining in Finland and surrender them to the Soviet Union. Airfields in southern and southwestern Finland were to be put at the disposal of Soviet forces for operations against the Germans in Estonia and the northern Baltic. Finland's armed forces were to return to peace-time status within two and a half months. Petsamo and the Porkkala area, 380 square kilometres located southwest of Helsinki, were to be turned over to the Soviet Union. Porkkala was to be leased to the Soviet Union for 50 years. 300 million dollars in war reparations to be paid in goods were also included in the terms. Finland agreed to cooperate with the allies in detaining and sentencing persons guilty of war crimes and in breaking up all organizations of a "fascist nature". An allied control commission under Soviet leadership was set up to enforce the truce.

The final peace treaty was signed in Paris on February 10, 1947. In previous negotiations the Finnish delegation had attempted to have the reparations reduced. These attempts were unsuccessful, and the terms of the truce were not modified. The treaty also reaffirmed the demilitarization of the Åland islands and determined the size of Finland's armed forces.

Finland's involvement in the maelstrom of great power politics led to defeat in two wars. In the second she lost 60,000 men; another 50,000 suffered permanent injuries. Approximately 2,000 civilians were killed. But independence was preserved and the country was spared occupation. She was able to chart her own course under completely different circumstances, both at home and abroad.

CHAPTER IX

Finland and the Cold War, 1945–1955

By the time Finland had concluded the truce with the Soviet Union, Germany's defeat was clearly inevitable. Germany and her allies gained additional enemies and the unscrupulous regimes established in occupied territories met resistance.

The most important event in the Second World War after the German attack on the Soviet Union was the involvement of the United States of America. Japan signed the anti-Comintern pact with Germany in 1936 to secure territorial gains made since 1933 on the Asian mainland and to counterbalance cooperation between China and the Soviet Union. Italy joined Japan and Germany the following year and the pact became a tripartite alliance in 1940. Japan sought to solve the problems of its growing population by creating the so-called "Great East Asia Co-prosperity Sphere" to be composed of China, Manchuria, Indochina, and the Dutch East Indies. Japan's aim was hegemony in the western Pacific. Two powers posed an obstacle to Japanese ambitions: the Soviet Union and the United States. Japan entered a non-aggression pact with the former in April 1941. The latter realized the nature of Japan's plans for East Asia in June of the same year, after the occupation of French Indochina. Talks between the United States and Japan stalled, and on December 7, 1941 Japan launched a devastating surprise attack against the American fleet stationed at Pearl Harbor. The aim was to paralyse the American striking force in the western Pacific, thereby providing the security necessary for the creation of the "Co-prosperity Sphere" mentioned above.

From the very beginning of the Second World War the United States supported the enemies of the Axis powers with money and arms including warships. By declaring war against Japan, Germany, and Italy, the United States put all her resources at the disposal of the war effort. America's greatest contribution was in military supplies and by

1944 U.S. production of armaments exceeded that of the rest of the world combined. The Axis powers, their allies, and those who fought alongside them faced the combined military and economic resources of the rest of the world.

The Soviet Union made the decisive contribution to the defeat of Germany, the most important Axis power. Stalin had long felt – with a good measure of justification – that western military leaders hoped that the Second World War would proceed much like the First. Germany would defeat the Soviet Union and the western allies could then destroy an exhausted Germany. The invasion of the Soviet Union indicated that Hitler had learned nothing from history. Germany could not withstand a war on two fronts and Russia was too vast to conquer, even with modern weapons. Germany suffered a crushing blow at Stalingrad and Soviet pressure increased month by month while western air power paralysed German industry and transport and wore down the morale of the populace. Stalin opposed British plans for a second front in the Balkans; he had his own conception of the future of south-eastern Europe. He in turn demanded efforts on the part of the western allies to open a second front in western Europe. President Roosevelt (1882–1945) and Prime Minister Churchill (1874–1965) were prepared to do this but insisted on thorough planning. They hoped to save the lives of allied troops by wasting steel.

The British defeated the combined German and Italian troops striking toward Egypt at El Alamein in the autumn of 1942, paving the way for an allied landing in North Africa in November. North African bases permitted the allies to attack Italy, the weakest link in the Axis chain. Sicily was conquered in July 1943, although Germany occupied Italy after Italian soldiers and politicians recognized defeat and overthrew Mussolini. The allied march into Central Europe ground to a halt, and the Italian peninsula remained a relatively quiet theatre of war for nearly two years. Allied operations in the south did not constitute the second front demanded by Stalin. This front was not created until the allied invasion of Normandy on June 6, 1944. A joint Anglo-American force established a bridgehead with the aid of air and naval support. The breakthrough began at the end of July; the race to Germany from the west had started. German resistence continued until May 1945.

In August 1945, atomic bombs, products of the most advanced

scientific research, were used to bring Japan to her knees. Harry S. Truman (1884–1972) succeeded to the presidency after Roosevelt's death. He ordered the bombs to be dropped on two cities. Civilian casualties were terrifying, and Japan surrendered.

This marked the end of the Second World War. The losses were enormous. The Soviet Union suffered most; over 20 million lives were lost (11.6 % of the population). Germany sustained a loss of $6^1/_2$ million (10 % of the population). The efforts of the United States and Great Britain to reduce their own losses paid off; the former lost 400,000 and the latter 325,000.

Churchill, Stalin, and Roosevelt solved the major strategic problems and made decisions that would affect the nature of the postwar world during negotiations held while the fighting was still in progress. Disagreements were so great that the three powers were content to deal in generalities; disputes over the details might have hindered the war effort. The essential weaknesses of the alliance became apparent after the defeat of the Axis powers. Final peace treaties with the smaller states that had fought alongside Germany were signed in Paris in 1947. A treaty offering rather generous terms to Japan was concluded in San Francisco in 1951, overriding Soviet opposition.

Agreement was not reached concerning the fate of Germany, the principal adversary. Germany was divided into zones of occupation controlled by the victors. The same system was applied to Berlin, located deep within the Soviet zone. Mutual suspicion between the Soviet Union on the one hand and Britain, France, and the United States on the other, prevalent before the war, had been largely ignored during the fighting. It came to the fore at the end of the war. Discord arose immediately after the defeat of Germany in attempts to solve the world's numerous difficult problems. Tensions between East and West, beginning in 1947, led to a new arms race known as the Cold War.

For Finland the situation in Europe created by Hitler's wars of conquest was comparable to that created by Napoleon. There is reason to extend this comparison. The role of Russia under Alexander I in defeating Napoleon was primarily in battles fought on land. Russia became the leading power in Europe when Britain, Napoleon's toughest adversary, withdrew from European affairs. The balance of power in Europe was preserved since Russia had rivals and the victors did not crush France. The role of the Soviet Union in defeating Hitler was the same as that of Russia in the Napoleonic wars. Stalin, however, did not achieve the status of Alexander I, even though the Soviet Union did become the dominant power in Europe by virtue of the strength it displayed during the war.

Europe set the course for great power politics in the First World War. It served both as the most important battlefield and the focal point of international politics. The United States provided important support to the Triple Entente and hastened the defeat of Germany. Then she isolated herself from Europe's quarrels. A combination of American material and Soviet manpower won the Second World War. After Hitler's defeat the United States offset the power of the Soviet Union, thus providing a balance of power. The United States could not withdraw without leaving Europe to deal alone with the superior forces of the Soviet Union; America also sought to safeguard her own interests during the Cold War. A balance of power throughout the world has set the course of international affairs in the postwar years.

1.

After signing a peace treaty with the Soviet Union, Finland was obliged to take these factors into account in providing for her own security. The transition to peace itself was a crisis, since the Germans, Finland's former comrades in arms, had to be driven out. Germany had no intention of withdrawing, much less of surrendering without a struggle.

The result was a costly war in Lapland in which Finland lost 1,000 men. To make matters worse, the Germans initiated a "scorched earth" policy. Neither the operations against the Germans nor the establishment of relations with the Soviet Union would have proceeded without friction had it not been for Mannerheim's prestige. The president was a living legend among the "whites" of the Civil War days. Hostility among the "reds" had cooled considerably over the years. The Winter War made most of the latter forget their grudges against the commander-in-chief. The initial success in the renewed hostility of 1941 increased his prestige as a military leader and respect for him grew when he became head of state in the dark days of August 1944.

Whatever Mannerheim decided was accepted without question.

Mannerheim was not a brilliant military planner. His talents lay elsewhere. He was the man who pondered other men's schemes and then determined the course of action. Neither was he a creative statesman during his term as president, although he was capable of exercising sound political judgment. He chose Enckell to serve as foreign minister and in mid November 1944 he picked Paasikivi for the post of prime minister. These two statesmen determined the approach to be used in dealing with the Soviet Union and outlined Finland's future foreign policy. Both made a significant contribution, although the basic policy bears the latter's name. Enckell had written as early as 1926 that "we must work to convince both Russia and the rest of the world that we want to consolidate our independence through peaceful cooperation with our eastern neighbour for our mutual benefit. But at the same time we must inform the whole world – and the *Russians* – that conditions in Finland differ enormously from those in Russia in every respect."

The men most responsible for relations between Finland and Russia have been either jurists or historians. Leo Mechelin, P.E. Svinhufvud, and J.K. Ståhlberg were among the former; the latter included Yrjö Koskinen and J.R. Danielson-Kalmari. During the Russian era these two groups represented different approaches. The jurists viewed relations between the two states mainly in terms of rights, and were therefore unyielding in their opposition to the era of oppression. In contrast, the historians viewed the problem with a greater depth of understanding, recognized the facts, and recommended a greater degree of flexibility. Jurists led the struggle for Finland's constitutional rights; the historians were among those who advocated a policy of conciliation.

Paasikivi was a jurist, but was active in the field of financial law and its history and soon shifted to economics and sociological research. While still a student he came into close contact with Danielson-Kalmari, the inspector of his student union. Like many other students from the province of Häme, Paasikivi was much impressed by Danielson-Kalmari's comprehension of politics in those days. Thus he adopted the "historical" approach at a fairly early age. Paasikivi maintained his interest in historical literature through the years and this in turn deepened his respect for it.

Paasikivi was a student during the period when imperialism and the great powers became the dominant factors in international politics. He also experienced the upheavals of the First World War. Although numerous small states received their independence at that time, the interests of the great powers, backed up by military might, still dominated world affairs. Paasikivi condemned disrespect for legalistic points of view. But realism was essential in foreign policy and geography made relations with Russia crucial. Peace and the restoration of mutual confidence were essential. Cooperation beneficial to both countries on the basis of friendship and mutual respect was the key to a successful relationship. Since Finland's position also depended on contacts with other countries, friendly relations had to be maintained with them. Paasikivi advanced a foreign policy that aimed both at strict adherence to treaties and non-involvement in conflicts between the great powers. He also succeeded in winning the approval of the Soviet leadership for his policy.

Paasikivi's knowledge of international politics enabled him to view events from a big power point of view and permitted him to understand Soviet demands for security. In directing Finland's foreign policy in the immediate postwar years, he argued that Finland had absolutely no intention of starting a war against the Soviet Union. Although Finland did wish to remain outside great power conflicts, she would fight if her national interests were in jeopardy. In an interview granted to an American magazine in February 1947, Paasikivi made it clear that Finland would fight an aggressor that launched an attack on the Soviet Union through Finnish territory. By the same token, he was prepared to accept Soviet aid in the event that Finland could not repulse the attack alone.

Paasikivi opposed Stalin's proposal for a treaty of friendship and mutual aid on the model of bilateral agreements previously concluded between Hungary and Romania and the Soviet Union. Treaties of this kind would have meant excessive involvement. Finland had no enemies and therefore Paasikivi argued that the principles in the statement mentioned above were sufficient to guarantee Soviet security. Here Paasikivi's analysis was quite natural. The Soviet Union sought to safeguard its own interests in foreign affairs, and made proposals to

Finland in accordance with these interests. Paasikivi was obliged to examine these proposals in the light of Finland's own interests and independence and make only those concessions which would not violate them. Consequently the Soviet Union might propose whatever it desired, but if it went beyond what Paasikivi considered justifiable, he would simply decline to go along. Since the Soviet Union did not wish to make excessive demands, a treaty between the Soviet Union and Finland was concluded in 1948, in accordance with Paasikivi's principles. From then on this agreement, along with the peace treaty, formed the foundation for improving relations between the two neighbours.

The Treaty on Friendship, Cooperation, and Mutual Aid, approved by parliament with considerable misgiving in April 1948, requires the contracting parties to develop friendly relations and work together to maintain international peace and security in accordance with the principles and objectives of the United Nations. If either country becomes the object of armed aggression through Finnish territory, Finland, as an independent state, will attempt to repel the attack. Finland agreed to concentrate all the resources at her disposal to defend her territorial integrity, if necessary with aid provided by the Soviet Union in a mutually acceptable manner or by means of joint operations. Both parties agreed to refrain from making or joining alliances that might be directed against the other, stated their desire to develop and strengthen economic and cultural ties in the spirit of cooperation and friendship, and agreed to respect each other's sovereignty and independence and the principle of non-interference in each other's internal affairs. The treaty was made for ten years. As long as neither party gave notice before the termination of the period specified, the treaty was to remain valid for five-year periods, until either party gave written notice of its intention to terminate the treaty one year before the end of the five-year period in progress.

The cornerstone of Paasikivi's policy was mutual confidence. Mistrust had to be relegated to the past. Finland could be certain that the Soviet Union threatened neither her independence nor her political system. For its part, the Soviet Union could consider its north-western frontier secure. Finland would not become involved in any ventures directed against the Soviet Union. An essential part of Paasikivi's policy was to convince those foreign powers who might plan an attack against the Soviet Union that Finland would honour her agreements, whether it was a question of the obligations involved in the peace treaty or in the pact concluded in 1948. Once suspicion was no longer prevalent, there would be no obstacles to either economic or cultural cooperation. Cooperation of this kind would only serve to strengthen ties of friendship and mutual confidence. Thus Finland's eastern border, the source of unrest and wars for centuries, would become a border of peace.

2.

Parliament had remained in session throughout the war by means of emergency legislation. Elections would have been particularly difficult to hold in wartime, especially for the displaced segment of the population. Demands for new elections were made as soon as the country returned to peacetime status. The Communists were especially strong. They founded the Finnish People's Democratic League (SKDL)[1] in cooperation with elements to the left of the Social Democrats in the political spectrum. Elections were held in March 1945.

Defeat shook Finland's party system severely. The effect was somewhat less drastic in the organizations themselves, but the situation at home and particularly that in the world at large had to be reassessed and party programmes altered accordingly. For the Communists peace meant the beginning of legal, public operations under relatively favourable conditions. The Patriotic People's League had already ceased to function during the war, even before it was officially banned according to the terms of the truce of 1944.

During the war an attempt was made to maintain the country's national unity through coalition governments which included the leaders of all parties. Due to the situation at the end of the war, most of those who had participated in government during the fighting stepped down. When demands of this kind were extended to service in

1 Hereafter referred to as the SKDL.

Parliament, protests were made and people began to back the party leaders who had borne responsibility during the war. Politicians who had remained outside the government during the war, particularly members of the peace opposition, could participate in foreign policy without suffering from the burdens of the past. They attempted to exploit this advantage and forced those who had served in government during the war to step down. Thus internal power struggles began in all parties, with the exception of the Conservatives and the Progressives. These conflicts were to influence party activity, orientation, and the selection of leaders for years to come.

Earlier support of monarchy did not shake the voters' confidence in the Swedish People's party. The achievement of independence and the potential it provided were taken into account in bringing the party programme up to date as were the dangers the majority might pose for the Swedish-speaking minority. Independence opened the way for unhindered contacts abroad, primarily with Sweden. Sweden's neutrality during the Civil War, and the Åland question in which the residents of mainland Finland energetically opposed annexation of the islands, disrupted relations between the two states. The issue was decided in favour of Finland. The Swedish People's party began to support the special status of the Åland islands, mainly because it suited the party's plans for obtaining autonomy for the country's entire Swedish-speaking population.

The Swedish People's party faced another challenge after the Second World War. The natural course of development did not further its interests. The growth rate of the Finnish-speaking population was more rapid and the proportion of Swedish-speakers declined continually. 60,000 votes were cast in the first elections after independence was achieved, 1,300,000 in 1939, 2,000,000 in 1954, and 2,370,000 in 1966. The corresponding turnout for the Swedish People's party was 117,000, 124,000, 140,000, and 135,000. Representation in Parliament was 22 in 1919, 18 in 1939, 13 in 1954, and 12 in 1966. The party's prestige has declined, although its M.P.'s have often played an important role in Parliament, indicating which way the legislature would vote on a given issue. During the first two decades after independence the non-socialist parties were strongholds of nationalism and friction arose between such groups and the Swedish minority. The

Swedish People's party went along with legislation aimed at putting a stop to Communist political activity. The party defended the parliamentary system, albeit cautiously, since a segment of the membership backed the Lapua movement. True to its principles, the party permitted its members to follow their own convictions with regard to reform programmes. Enthusiastic supporters of reform, the more cautious, and conservatives as well, have all found a home in the Swedish People's party. The party's principal concern is support of Swedish nationalism.

In foreign affairs the party took its lead from Sweden, advocating neutrality. Although it strongly opposed Bolshevism and the terror of the Stalin era and although its members supported efforts to intervene in Russian internal affairs during the Russian Civil War, the party opposed territorial expansion and accepted the Treaty of Tartu. Its M.P.s were consistent. They opposed the borderland policy and the 1922 Treaty of Warsaw. They put little trust in any guarantees for national security the League of Nations might provide, although they were prepared to support Finnish participation in the international organization.

Conflict arose with regard to National Socialism. There were those who felt it could be applied in Finland; they believed a similar system could save Finland from the decadence of a parliamentary system. Others regarded Germany as the only power capable of counterbalancing the growing might of the Soviet Union. Neither group ever constituted more than a small minority within the Swedish People's party. The vast majority supported the nation's general approach to foreign policy which included opposition to National Socialism, neutrality designed to safeguard independence, and closer relations with the other Scandinavian countries.

The Swedish People's party participated in coalition cabinets during the war, although there were party members who played a role in the peace opposition. These attempts circumvented the party's representatives in the cabinet. Although the most active members of the peace opposition were from the ranks of this party, the majority felt that the government was sincerely seeking peace. The action of the party toward the end of war and the internal quarrels that disrupted it after peace was restored weakened its position but did not destroy party unity.

Due to the diversity of its membership, the Swedish People's party had to solve the crisis with as much flexibility as possible. Since the leadership had generally acted with extreme caution during the war, adapting to the new situation did not rend the party fabric. The new problems themselves facilitated transition; they tended to draw attention away from the recent past. An example was the resettlement of the Karelian refugees, which threatened to disrupt the proportions between the two language groups in Swedish-speaking districts. Another was the language issue in the universities and a third involved safeguarding the rights of the Swedish-speaking population in the Porkkala area, which was leased to the Soviet Union. Under threat of war, and particularly during the hostilities, the language conflict declined in importance. The preservation of independence was the only goal. The settlement of refugees in Swedish-speaking districts evoked considerable opposition from the party following the Winter War; resistance was even stronger in 1944. The party's opposition was successful; legislation was passed preventing resettlement that would disrupt the existing proportions between the two language groups. Concessions which would meet the demands of Swedish-language culture were also called for and the Finnish-speaking majority in Parliament agreed to boost the number of Swedish-language professors at the University of Helsinki from 15 to 23.

The "war guilt" issue also caused discord within the Swedish People's party. There was a tradition of uncompromising insistence on legality among the Swedish-speaking educated classes. It dated back to the era of oppression. The idea that someone should be punished for an act which was not a crime when it was committed was abhorrent. Bringing the country's wartime leaders to trial involved this principle. As a result, only those members of the party who had belonged to the peace opposition actively supported the "war guilt" legislation. The others merely bowed to the inevitable.

The Swedish People's party took a realistic stand in foreign affairs in the postwar years. Friendly relations with the Soviet Union had to be established, although not at the expense of relations with other countries. Closer ties with Sweden, a country which had remained neutral during the Second World War and which intended to continue this policy, were considered important. The party also advocated

Finnish membership in the Nordic Council, an organ composed of members of Scandinavian parliaments and governments designed to promote cooperation.

The position of the party deteriorated in proportion to the decline in strength of its parliamentary group. Perhaps the reason for this decline lies in the dwindling attractions of power. The best brains sought out fields where Swedish-speakers had the most opportunity: business, science, scholarship, and the arts. The number of Swedish-speakers in all these fields has exceeded their proportion of the total population. The party has also participated in the government; its leader, Ralf Törngren (1899–1961), served as prime minister for a few months in 1954. But the party has been quick to remove its members from the cabinet due to the wide variety of views its members hold. It is impossible to find a consistent line of approach in domestic politics that would not offend some faction of the party.

Until the 1930s the Conservatives and the Progressives were almost constantly represented in the cabinet and thus took the lead in determining policy.

The basic principles of liberalism were taken into account in drawing up the 1919 Constitution and the practical aspects of liberal doctrine were gradually implemented. Support for the Progressive party, built on the principles of liberalism, decreased continually. The party's parliamentary group decreased to 6 by 1939, from a peak of 26 in 1919.

In contrast, the Conservative party gained a firm foothold in Finnish politics. Its support grew as that of the Progressive party dropped off. It reached its peak in 1930, when 42 Conservative M.P.'s were returned. The party achieved this success partly due to the coincidence between its programme and popular feeling in those days – it was the heyday of the Lapua movement – and partly because those voters who had lost faith in the parliamentary system backed Conservative candidates. When the latter founded the Patriotic People's Movement in 1932, the forces of conservatism split, the Conservative party winning 18 seats and the Patriotic People's Movement 14. The normal number of Conservative M.P.'s was returned in the following elections: 25 representatives or one-eighth of the total.

Both parties were founded in 1918. They adopted the national character of their predecessors, the language parties, and this also appeared in their programmes. The founders of these two parties were experienced politicians and as a result their positions in the language conflict were moderate. Thus the Constitution included provision for making both Finnish and Swedish official languages and the legislation created on the basis of these provisions took the interests of the minority into account. Finnish-speaking students and a segment of the educated classes began to demand improvements to meet the growing demands of the Finnish-language population in the 1920s. The Conservatives and the Progressives responded by incorporating proposals to Finnicize the state university into their programmes.

Both parties supported private enterprise. The participation of the state was acceptable in those areas in which private capital was insufficient or where foreign investment might eventually pose a threat to the country's economic independence. Thus both were prepared to approve a dominant role for the state in mining operations and in developing electric power. National defence was also a part of the programme of both parties. In this case the Conservatives were the more consistent of the two; they were persistent and energetic in their effort to strengthen Finland's defences. There were also Progressives who considered defence of primary importance, although the majority stressed social reforms.

Both made the same appraisal of the international situation. They feared a Soviet invasion and Communist infiltration. In order to put an end to the latter, they were both prepared to accept legislation in the early 1930s restricting Communist activity. But there were differences in approach which prevented the parties from cooperating. The Progressives were a party of the centre and demanded moderation; the Conservatives were further to the right and reacted more sharply to Communism.

The rivalry between the Conservatives and the Progressives began as early as the 1919 presidential elections. As the leader of the republican forces in the constitutional struggle, Ståhlberg had earned the disfavour of the Conservatives; the defeat of Mannerheim, the Conservative candidate, only increased their dislike. The presidential elections of 1931 and 1937 also tended to worsen relations between the two parties since Ståhlberg and Svinhufvud ran against each other and the campaign reached a level of intensity more typical of southern countries. Svinhufvud won the 1931 elections but he trusted in T.M. Kivimäki, a Progressive, who served him as prime minister. When Kallio was elected president in 1937, cooperation between the Social Democrats and the Agrarian Union began. The Conservatives were left out of the cabinet. Opportunities for Progressives to influence the course of political affairs decreased, although Cajander, one of their number, served as prime minister from 1937 to 1939.

Ståhlberg played a major role in internal affairs immediately after independence. He frequently set the course of future developments through his efforts to create a parliamentary tradition. This was the case when the imprisoned insurgents were pardoned. Here the Conservatives felt that he paid insufficient heed to legality and treated the guilty with excessive deference. In 1923 Ståhlberg acted against the wishes of the majority of the cabinet by dissolving Parliament and called for new elections when arrests of Communist M.P.'s denied Parliament a quorum. The actual breach between the two groups did not take place until the beginning of the 1930s, first with regard to the parliamentary system, and then with regard to democracy itself.

Conservatives were critical of developments in Finnish politics after independence and the predominance of "horse-trading" or compromise. The Progressives were more tolerant. This was both a matter of principle and the result of Ståhlberg's efforts to create political traditions. At the outset Progressives were behind systematic efforts to suppress Communist activity. Support among Progressives withered when the movement began to attack democracy. The kidnapping of Ståhlberg was the final blow.

Conservatives maintained for a long time that the Lapua movement would have a beneficial effect on politics and the party offered its support. Paasikivi led the Conservative party in breaking with the movement as it became increasingly violent. Both the Progressives and the Conservatives took the same stand after the Patriotic People's Movement became an independent party.

Conservatives and Progressives viewed the everyday conduct of foreign affairs differently, although they agreed – as was mentioned above – on the basic premises.

Holsti was the principal architect of the Progressive party's foreign policy. He favoured alignment with the West and the borderlands. Progressives considered alignment with the latter a means of opposing the Soviet Union, since close relations existed between France and Poland. The Conservatives denied their support once they were convinced that the Progressive policy would lead to involvement in conflicts between the great powers. They also disliked what they considered an anti-German bias. The League of Nations sought to preserve the status quo resulting from the war; this meant keeping Germany weak. Progressives had nothing against these aims, and backed the League. The anti-German attitude of the League made the right-wing friends of Germany wary. The Conservative party accepted Finnish membership in the League, but with considerable reservations.

Conservatives and Progressives agreed on the necessity of preserving neutrality. They also backed a policy of Scandinavian neutrality as international tension grew in the 1930s. Kivimäki, a Progressive, was prime minister and the Conservative Hackzell was foreign minister when this decision was made. However, the Conservatives had less faith than the Progressives in collective security and were more persistent in demanding increased military spending. There was a shade of difference in the attitudes of the two parties toward National Socialist Germany. The Conservatives were more moderate in their criticism of the regime and advised against permitting the nature of Hitler's Germany to affect Finland's foreign policy. Both parties took the same position on the demands made by the Soviet Union in autumn 1939 and on foreign policy at the outbreak of the war. In both parties there were those who were cautious and those who espoused a bolder line. In general, Conservatives and Progressives gave the government their unqualified support.

The decline of the National Progressive party was no accident, although the party's unwavering insistence on legality in the rather confusing period of reappraisal after the war did lead to a brief upturn; nine progressive M.P.'s were returned in the 1945 elections although the party won only five seats in the next elections.

As the party lost its significance, its members faced a tough decision; should they continue as they had before, affiliate with another party, or seek a new point of departure? Disbanding the party was especially hard for the older Progressives to swallow. Thus there was considerable support for preserving the status quo. The Progressive and Conservative programmes had been similar since independence; after the war there was virtually no difference at all. In the end those who favoured the third alternative – terminating the existing party and setting out on a new course – carried the day. In 1951 they founded the Finnish People's party. The party's new programme was up-to-date and appealed mainly to civil servants and businessmen, although it also drew on working class support. The Finnish People's party doubled its representation in Parliament in 1951, increased it to 13 in 1954, and to 14 in 1962 under the name of the Liberal People's party. In 1966 the party again suffered a setback, losing 6 seats.

Support for the Conservative party remained constant after the war. Aproximately one-eighth of the electorate voted Conservative, electing 28 representatives in 1945, 24 in 1954, and 26 in 1966.

The Agrarian Union had been a moderate party during the aftermath of the Civil War with certain exceptions; personal experiences led the party to take a hard line on the insurgents and call for more severe punishment. The Agrarian Union took an extremely negative view of Communism. A cabinet led by Kyösti Kallio was responsible for imprisonment of the Communist members of Parliament in 1923. As long as the Lapua movement directed its wrath exclusively at the extreme left, it retained the sympathy of the Agrarian Union. But the movement's opposition to Parliament and democracy quickly drove the Agrarian Union into the ranks of those who opposed it. Opposition to the Lapua movement was clearly a major factor in the development of cooperation between Agrarians and Social Democrats. This, along with Social Democratic efforts to defeat Svinhufvud in the 1937 presidential elections and the "red-green" cabinet headed by Cajander that followed, furthered these efforts.

The ranks of the Agrarian Union expanded in the early 1930s during the crisis of democracy, as young members of the educated classes joined the party. This trend was strongly national in character, and there was no difficulty in winning party support for Finnicization of the university. A programme of this sort was obviously in keeping with previous stands taken by the Union.

In view of the nature of the party and the attitudes of its members, the Agrarian Union could not have developed an original foreign policy.

The party lacked experts in the field. The preservation of independence was a basic tenet of Agrarian Union ideology and the party backed whatever policy appeared to promote it. When nothing else seemed effective, in times of crisis, the party actively supported national defence. However, the maintenance of a large defence establishment did present problems for the Agrarian Union. National defence entailed high taxes – something the party had always opposed. A lengthy period of service deprived farm families of manpower. As a result, the Union was chary of defence programmes. When war came in 1939, the Agrarian Union took a firm stand. Some of its leaders were prepared to continue the struggle in March 1940 with western aid. The Union had a strong foothold among the Karelian refugees and Juho Niukkanen (1888–1954), a Karelian, was a party leader. Thus the Union did not view Finland's role in the attack on the Soviet Union a disaster.

Support for the Agrarian Union remained basically constant during the postwar period and since its voters had a majority in areas where families were large, it benefited from an additional advantage; seats in Parliament were allotted to election districts on the basis of population. The Union elected 49 M.P.'s in 1945, 53 in 1954, and 49 in 1966.

The Social Democratic parliamentary group favoured a republican form of government in which Parliament was supreme, although it was forced to compromise with the centre when the rightist minority demanded an increase in the powers of the president and cabinet. During the early years of independence Social Democrats worked actively to secure passage of the numerous reforms proposed in those years. They either initiated the reforms themselves, as was usually the case in social affairs, or supported the efforts of progressive forces in Parliament to unify the nation, develop the economy, and improve educational institutions.

In 1918 the party joined the opposition and refused to participate in the government. It soon abandoned this negative approach, and in 1926 formed a cabinet headed by Väinö Tanner. Relying on minority support, the Tanner cabinet had difficulties, although it did succeed in passing certain social reforms with the help of the centre. Opposition stiffened as the Lapua movement struck out against anything that smacked of Marxism, including Social Democracy. Svinhufvud's refusal to prevent Social Democrats from serving in the cabinet destroyed any opportunities for cooperation between right and left that might have existed. This was particularly apparent in the 1937 presidential elections in which the Social Democrats considered the defeat of Svinhufvud their principal objective. Their success paved the way for cooperation with the Agrarian Union.

Social Democrats had emphasized the necessity of peace from the very beginning. There were pacifist elements in the party and those who believed that independence could be best preserved by declaring Finland's neutrality. There was also support for disarmament. But the facts were not forgotten in declaring these principles; as long as world-wide disarmament remained a mere hope, a small nation was obliged to maintain its own armed forces. The Social Democrats were extremely wary of long periods of service and large appropriations for defence. Tactics were at least partly at stake. The party wooed working class voters by opposing defence spending. Here there was little risk of damaging national interests; the non-socialist majority made certain the country's defences were not neglected. Social Democratic opposition to the military establishment appealed to the masses since the hated Defence Corps was part of the country's armed forces.

Social Democratic attitudes toward defence of the country changed after the Nazis came to power in Germany and the Soviet Union became militarily strong. Increasing international tension encouraged this gradual reappraisal. Social Democrats entered government in 1937 and this gave them partial responsibility for maintaining Finland's defences. Differences between Social Democrats and Communists combined with the Soviet Union's role as leader of the world Communist movement furthered this trend.

The Social Democratic party advocated a foreign policy based on collective security and non-interference in the internal affairs of other countries. Leaders like Väinö Voionmaa (1869–1947) were involved in plans for the establishment of a "Greater Finland" after independence had been won, at a time when Russia seemed to be disintegrating. But those who determined party policy had consistently favoured recognition of the Soviet Union and a peace treaty that would guarantee Finland's historical frontiers. As a member of the negotiating team headed by Paasikivi at the Tartu talks, Tanner worked hard to make the basic line of the Social Democratic party part of the treaty. Later on the party opposed all interference in the internal affairs of the Soviet Union and any policies that might be interpreted as anti-Soviet; this was the case in deciding whether or not to ratify the Warsaw treaty. The party was somewhat uncertain about the League of Nations, but gave unqualified support to the so-called Scandinavian orientation. Differences of opinion regarding the demands made by the Soviet Union in 1939 did arise. Some were ready to rule out territorial concessions altogether; others were prepared to compromise. The party leadership took the latter, more realistic stand. In a world on the brink of war Finland could ill afford to be obdurate. Thus Tanner agreed with Paasikivi during the Moscow talks. Concessions had to be made as long as they did not jeopardize Finland's neutrality or her defences.

The Social Democratic party bore substantial responsibility during the war. It is obvious that without Social Democratic cooperation, Finland would not have survived the trials of those years.

Individuals with Communist inclinations who had infiltrated Social Democratic organizations in the 1930s opposed both Finland's official foreign policy and that recommended by the Social Democratic party. They were very sympathetic toward the Soviet Union, regarding it as the only power capable of standing up to National Socialist Germany. Caught off guard by the agreement between Nazi Germany and the Soviet Union concerning spheres of influence, these individuals supported the government during the prelude to the Winter War and during the actual hostilities as well. No essential change in their attitudes occurred until after the conclusion of the Treaty of Moscow in 1940, when they began to handle relations with the Soviet Union on their own, relying on support from the Soviet embassy. This led many Finns, including the leaders of the Social Democratic party, to anticipate a coup d'etat. Instead of improving relations between the two countries, Communist efforts, which had considerable backing, only worsened the situation. In the end the government came to the conclusion that these activities were treasonable and moved to put a stop to them. The abruptness of the official Finnish reaction only served to increase suspicion in the Soviet Union. The Social Democratic party drove the opposition out of the fold. These same elements, whose leaders were in prison during the second phase of hostilities, tried to hinder the war effort. They had relatively little success. Toward the end of the war certain Social Democratic leaders also joined the peace oppositon mentioned earlier.

The Social Democratic party faced a serious crisis after the war. In addition to the expulsion of the Communist elements mentioned above, conflict between the supporters of Väinö Tanner and the peace opposition flared up. The former rejected the charges made against the party while the latter demanded that Tanner resign from the party leadership and be brought to trial for his role in leading Finland to war. These issues were closely involved with the problem of cooperation with the Communists. The peace opposition favoured cooperation, arguing that the Communists might thereby become a parliamentary party. Those Social Democrats who had cooperated closely with the other parties during the war rejected this view outright. This group, the so-called "comrades in arms," felt that cooperation of this type would lead to the establishment of a people's democracy.

This fierce struggle spread to sports organizations, the trade unions, women's groups, and youth associations. It also affected business enterprises operated by the labour movement. Only the cultural organizations remained united. The anti-Communist forces won the battle, although part of the Social Democratic party broke away, joining an organization of Communists and insurgent Social Democrats, the SKDL.

The struggle within the Social Democratic party, which went on throughout the 1950s, led to a decline in support. In 1945 35 of the 85 seats won in the 1939 elections were lost to the Communists. The party regained some of this support in 1948, obtaining 54 seats, mainly at the expense of the SKDL. Disunity and a poor start resulted in another setback in 1962. The Social Democrats wound up with only 38 representatives in Parliament. In the elections held in March 1966, the party matched its postwar peak, winning 55 seats.

The Finnish Communist party, founded by those revolutionaries who fled to Russia in 1918, was legalized in 1944. The insurgent leaders left Finland under a cloud of despair, under circumstances which easily led to both feelings of guilt and a desire for revenge. Hopes were kept alive all those years. In the beginning there was tension between those Communists that had fled and those who had remained in Finland; the latter accused the leadership of making a basic misinterpretation of the situation. The Communists who remained in Finland founded the Finnish Socialist Labour party. The party's entire parliamentary group was imprisoned in 1923 and the party was disbanded by the decision of a court of law. In 1924 the Communists resurfaced as the Workers' and Smallholders' party and elected 18 M.P.'s. In 1929 they increased their representation to 23 seats.

The Lapua movement introduced persecution of individual Communists and Parliament passed legislation making both the party itself and the organizations and associations under its jurisdiction illegal. The same legislation obliged the authorities to make certain that Communists would never again participate in politics. Although the Communists then proceeded to infiltrate Social Democratic organizations and support radical candidates of the latter, operations were also carried on underground. Trials in Finland against Communists were commonplace since the party sought to overthrow the existing political system and since its members were frequently charged with spying on behalf of the Soviet Union, where their instructions originated. As a result, numerous Communists were imprisoned, becoming martyrs in the eyes of their idealistic supporters.

Radical changes had to take place before Communist leaders, particularly those living in voluntary exile, would have been willing to return home. Thus the party operated on two levels. In Finland it worked to create an atmosphere conducive to revolt and in the Soviet Union it sought to promote the world Communist movement. Communist leaders living abroad ignored the true nature of economic and social developments in Finland and the increasing appreciation for independence on the part of the working class. The information they received and passed on to the Soviet government was incorrect. It boosted their own hopes for revolution and encouraged Soviet distrust of Finland. Thus the nation's morale during the Winter War, and particularly the participation of Communists in Finland in the war effort, came as a surprise to both the Finnish Communists living in the Soviet Union and to the Soviet government, who had relied on the former as an important source of intelligence.

The Communist party derived a certain advantage from its past after it was legalized by the truce of Moscow. The loyalty of party supporters had endured the trials of underground operations and provided a reliable nucleus once permission to function openly was obtained. Friendly relations with the Soviet Union, a policy the party had backed all along, became generally accepted. This in turn increased the party's prestige among non-Communists. Since Finland's own future was uncertain, the party also attracted those who tend to jump on the band wagon. But ignorance of Finnish conditions and a lack of information on the mood of the country, combined with insufficient political experience, prevented the party from exploiting the paralysis affecting other groups in the years immediately after the war. The outcome of the 1945 elections was extremely promising; 49 Communist M.P.'s were returned. The Agrarian Union also won 49 seats and the Social Democrats 50. But the finesse necessary to make use of the victory was missing. Since the existing conditions were not thoroughly understood, mistakes were made. Goals were set too high, and the party behaved as though the election outcome was just a beginning. Internal divisions prevented agreement on a single course of action. The experience gained in establishing people's democracies in the occupied countries of eastern Europe was apparently not applicable to Finland. The opportunity was lost. Other parties gained the time they needed to regroup. The defeat of those Social Democrats who favoured cooperation with the Communists represented a serious setback. In the 1948 elections the party lost 11 seats. The outcome of the elections put an end to the party's participation in government and reduced opportunities to exert influence on the course of public affairs. Party fortunes remained low in the elections of 1951 and 1954, when 43 Communists M.P.'s were returned. The 1958 elections marked a sharp upswing in support; the SKDL won 50 seats. A steady decline followed, partly due to strife within the party and partly to unfavourable election alliances. The party won 47 seats in 1962 and 41 in 1966.

Regardless of election results, the role of the party remained basically unchanged. In competing for the votes of workers and smallholders, the Communist party was sharply critical of the status quo. It pointed out shortcomings and proposed reforms that were beyond the capacity of the national economy. Rival Social Democrats and Agrarians were forced to take a stand on these issues. The consequence was a wage-price spiral which only added to the inflation caused by the

206

economic strain of the war.

The party's position on foreign affairs was consistent; good relations with the Soviet Union were vital and had to be improved heedless of Finland's status with regard to the rest of the world. Here the Communist programme departed from official foreign policy, which was based on neutrality and good relations with all countries. Communist efforts to take the lead in improving relations with the Soviet Union slowed the process of building strong ties.

An attempt was made after the war to unite the entire nation behind a single foreign policy. Good relations with the victorious powers were absolutely essential, particularly in the case of the Soviet Union. The latter was capable of exerting pressure while the war reparations were being paid. The role of Finnish Communist leaders in relations with the Soviet Union and the favourable response of Soviet diplomacy prevented a manifestation of public unanimity. Now and then the Conservative press complained that Finland was not treated as an equal of the victorious powers in accordance with the terms of the treaties, although in general it too recognized the necessity and essential correctness of the Paasikivi line.

For the Agrarian Union conversion to peacetime status occurred rather rapidly. Party leaders had been in the cabinet and had accepted the government's foreign policies, although they actually played no role in determining policy. Nevertheless, two Agrarian ministers were sentenced for their role in the war. Upheaval within the Union after the war led to the departure of the old guard from positions of leadership.

The Agrarian Union, under the leadership of Urho Kekkonen, adopted Paasikivi's approach to foreign policy. Cooperation between these two men began before the end of the war when the former joined the peace opposition and the latter outlined a postwar foreign policy that stressed national security. When Paasikivi took over he expressed his confidence in Kekkonen.

Efforts to ensure an adequate food supply in the postwar years led to strict price controls and an intricate system of subsidies and protective tariffs. Continued shortages after the postwar years and a lack of foreign currency, which frustrated efforts to free foreign trade, perpetuated these controls. Eventually the index of agricultural income was linked to the wage scale. Parties representing large interest groups began to look out for their own economic advantages, as continued inflation created the impression of an abundance of money and a rapidly rising standard of living. This was the focal point of Agrarian policy in the postwar years. It linked agricultural profitability with the problem of migration from farms to the town caused by industrialization. Migration to towns and population centres had to be slowed by improving economic and cultural opportunities in the countryside and by locating industries in rural areas. These efforts, based on the philosophy of the Union's founder, Santeri Alkio, did not succeed and the Union changed its name to the Centre party in 1965.

3.

The illegal intervention of Prime Minister Paasikivi and certain other authorities — which they felt the situation demanded — and attempts to persuade wartime leaders not to run and thus make way for "new faces," were partially responsible for the impressive Communist victory in Finland's first postwar elections. General uncertainty and pessimism about the future also had an effect.

The "big three" dominated Parliament: the Social Democrats, the Agrarian Union, and the People's Democrats or Communists. Paasikivi formed a government in April 1945, largely with the support of these groups. Each received approximately equal representation in the cabinet. Enckell continued to serve as foreign minister.

Reconstruction of Finland's foreign policy proceeded apace. The war against Germany in northern Finland was brought to an end in April 1945. Those organizations banned according to the terms of the peace treaty ceased operations. The most important of these were the Lotta Svärd, the veterans' organization, and the Academic Karelian Society. In the autumn of the same year Parliament passed emergency legislation providing for punishment of those responsible for starting the war.

On the basis of this retroactive act, former President Ryti, Rangell, Tanner, Linkomies, and Kivimäki, all former prime ministers, and Antti Kukkonen (born 1889) and Tyko Reinikka (1889–1964), both former ministers, were given prison terms of varying length. They were convicted of playing a significant role in the decision to take up arms in

1941 or of preventing the conclusion of peace during the course of the war, while serving in the government or in diplomatic posts abroad. The allied control commission had demanded the emergency legislation and the sentences.

Finland experienced a rapid economic recovery. The nation's productive capacity remained intact, except for industry in the ceded areas and shipments of machinery made to the Soviet Union in the form of war reparations. World markets for Finnish products opened up just as they had after the First World War. The wood processing industry achieved immediate success in regaining the markets it had lost during the war. The demand was great, and price levels rose. The peak of the business cycle caused by the Cold War and the arms race was reached in 1951 and 1952, due to the Korean War. As a result, Finland's foreign trade expanded and the balance of trade became favourable.

The state was burdened with heavy expenditures, both those caused by war and those paid to the refugees. The war reparations, which swelled from the 300 million dollars stipulated in the treaty to 550 million dollars in 1952, even though the Soviet Union reduced the payments by 73.5 million dollars in virtue of the fact that the goods were delivered at 1938 world market prices, were the major factor. The strain on both the national budget and the economy was so great that devaluation was unavoidable. Most of these expenditures were financed by means of state loans and, as the value of money decreased, with public savings capital. Organized labour rapidly grew in strength after the war and was in the position to demand compensation both for inflation and for increases in productivity. Finland's ability to compete abroad suffered as a result of the growth in costs of production. This led to two devaluations of the mark with respect to foreign currencies in 1949, the first amounting to 17.7 %. The second followed the devaluation of the pound sterling, and amounted to an additional 44 %. The value of the mark in 1955 was one-fifteenth of its 1938 value and in 1966 one twenty-fifth.

Mannerheim resigned in mid-term, in March 1945. Parliament elected Prime Minister Paasikivi to complete the remaining 4 years of the term, by means of emergency legislation. Paasikivi called on Mauno Pekkala (1890–1952), the director of the Board of Forest and affiliated with the People's Democrats, to serve as prime minister. The new government relied on the support of "the big three," just as its predecessor had. Enckell remained in the post of foreign minister. Communist efforts to seize power were made while the Pekkala government was in office. There were rumours of a coup d'etat in the spring of 1948 and Parliament issued a statement of no confidence in Yrjö Leino (1897–1961), the minister of internal affairs. The president dismissed him at once.

The Conservatives, the Progressives, and the Swedish People's party backed Paasikivi in the 1950 presidential elections. The Agrarian Union supported one of its own, Urho Kekkonen (born 1900), a realistic postwar leader. Kekkonen, who holds a doctorate in jurisprudence, had served in several governments, beginning in 1936. The SKDL put up Mauno Pekkala, who had served as minister of agriculture under Tanner and subsequently in various ministries during the war years and as prime minister from 1946 to 48. The Social Democrats did not have a candidate of their own, but announced in advance that they desired the re-election of Paasikivi. Paasikivi's extensive support brought him victory in the first round of voting.

Relations with the Soviet Union remained the focal point of Finnish diplomacy. Closer relations with other countries developed as relations with the Soviet Union improved. Neutrality, however, remained the ultimate objective.

The metal industry, which had expanded to make the war reparations deliveries, was now a vital sector of the economy. Long-term trade agreements with the Soviet Union were concluded in 1950 providing for an exchange of goods at world market prices and guaranteeing the future of the metal industry. The agreements gave Finland an opportunity to maintain industrial production and import grain, raw materials, manufactured goods, and certain heavy industrial products from the Soviet Union. For a long time Finland exported more than she imported from the Soviet Union and the achievement of equilibrium was a constant goal.

The confidence built up between the two countries was put to the test at the end of 1954 when a security conference was held in Moscow. The western powers did not send any representatives, and thus the conference consisted solely of talks between the nations of the eastern bloc. As a neutral, Finland declined to participate. The Soviet Union was content merely to complain about the Finnish stand in a diplomatic note.

In the autumn of 1955, President Paasikivi received an invitation to visit Moscow together with Urho Kekkonen, then serving as prime minister for the fifth time. These talks resulted in the return of the Porkkala area, which had been leased to the Soviet Union. This action was a display of confidence in Finnish foreign policy, and an example to the United States, which maintained a network of bases in foreign countries surrounding the Soviet Union. An agreement to continue the Treaty on Friendship and Mutual Aid for twenty years was also concluded during the talks.

Finland had attempted to join the United Nations in order to obtain international recognition for her neutrality. Paasikivi himself was reluctant and somewhat suspicious of such attempts. In a world dominated by the Cold War, expansion of the organization's membership became a vehicle for political manœuvring. If a country approved by the eastern bloc became a member, then membership for a nation with a western orientation was necessary in order to preserve the balance of power. These tactics blocked Finland's entry until 1955.

After Stalin's death in 1953 the Soviet Union was ruled for two years by a group of five within the council of ministers. N. Khrushchev (1894–1971), elected first secretary of the Communist party in 1955, exploited this position and the party machinery and became prime minister in 1957. He then led the Soviet Union until 1964. Khrushchev did not re-establish the rule of iron practised by Stalin. He increased the freedom to criticize and appeared in person to explain his policies. He continued the policy of peaceful coexistence adopted by the collective leadership. In a speech made in 1956 he rejected the Leninist doctrine on the inevitablity of war between the Soviet Union and the capitalist countries, insisting that countries with differing social and economic systems could live at peace with one another if they so desired and if peaceful coexistence proved mutually beneficial.

Paasikivi gave foreign policy priority over domestic affairs, leaving the latter to his ministers. Thus his prestige did not serve to stabilize domestic politics.

The most significant political phenomenon in postwar Finland was the growth of working class influence on the course of public affairs. Here the trade unions assisted the political parties. In 1940 there were 66,000 members in the Finnish Association of Trade Unions. This number had grown to 300,000 in 1945. In 1965 there were 250,000 members in the Confederation of Trade Unions (SAK) and 105,000 in the Organization of Trade Unions, a rival federation founded in 1960.

Since politics and economics went hand in hand, efforts to use the trade union organizations as an extraparliamentary pressure group began. The threat of a general strike became especially popular, and was employed in March 1956. Such threats did not cease until the power struggle that arose within the Social Democratic party in the 1950s succeeded in driving the political and professional groups of the movement apart, the latter coming under the leadership of opposition forces within the party.

An extensive study on nationalization was initiated while the "big three" parties were in power. The project went on for years. It was blocked by different groups at various times and the nationalization programme carried out by the British Labour party proved unsuccessful before the research was completed. In the end the project turned out to be unnecessary. Nevertheless, the Communist party, faithful to its principles, demanded nationalization of the means of production. The Social Democratic party was a strong advocate of a planned economy in which the state would play an increasingly large role in business, particularly in the industrial sector. Democratic socialism was the goal. The parties of the centre, to say nothing of the right, continued to stress the importance of a free market economy as the basis for economic growth.

Despite all the difficulties Finland faced both at home and abroad in these years, and while the programmes mentioned above were being carried out, far-reaching social reforms were implemented which greatly increased outlays by the state. Social security for the aged, for children, and for invalids was increased, the arts and sciences were promoted, educational institutions were improved and a network of roads was constructed, particularly during periods of unemployment. There was general agreement in Parliament on the necessity of these reform programmes, since each party felt the pressure of the electorate.

Campaign promises grew as democracy developed during the 1950s.

So did the gap between party programmes and the chances for implementing them. The power of pressure groups, particularly economic ones, became more and more apparent. Cooperation between the Agrarian Union and the Social Democrats, a factor that tended to stabilize conditions after the war, became increasingly difficult as rivalry between the parties became more acute. Election campaigns led from one crisis to another and the permanent parliamentary majority envisaged by President Paasikivi, which would have paved the way for steady development, never materialized. Thus opportunities for consistency and long-term programmes did not arise.

Paasikivi's departure from politics after the end of his second term on March 1, 1956, marked the end of an era in Finnish history. The last major political figure of the generation that had taken part in the struggles of the era of autonomy, in the achievement of political independence, in preserving that independence in two wars and in consolidating these gains after World War II, had stepped aside, making room for those who had acquired their experience since Finland had won her independence.

CHAPTER X

Neutral Finland and the Balance of Power, 1955–1966

Indications of a new era in Finnish politics were apparent in the election campaign. Prime Minister Urho Kekkonen's government resigned in January 1956, but continued in office. Kekkonen had actually launched his campaign as early as 1952 with speeches made all over Finland, setting an example for other candidates as he "Americanized" the campaign. The campaign was lively – to some extent a contest between personalities. This was particularly clear in the efforts of Social Democrats and Conservatives to defeat Kekkonen.

Kekkonen's alliance received the votes of 88 electors, Fagerholm's (born 1901) 72, Sakari Tuomioja's (1911–64) 57, Eino Kilpi's (1889–1963) 56 and Törngren 20. The only serious candidates were Kekkonen and Fagerholm, political rivals for at least two decades. Paasikivi, whom the Conservatives persuaded to run in the second round, came in third. Kekkonen defeated Fagerholm by a vote of 151 to 149.

The new president's rise to the highest office in the land was the result of a long political struggle. Unlike Paasikivi, Kekkonen was active in domestic politics throughout his career. His political opponents even claimed that he worked to split the Social Democratic party after he became president.

Disunity – the product of mistrust and suspicion – characterized the beginning of this new era in Finnish politics.

1.

Kekkonen's fifth cabinet was a coalition of Social Democrats and Agrarians. The former turned in their resignation after the cabinet voted to raise agricultural prices in January 1956. The SAK threatened a general strike while Parliament was in session, demanding that prices be restored to previous levels. Agricultural employers responded with a threat of their own, announcing that deliveries would stop on March 1, the day set for the beginning of the general strike.

Since the government had resigned and the former prime minister had been elected president, the country was without a government at the end of February, the deadline set by the SAK. The new president, however, lost no time and succeeded in appointing a cabinet on March 3. Fagerholm formed his second cabinet and named Törngren foreign minister. Törngren represented the Swedish People's party until August 1956 and then continued as a non-party minister. In addition to the prime minister there were five other Social Democrats in the cabinet, six Agrarians and one member of the Finnish People's party. There was one non-party minister while the cabinet was being formed.

At the outset the government did not intervene in the general strike. This permitted extremist elements to take the law into their own hands. Public opinion forced the government to take action that would restore order. The three-week strike led to the wage rises called for by the SAK and an even faster rate of inflation. The strike organized by agricultural employers proved ineffective.

The leadership of the national trade union organization fell into the hands of the opposition faction within the Social Democratic party. Trade union members who supported the party leadership did not approve of the strike. The result was further discord within the Social Democratic party, first with regard to trade union affairs and later on in the realm of politics. Certain Social Democratic unions broke off from the national organization permitting disunity to continue into the mid 1960s, when talks aimed at reunification began.

A power struggle between the Social Democrats and the Agrarian Union, disagreements concerning economic policy, and the economic and legal questions that arose from the general strike made life difficult for the second Fagerholm government. Rent by dissension, this government turned in its resignation in April 1957. Since there was no apparent solution to the crisis, the cabinet withdrew its request in response to the wishes of the president and remained in office as the Pekkala cabinet had done. But the cabinet was no longer effective and resigned again in May, this time for good.

V. J. Sukselainen (born 1906) was appointed to head a minority government composed of representatives of the Agrarian Union, the Swedish People's party, and the Finnish People's party. Johannes Virolainen (born 1914) became minister of foreign affairs. Sukselainen tried to put an end to years of fiscal irresponsibility. The situation had deteriorated to the extent that the state not only had to postpone payments, but also suspend them at regular intervals. But the government did not receive parliamentary support for the remedies it proposed, nor was there general agreement within the cabinet itself on these matters. The two ministers representing the Swedish People's party resigned only a little more than a month after the government took office and were replaced by members of the two parties remaining in the cabinet.

The cabinet was left with the support of a mere one-third of Parliament and found its troubles multiplying. Efforts were made almost immediately to work out a formula for a broad-based five-party government. But Prime Minister Sukselainen felt that the talks held in August did not offer any prospects of success. Rather than permit the entire government to resign, two non-party ministers from the business world and five Social Democrats who belonged to the opposition faction were appointed to replace three Agrarians, two members of the Finnish People's party, and one non-party minister.

Thus the government's backing in Parliament dwindled further. It enjoyed only the support of the Agrarian Union and an undetermined number of Social Democrats who were members of the opposition within the party. It was unable to persuade Parliament to pass its economic programme. Consultations were not held with the parliamentary groups during the critical phase of the talks leading up to the formation of the government, and this produced bitterness, particularly among Social Democrats in Parliament. This also hurt the government.

When Parliament convened in the autumn of 1957 the Social Democrats called for a vote of no confidence. They asked the ministers if parliamentary procedure had been observed in forming the cabinet. The government toppled accidentally, after a heated discussion and some rather intricate manœuvring. It was defeated by one vote on a resolution put forward by the People's Democrats. This resolution blamed the right for the country's economic difficulties and demanded more representation for the working class in government. The crisis that arose in the middle of October was resolved in record time: 42 days.

A caretaker government was named on November 29, 1957 after the Agrarians and the Social Democrats could not come to an agreement on the qualifications of members of the opposition faction of the latter party. Rainer von Fieandt (1880–1972), director of the Bank of Finland, became prime minister. A retired ambassador, P. J. Hynninen (1883–1960), became foreign minister. Otherwise, the cabinet was composed of high-ranking civil servants and university professors, affiliated with the Agrarian Union and the Social Democratic party.

The government applied its skill to the country's economic problems, but failed due to a lack of parliamentary support. A dual pricing system, part of a complicated system of supports for agriculture and consumers, was the government's target. Under the terms of this programme, farmers sold their crops to the state reserves and were able to buy the grain they needed at a reduced price. The government sought to simplify this procedure. This proved a political mistake; the Social Democrats and the Agrarians agreed to bring down the government. The caretaker cabinet stepped down when the People's Democrats joined forces with the other two major parties.

Cooperation between Social Democrats and Agrarians to bring down the von Fieandt government was tactical. Deeprooted mistrust remained and efforts to form a majority government seemed out of the question. On April 28, 1956 a cabinet headed by Reino Kuuskoski (1907–1965) was appointed. Hynninen continued to serve as foreign minister. Not one party agreed to support the government. The Social Democratic opposition had the largest representation; four ministers affiliated with this faction served in the cabinet.

The muddled state of Finnish politics and personal animosities among the leading politicians led to seven crises between 1956 and 1958. In one case the cabinet agreed to stay on after turning in its resignation. Changes in the make-up of the government occurred on three separate occasions and two caretaker governments in succession ruled the country.

Relief was anticipated from parliamentary elections held in July 1958. The left gained a narrow majority of 101 seats. The People's

Democrats won seven additional seats, raising their total to 50, thereby becoming the largest party in Parliament. The Social Democrats lost six seats, holding on to 48. Ten of these members joined the opposition. Since the latter gained three seats from their own election alliance, there were 13 opposition Social Democrats in Parliament and 38 regulars. The most important change within the non-socialist minority was a loss of five seats sustained by the Agrarian Union. The Finnish People's party lost five seats and the Conservatives picked up the same number.

The resultant balance of power proved barren. Relations between the Social Democrats and the People's Democrats were severely strained. Nevertheless, efforts were made to establish the broadest possible backing in Parliament for the new government. Negotiations were of record length. The isolation of the People's Democrats continued, despite their election victory. On the other hand, every effort was made to bring the Social Democratic opposition, now outside the party, into the coalition cabinet headed by Fagerholm. This attempt failed, and Fagerholm's third government was appointed on August 29. In addition to the prime minister there were four other Social Democrats, five Agrarians, three Conservatives, and one minister each from the Swedish People's party and the Finnish People's party. Virolainen was named foreign minister.

Although the government had two-thirds of Parliament behind it, the president doubted its ability to handle foreign affairs as early as the negotiation phase. In accordance with parliamentary principles, he did not let his doubts influence his decision. In contrast to the action he took after the appointment of the first Fagerholm government, he declined to lend the prestige of his office to the government's conduct of foreign affairs. This lack of support along with the composition of the government and the relegation of the People's Democrats to the opposition led Soviet leaders to expect a change in Finland's foreign policy. Foreign Minister Virolainen tendered his resignation on December 4, along with the other Agrarian ministers. The prime minister then did the same in the name of the entire cabinet.

In the months leading up to the crisis, and during the crisis itself, the Soviet Union observed a policy of "watchful waiting" in its relations with Finland. Communications between the two states gradually came to an end. The problem was resolved on January 13, 1959, when the third cabinet headed by Sukselainen was appointed. It was composed of Agrarians, except for Törngren, the foreign minister, who was a member of the Swedish People's party. Assisted by the president, the government succeeded in restoring normal relations with the Soviet Union. Otherwise it was not nearly so successful. It was a non-socialist minority government and confronted a socialist majority in Parliament. This prevented it from carrying out an energetic economic policy, although in comparison with the short duration of most Finnish governments, it was remarkably long-lived.

The Sukselainen government resigned at the end of June 1961. Martti Miettunen (born 1907), appointed a provincial governor in 1958, formed an Agrarian minority government. Only slight alterations were made in the previous cabinet. The most important was the departure of Törngren, who had served as foreign minister. Ahti Karjalainen (born 1923), appointed director of the Bank of Finland in 1958, succeeded Törngren as foreign minister.

The Miettunen government was another in the series of minority cabinets which handled foreign affairs successfully, but which were unable to come to grips with domestic problems. Although relations between Finland and the Soviet Union remained good, power politics on the European continent led to the so-called "note crisis", which began on October 30, 1961. The president dissolved Parliament in order to resolve the crisis. The Agrarian Union made good its previous losses in new elections held in February 1962, increasing its representation from 48 seats to 53. The Conservatives gained three seats, increasing their representation from 29 to 32 and the Finnish People's party gained an additional 5 seats for a total of 13. The Social Democrats won an additional seat, while the Social Democratic opposition, now the Socialist Union of Workers and Smallholders (TPSL), lost 12 seats and retained 2. Since the SKDL lost three seats, the one-vote socialist majority became a minority of 87.

Efforts to form a new government began after the elections and the resignation of the Miettunen government. A government headed by Ahti Karjalainen, a doctor of political science, was appointed on April 13, 1962, after two months of negotiations. Veli Merikoski (born 1905), a professor of administrative law at the University of Helsinki, became foreign minister. The SAK agreed openly to permit three of its leaders to join the cabinet. Five of the remaining posts were given to the Agrarian Union, three to the Conservatives, and two each to the Swedish People's party and the Finnish People's party. The cabinet had the backing of a considerable majority in Parliament. Discord on the left also made the government's work easier. Since no party wanted to work with the People's Democrats, Paasikivi had considered it fitting to leave out the party of the right as well. Deviation from this pattern in forming the third Fagerholm government in 1958 had proved to be a mistake. After the Conservatives entered the government, the Social Democrats, who had been denied a role in foreign affairs, served to maintain an equilibrium in accordance with the political pattern for the parliamentary term from 1962 to 1966.

The most serious difficulties faced by the Karjalainen government were domestic. They were the result of both disunity among the parties that supported the government and of the conflicts within these parties. Disagreement over economic policy between the non-socialist ministers and those representing the SAK was another source of trouble. However, despite numerous crises, the government remained in office until the end of August 1963. A 90 million mark increase in consumer prices stipulated by the agricultural income act was the last straw. The SAK representatives in the cabinet could not accept this measure and resigned. Although the government replaced them with members of the Agrarian Union and non-party appointments, differences of opinion caused by efforts to balance the budget led to the cabinet's downfall in December 1963.

The president acted quickly. He appointed a caretaker government headed by Reino Lehto (1898–1966) on December 18, 1963 after a 24-hour crisis. Jaakko Hallama (born 1917), secretary of state, became the foreign minister. Despite its skill, the Lehto government had no more luck than any other caretaker cabinet. It managed merely to deal with day-to-day matters which could not be postponed.

Talks aimed at establishing a majority government began, in anticipation of new elections. A government headed by Johannes Virolainen was appointed on September 12, 1964. Karjalainen became foreign minister. Karjalainen's simultaneous appointment as the prime minister's deputy indicated the growing supremacy of the Agrarian

Union. In addition to the ministers mentioned immediately above, there were five other Agrarian representatives, three Conservatives, and three ministers each from the Swedish People's party and the Finnish People's party.

The Virolainen government resumed the tradition of Agrarian dominance broken by the caretaker cabinets. After the 1962 elections the president was an Agrarian and Kauno Kleemola (1906–1965), an Agrarian, was speaker of Parliament from 1962 until his death. Agrarians also occupied the posts of prime minister and foreign minister. This proved to be a windfall for the parties which did not participate in the cabinet, particularly for the Social Democrats. The determined opposition of this party, which was at times almost feverish, proved an important asset in the 1966 election campaign. The party had been denied a role in foreign affairs, although it had modified its previous stand. This turned out to be an additional advantage.

2.

The ground work for Finland's foreign policy in the postwar world was laid in 1947 during Paasikivi's term of office, at the outset of the Cold War. Paasikivi's appraisal was correct, and served as a guideline for future policy. The basic validity of the Paasikivi line has remained, although the Cold War varied considerably in intensity and caused political speculation about Finland from time to time.

Mutual suspicion between the two camps led by the Soviet Union and the United States continued and even intensified. The arms race picked up speed as the Second World War grew increasingly remote. The rivalry spread to the farthest corners of the earth, and even into space. Political and military conflict had some effect everywhere, especially in areas located on the border of the two opposing blocs. Repercussions caused by such conflicts were considerably weaker in more remote areas, except when there was an immediate threat of a Third World War, as there was during the Cuban crisis of 1962.

Profound changes in thinking occurred after the Second World War. The development of military technology was a crucial factor. In an age of missiles, small land areas lost much of the significance they had when land operations were the principal form of warfare. After the Second World War, the United States and the Soviet Union, together with their allies, controlled the territory needed for land operations. The inviolability of a nation's air space also declined in importance. In an age of missiles nations could defend their air space solely by striking back or threatening to do so. There were no other means available. Although technologically advanced warfare reduced the interests of the great powers in the territory of small states, it did not make military vacuums secure. The arms race forced the great powers to make every effort to protect their gains and thus prevent attempts to expand on the part of a rival group by diplomatic, economic, or military means. Small states, however, could not base their security on these conflicts of interest.

The most important new factor in the postwar years was the threat of a Third World War. Civilization itself was in danger. The consequences of defeat served as another deterrent. Here the sentences meted out in the Nuremberg trials held from 1945 to 46, after the collapse of Nazi Germany, were a sobering reminder. Both major world powers had nuclear stockpiles sufficient not only to destroy each other, but mankind as well. In the mid 1950s the "balance of terror" became the basis for peace, or at least for the postponement of a Third World War.

But neither the development of military technology nor the balance of terror diminished the importance of a nation's geographical position in determining its foreign policy. Geography remained the most important factor, determining the extent of a nation's defence requirements and dictating the measures needed to provide security.

Under Paasikivi, relations with the Soviet Union were the most important element in Finland's foreign policy. The sensitivity of this question was directly proportional to the threat felt by the Soviet Union in each international crisis. The Cold War was extremely intense while Paasikivi was in office. This was due to the supremacy of the United States in nuclear weapons, which continued throughout most of the 1950s. The Soviet leadership was obliged to follow the foreign policy of neighbouring countries with the utmost care. Would the United States attempt to use its military might to alter the balance of power achieved after the Second World War? Paasikivi understood this, and sought to avoid involvement in anything that might disturb the Soviet Union. The principal danger was the network of bases the United States and its allies had established around the Soviet Union. Any one of these was in range of important targets within the Soviet Union.

Germany seemed to be the greatest threat. Two states were formed from the nation that started the Second World War and then suffered defeat and occupation. There were forces in the larger, more powerful of the two that were susceptible to demands for revenge and harboured a desire to reunite the country. Soviet diplomacy considered these elements a menace. Finland had important commercial interests in both Germanys; West Germany accredited Finnish trade representatives in 1952. East Germany did likewise in 1953 in return for similar recognition from Finland. By adopting this policy, Finland decided to treat both German states according to the same principle. Formal recognition of both would occur later.

West Germany rearmed with the assistance of the United States, East Germany with the help of the Soviet Union. Although the Soviet government attempted to block German rearmament with a threat of war, the United States had its way, and West Germany joined NATO, becoming the Federal Republic of Germany.

Although the Soviet Union exploded a hydrogen bomb in 1953 and orbited a satellite around the earth in 1957, before the United States succeeded in doing so, it still considered its position insecure in the early 1960s. Hitler's Germany had fought the Soviet Union single-handed while it was engaged in hostilities with the western powers. Nevertheless, it brought the Soviet Union to the brink of destruction. According to the Soviet view, a Germany bent on revenge and supported by the Soviet Union's wartime allies, particularly the United States, posed an even more serious threat. After the death of Stalin and the establishment of a nuclear balance of power, the Soviet government, first under collective leadership and then headed by Khrushchev, adopted the policy of peaceful coexistence set out by the former in a speech given in 1956. Since the West regarded peaceful coexistence as a mere tactical stratagem, designed to lull the rest of the world into a sense of false security and pave the way for the destruction of the free world, the effect was scarcely soothing.

The transition period in which the Soviet Union overcame this fear caused crises in Europe and the world at large. These difficulties were also reflected in relations between Finland and the Soviet Union.

In general, European crises did not affect Finland's postwar position unless there was a clear threat of general war, as was the case during the Cuban crisis. Neither the Korean war nor the conflict in southeast Asia, tensions between the United States and the People's Republic of China or between these two states and the Soviet Union, the Suez war, nor changes in the military and political situation in the Middle East had any effect in northern Europe. On the other hand, the uprising in Hungary in 1956 and events in other people's democracies did have an unsettling influence. They ended discussion in Denmark and Norway aimed at reducing ties with NATO.

The German problem did make itself felt in relations between Finland and the Soviet Union throughout the 1950s and into the following decade. Relations between the two countries went through a series of crises before cooperation could proceed without friction. This did not occur until the 1960s, when the Soviet Union became convinced of the sufficiency of her armed forces, the continuity of Finnish neutrality, and the durability of the Treaty on Friendship, Cooperation, and Mutual Assistance.

After rearmament and a period of rapid growth which made her an economic power, West Germany gained her independence, becoming the Federal Republic of Germany, a name which alluded to a reunited Germany. The Soviet Union had granted the eastern zone independence in the previous year. Although the German Democratic Republic joined the Warsaw Pact, thereby increasing the latter's effectiveness, the Soviet Union directed its attention to the dangers posed by the growing might of the Federal Republic. In the mid 1950s the Soviet Union began to demand recognition of the sovereignty of the German Democratic Republic and the conversion of West Berlin into a free city. The western powers rejected both demands and international tension increased. This occurred in the autumn of 1958.

Technological achievements helped consolidate Soviet policy, although the rise of Khrushchev to the leadership of both state and party after the demise of the collective leadership was an even more significant factor. In the years following the death of Stalin, Khrushchev had favoured conciliation in international politics. Numerous setbacks, such as events in Hungary and the consolidation of his own position led him to adopt a hard line.

Finland was extremely important in efforts initiated by the collective leadership in the mid 1950s with the goal of expanding the sphere of peaceful coexistence to embrace all of Scandinavia. Khrushchev's policy did not bear fruit, Denmark and Norway did not reduce their ties with NATO, and as a result of the events in Hungary, public opinion in traditionally neutral Sweden became anti-Russian.

Governments usually conduct foreign policies without regard to fluctuations in public opinion, in accordance with what they consider the nation's interests. Nevertheless, discussion based on both ideals and emotions and changes in public opinion does take place in democracies and Communist countries alike. There is an essential difference; in democracies articles are written which take no heed of the government's stand. Such articles are often harmful. In contrast, the press in a one-party state never writes anything that might contradict the official line, even though the communications media are not under the direct control of the state or party.

The Soviet press followed the 1958 election campaign closely, and did not conceal its sympathy for the People's Democrats in their efforts to win back the gains made in 1950 which were subsequently lost in the next elections. The SKDL achieved what it set out to do, increasing its representation in Parliament from 43 seats to 50, thereby becoming the largest party in the legislative body. Satisfaction was expressed publicly in the Soviet Union. Lacking an understanding of Finnish politics, the Soviet leaders were confident that the outcome of the elections would mean a role for the victors in the cabinet. This was not the case. The People's Democrats were not included in the talks leading up to the formation of the new cabinet, although politicians known for their anti-Soviet views did take part. Soviet newspapers expressed disappointment, dissatisfaction, and suspicion that the new government intended to re-orientate Finnish foreign policy.

Relations between the Soviet Union and Finland at the beginning of Kekkonen's first term appeared to follow the lead set by Paasikivi, which called for sufficient mutual confidence to avoid recurring crises. President Kliment Yefremovich Voroshilov (1881–1970) came to Finland in August 1956 in response to a visit made by President Paasikivi the previous year. In late January and early February 1957,

Prime Minister Fagerholm visited Moscow at the invitation of the Soviet government. The statement issued in conjunction with this visit stressed the importance of good relations between the nations of northern Europe in preserving world peace. Prime Minister Nikolai Aleksandrovich Bulganin (born 1895) returned this visit in June of the same year, accompanied by the first secretary of the Communist party. The atmosphere remained friendly. In autumn 1958 the Soviet Union adopted an unfavourable attitude toward the third Fagerholm government. Although no breach of international practice was involved, the Soviet government clearly displayed a lack of confidence in the Finnish cabinet. It appealed to the recently concluded trade agreement, criticizing Finland's failure to import the goods stipulated in the agreement. Neither had Finland made use of a loan granted by the Soviet Union for this purpose. The Soviet Union regarded this failure as an expression of intent which did not correspond to Finland's previous foreign policy.

The Finnish government disagreed. It denied the connection between this or any other action and a change in foreign policy, pointing out that it had no control over foreign trade. It could only make purchases destined for reserve stores and make recommendations to the business world. Restrictions were removed in 1958 which released large quantities of currency and purchasing power sought out those markets which offered the most economical commodities. The Soviet loan had actually been intended for long-term investments involving large projects.

Although the Soviet government was informed of all this, it persisted in believing that Finland was abandoning the Paasikivi line. The Finnish government argued that its postwar diplomacy had won such widespread approval that a change of course was out of the question. Only a serious misunderstanding of the international situation could lead to action of this kind. A new course in foreign policy would also represent a violation of treaties between the two countries, a move that would not be consistent with traditional Finnish conduct with regard to international agreements.

Despite these explanations, relations between Finland and the Soviet Union were strained to the breaking point. The Soviet ambassador in Helsinki was called home in October and the post was left vacant.

Strained relations led the Agrarians, headed by Virolainen, to resign in December. The prime minister and the rest of the cabinet soon followed suit.

Efforts were made to find a new basis for the government under circumstances in which Finland's room to manœuvre was clearly reduced. A cabinet with the backing of a substantial majority in Parliament could restore normal relations with the Soviet Union. After weeks of negotiations which did not produce the necessary harmony, an Agrarian minority government was formed at the expense of parliamentary procedure. The new government was capable of handling foreign affairs.

In order to ensure that relations had been normalized, President Kekkonen made an unofficial visit to Leningrad at the end of January 1959 and met with Khrushchev. Khrushchev noted that relations had cooled while the Fagerholm government was in office, but expressed his belief that they would improve once the crisis was over. He also stated his hope that relations between Finland and the Soviet Union might serve as an example of peaceful coexistence between a large socialist state and a small non-socialist state.

Good relations between the two countries were restored after the appointment of the Sukselainen cabinet and the president's visit to Leningrad. A new Soviet ambassador left his credentials at the end of February 1959. A policy of peaceful coexistence based on mutual confidence, friendship, and increasing cooperation continued for the next two years. But in the autumn of 1961, a new, more serious crisis took shape.

In June 1961 Prime Minister Khrushchev met John F. Kennedy (1917–1963), the president of the United States, in Vienna. The Soviet prime minister wished to meet Kennedy personally and exchange opinions on matters concerning both countries. He put his inexperienced opponent to the test and proceeded to increase tension after the talks in Vienna proved unproductive and neither recognition of East Germany nor the conversion of West Berlin into a free city won any backing in the West.

The Soviet Union interrupted reductions in its armed forces undertaken previously and began to tighten up its defences. It resumed nuclear testing and Soviet politicians and the Soviet press brought up the possibility of a new war. Traffic between East and West Berlin was stopped on August 13, 1961, and Soviet forces closed off the border zone. In order to stem the flow of manpower from East to West through Berlin, the government of the German Democratic Republic began work on a wall along the border between the two zones.

These tensions meant a renewed strain on relations between Finland and the Soviet Union. While President Kekkonen was on a successful visit to the United States, the Soviet government sent Finland a long and carefully prepared note on October 30, in which it referred to the international crisis in progress and appealed to sections of the 1948 treaty on Friendship, Cooperation, and Mutual Aid which provide for consultations. The Soviet Union called for consultations. Fear of West Germany and its allies was one factor. The rapprochement between France and Germany which Khrushchev had attempted to prevent by accommodating the latter and which was already a reality in 1961 also contributed to the Soviet move.

In assessing the Berlin crisis from the western point of view, the crucial role of West Germany in NATO had to be taken into account. After the NATO defence lines were shifted to the West German border, the significance of the Federal Republic increased greatly. The United States considered Germany her most effective ally. Although West Berlin was located deep within the German Democratic Republic, lacked political significance, and was impossible to defend, it was an important factor in great power politics. From time to time the western powers repeated their pledge to remain in West Berlin even at the risk of a Third World War, since failure to honour the alliance might set off a chain reaction necessitating reappraisal in all countries along the border between the two groups and in those nearby as well. Those countries which had built their foreign policy on the basis of western military support might begin to doubt the wisdom of their decision and consider safeguarding their security and independence with a policy of peaceful coexistence similar to that practised by Finland. The western powers felt that concessions would weaken their prestige and military preparedness. As Khrushchev kept international tensions high, West Berlin became a touchstone of western policy, particularly for the United States. Alongside recognition of sovereignty, the Berlin question had become a crucial factor in relations between the German

Democratic Republic and the Soviet Union by 1961. Located within the Democratic Republic, West Berlin formed a Western propaganda centre and a gateway to the West for East Germans who had grown weary of the system. It therefore warranted a close watch. An overall settlement of the Berlin crisis was important to the German Democratic Republic as it sought to promote its sovereignty, although it did not seek to incorporate the western sector of the city.

Thanks to great power politics and numerous national factors, a centre of unrest had formed in the heart of Europe, keeping the threat of a new war alive. When ideological disputes and world-wide rivalry between Communist countries and those with free market economies are taken into account, the fact that all means were used in 1961 is perfectly understandable. The articles of the 1948 treaty providing for consultations between Finland and the Soviet concerning the threat of war were used by the Soviet Union.

In proposing such consultations, the Soviet leadership demonstrated just how hot the Cold War had become. It was clear from the note presented by the Soviet government that it did not lack confidence in Finland's leadership nor did it suspect that Finland was not prepared to fulfil its obligations according to the 1948 treaty.

This analysis coincided with the Finnish position. Since the end of the Second World War Finland had come to believe that its south-eastern and eastern frontiers were borders of peace and friendship like her western one. Finland was determined to defend herself in the event of an attack on the Soviet Union launched through Finnish territory. To the extent possible, defensive operations would be performed with the country's own armed forces. But Finland's national security was built primarily on a policy of neutrality. Here Finland was persistent and received recognition from Kennedy during President Kekkonen's visit to the United States at the time when the Soviet note was presented. Finland again expressed her desire to remain outside conflicts between the great powers. She argued that this could be achieved by means of general recognition for Finnish neutrality. Relations characterized by mutual confidence built on the basis of the 1948 treaty were put to the test after the presentation of the Soviet note. In the West rumours and predictions of Finnish submission were rife and this added to the seriousness of the situation.

Foreign Minister Karjalainen set off for talks in Moscow after the president had returned to Finland from the United States. The Soviet foreign minister informed him that military consultations would be unnecessary if Finland would guarantee its present orientation and the continuation of good relations between the two countries in the future. The Finnish government took up the offer and set out to avoid military consultations. As such, these consultations would not have been in conflict with the treaty. But there was talk, mainly abroad, which would have destroyed the basis for continued good relations with the Soviet Union.

In conjunction with the presidential election campaign then in progress, all the parties had announced their support for the preservation of friendly relations with the Soviet Union, based on mutual confidence. But the principal aim of most parties was to displace Kekkonen, and the above assurance did not convince the Soviet leaders. Due to foreign pressure Finland could no more extend the president's term with emergency legislation – regular elections were approaching – than it could guarantee the government's permanence without abandoning parliamentary democracy. Dissolution of Parliament was the only constitutional alternative which might convince the Soviet Union that Finland's foreign policy would continue. President Kekkonen dissolved Parliament on November 14.

As the tension grew, foreign communications media showed increasing interest in Finland's position. The president journeyed to Novosibirsk to meet with Prime Minister Khrushchev, hoping to alleviate the crisis. In talks held there on November 24 and 25, Kekkonen admitted that war might break out in Europe, but also contended that the military consultations proposed by the Soviet leader might cause unrest and lead to a war psychosis in Scandinavia, thereby undermining Finland's neutrality. He suggested that the Soviet Union abandon its request. This would pacify public opinion throughout Scandinavia and would in turn lessen the need for security precautions in Sweden and in Norway and Denmark, both members of NATO.

At the conclusion of the talks Khrushchev announced that the Soviet Union supported Finnish neutrality. Trusting in the experience, good will, and ability of those responsible for Finland's foreign policy, the Soviet Union would drop the request for consultations. Khrushchev did

230

express the wish that the Finnish government "would follow the course of events in northern Europe and the Baltic closely and if it proved necessary, provide the Soviet Union with its opinion of what should be done."

As a result, Kekkonen's opponent in the presidential election campaign, Olavi Honka (born 1894), withdrew from the race and relations with the Soviet Union improved rapidly.

As early as June 1960, the Agrarian Union convention had chosen Urho Kekkonen as its presidential candidate. The Social Democrats headed by Tanner sought Kekkonen's defeat. This led to a search for the candidate with the broadest appeal possible. In February 1961 Honka, a retired attorney general, agreed to become the candidate of the six so-called "democratic" parties. But there were those who supported Kekkonen's re-election in all these parties, and due to Honka's inexperience in foreign affairs there was also some opposition to the latter's candidacy.

After the diplomatic crisis mentioned above forced Honka to withdraw his name, these parties named their own candidates. The Social Democrats chose Rafael Paasio (born 1903), a member of Parliament and a newspaper editor. The People's Democrats picked Paavo Aitio (born 1918), a member of Parliament, and the TPSL chose Emil Skog (born 1897). Kekkonen's election alliance included the Agrarian Union, part of the Swedish People's party, and most of the Finnish People's party. There were also numerous Conservatives and non-party candidates on Kekkonen's list. The Conservatives, the Swedish People's party, and the Finnish People's party did not choose candidates of their own.

Campaigns for both presidential and parliamentary elections were held at the same time. Foreign policy and the note crisis were the major issues. Kekkonen's alliance alone was prepared for the campaign. The others had to be content with the mere appearance of a campaign organization or a make-shift arrangement. Time was short. Kekkonen's alliance received 145 votes, Aitio's 63, Paasio's 36, and Skog's 2. An alliance of Conservatives and the Finnish People's party won 39 seats in the electoral college and the Swedish People's party 15. Urho Kekkonen was elected in the first round of voting with the support of his own alliance and the votes of the Conservatives and both the Swedish and Finnish People's parties. Left-wing electors voted for their own candidates.

The note crisis became a milestone similar to the return of the Porkkala area during Paasikivi's term of office. The former was proof that past hostilities were over; the outcome of the latter demonstrated Finland's determination to maintain a policy of peace and friendship and live up to her treaties. It also meant that a relationship of mutual confidence between Urho Kekkonen and Prime Minister Khrushchev had been established. Cooperation subsequently advanced, not only in relations between the two countries, but in evaluating the international situation as well.

Decisions made between Khrushchev and Kekkonen in bilateral talks which were binding on both countries undercut the authority of Parliament to some extent. Consequently decisions included in joint communiques were considered binding not only on the Soviet Union, but on Finland as well. The problem of leasing the Saimaa canal zone was resolved in this way. This issue had first come up in the 1940s, and was taken up again at Finland's request from time to time. Khrushchev agreed to lease the territory as a demonstration of confidence in Finland and of the friendship of the Soviet leadership.

Despite a short interlude following Khrushchev's fall in 1964, friendly relations continued under the new collective leadership composed of Leonid Illych Brezhnev (born 1906), Alexei Nikolaevich Kosygin (born 1904), and Nikolai Viktorovich Podgornyi (born 1903). The leaders of the two neighbouring states, particularly President Kekkonen and Prime Minister Kosygin, established the custom of exchanging views several times a year about mutual relations, economic and cultural ties, and the international situation.

Decreased tension in Europe and increasingly widespread recognition of Finland's foreign policy had a stabilizing effect. Concensus on foreign policy was achieved at home. A better understanding of world politics recommended a policy designed to safeguard national interests, and this was the chief criterion in determining attitudes toward armed conflicts or situations in which such conflicts might arise. But neutrality did not mean indifference and the Finnish public became increasingly concerned about world peace in the postwar years. Freedom of the press permitted ideological discussion and stands were taken.

The Finnish Communist party consistently called for an interpretation of neutrality that favoured the eastern bloc. It supported recognition of the German Democratic Republic and criticized the United States and the foreign, military, and economic policies of the western bloc. The People's Democrats had certain reservations about the work of the Nordic Council, but participated in it within the framework of the restrictions imposed by Finland's neutrality, as did the other parties. The TPSL adopted the same position. Under Väinö Tanner, the Social Democratic party was a staunch opponent of Communism. This opposition was also interpreted as anti-Soviet, putting the Social Democratic party in an awkward position with regard to foreign affairs. Distrust within the Soviet Union was not reduced when Social Democrats failed to reject the sharply anti-Communist and anti-Soviet resolutions of the Socialist International, of which the party was a member.

A change occurred after Tanner stepped down at the 1963 party convention and Rafael Paasio, free of the burdens of the former, became chairman. At the 1966 convention the Social Democrats declared their support of the country's official foreign policy. They went even further with respect to Germany, approaching support for recognition of both German states. Plans for cooperation with the Communists aimed at unifying the labour movement and promoting the common interest of the working class at all levels of government were also made.

The Agrarians consistently took the lead in foreign policy among the non-socialist parties, drawing on the Swedish People's party for support. Uncertainty about Finland's foreign policy among the other parties gradually disappeared, as was evident in the 1963 presidential elections. Personal differences with Kekkonen did affect the attitudes of certain individual politicians when foreign policy was at stake. Efforts were made to find shortcomings in Kekkonen's interpretation of neutrality. From time to time there was a lively ideological discussion, characterized by anti-Communism. This was particularly true during election campaigns. At times it meant success in domestic politics. As late as the 1960s it often denied the individuals in question any influence on the country's foreign policy.

3.

The growth in the amount of horsepower used is a reliable indicator of Finland's industrial growth. In 1920 Finnish industry had 300,000 horsepower at its disposal, in 1938 1,100,000, in 1950 1,550,000, and in 1964 4,650,000. In 1920 there were 117,000 factory workers and in 1964 350,000. Diversification of industrial production kept pace with increasing mechanization. A country dominated by the wood processing industry during the first quarter-century of independence became an industrial nation in the true sense of the word after the Second World War. In comparing gross production for two years, 1954 and 1966, diversification is obvious. In the former year the wood processing industry accounted for 31 % of the total while only 24 % in the latter. For the metal industry the figures were 24 and 23 respectively, for the textile and clothing industry 11 and 6, for the food, beverage, and tobacco industries 16 and 24, the chemical industry 6–6, graphics 2–4, and other industries 10–13.

In 1966 products of the wood processing industry accounted for 66.5 % of all exports, metals and products of the engineering industry 16.9 %, agricultural products and furs 4.4 % and others 12.2 %.

Concerted efforts have been made since Finland gained her independence to expand the area in cultivation and intensify agricultural production. As early as the 1920s certain agricultural products were important exports and efforts to achieve self-sufficiency in the production of food became essential as the Second World War approached. These attempts won the approval of the entire population. After the war it was natural that the farming population from Karelia should receive land elsewhere in Finland. Since 14 % of the country's arable land had been lost, new fields had to be cleared merely to fulfill the needs of the refugee population. In addition, government promises of land in East Karelia made to front-line soldiers during the second phase of the war had to be honoured. Consequently the farming population continued to grow after the war.

137,000 people were either freed from agricultural and forestry by mechanization or left the countryside in search of a better living during the five-year period from 1961 to 1966. But despite the fact that migration to the towns reduced the rural population by 25 %, special measures were still necessary to maintain rural incomes on the level of rapidly rising earnings in other fields. Since a mere 25 % of all the farms in Finland had more than 10 hectares under cultivation, the investments necessary for mechanization could not be justified, as equipment could not be used efficiently. Joint use of machinery did not appear to be feasible. Occupational training in agriculture was the principal problem in postwar Finland, where developments had not kept pace with those in the other Scandinavian countries. A transfer of income to this vital occupation was necessary. The controversy concerning the extent and nature of farm supports hindered cooperation between political parties and made agreement on other issues more difficult since sharp differences arose among the various political parties and population groups. Party tactics contributed to the existing muddle.

4.

In removing all vestiges of backwardness, Finland had to take human factors into account as well. She had to increase the security of each citizen and compete for the best manpower with a more advanced Sweden. Finnish wage levels were low. In the middle of the 1960s wage levels in Sweden were 140, when the index for Finland was 100. Efforts to narrow this gap were essential in order to safeguard the nation's interests.

Transfer of income from one group to another by means of legislation and voluntary agreements between organizations became a generally accepted tool in social politics in countries seeking to achieve economic growth during the postwar years. Social insurance programmes were consequently expanded. The system of pensions for the aged and the disabled founded in 1937 under the terms of the national pension act was revised in 1956. The number of people receiving pensions, which was 93,000 in 1950 and 375,000 in 1956, was 540,000 by the end of

1966. In 1956 100 million marks in pensions were paid out and in 1966 nearly 900 million. The average annual pension rose from 600 marks to 1,600 during the same period.

Health insurance was initiated in the 1960s, costing the state 200 million marks in 1966. Pensions for individuals with both long-term and short-term positions and family pensions, providing security for widows and orphans, were also introduced in the 1960s.

Other forms of social assistance also represented income transfer; they included child allowances, family allowances, special child allowances, maternity allowances, free school lunches and tax reductions for families with children. In 1966 expenditures for the benefits ran to 400 million marks.

A rising standard of living and the transfer of income through taxation mentioned above reduced the importance of public maintenance. Despite this trend, 200 million marks in welfare and institutional care were paid out in 1966.

Outlays for social service in Finland came to 246 million marks in 1948, 881 in 1956, and 2,490 in 1965. On a per capita basis these expenditures amounted to 63 marks in 1948 and 199 marks in 1965.

Despite these accomplishments, Finland was unable to catch up with the rest of Scandinavia. In Sweden expenditures for social welfare accounted for 10.6 % of the net national product in 1948 and 16.9 % in 1965. In Norway the corresponding figures were 7.2 and 14.8, in Denmark 9.7 and 14.5, and in Finland 7.4 and 12.1.

Differences in the standard of living also varied greatly from one part of the country to another, between industrialized southern and western Finland and the developing areas in eastern and northern Finland. The latter remained behind the rest of the country in terms of social services and other benefits.

Migration to population centres accelerated by economic difficulties in the rural areas has caused a housing shortage in addition to employment problems. Housing conditions in Finland have been crowded, except in the countryside where land and building materials are cheap. Diligent rural families have not faced intolerable living conditions. Postwar migration from the countryside to the towns has prevented housing standards from rising appreciably. Technology has, however, made standardization possible, although the rise in earnings that has taken place at the same time has increased the cost of land tremendously. Since it has been impossible to guarantee a supply of land at reasonable prices by means of legislation, housing in urban areas has been expensive in postwar Finland. Housing has been a major political issue. In areas where industrial growth is rapid, the shortage has prevented production facilities from expanding and has forced labour to move elsewhere, sometimes even abroad. In the 1960s increasing reliance on public funds was made in the construction of housing. Housing production was also encouraged by tax reductions and exemptions. These policies resulted in wave after wave of speculation without easing the plight of the renter. The result has been an even larger burden on the state with regard to the construction of blocks of flats.

Industrialization has created other problems, including those of regional and community planning and pollution. The appropriate use of leisure time created by shorter working hours and longer vacations is also involved here. Increasing attention was focused on these problems during the 1960s.

5.

An urban environment with a relatively large population is a prerequisite for the establishment of cultural institutions such as institutes of secondary and higher education, adult education prog-rammes, art schools, theatres and orchestras. Before radio and television became widespread the countryside lacked these services altogether. The development of a transportation network provided the rural population with access to cultural amenities. In 1956 there were 47,000 private cars in the countryside and in 1966 225,000. The corresponding increase in the towns was from 55,000 to 280,000. Rapid industrialization and the simultaneous mechanization of agriculture drove the rural population to the towns and cities where the growing needs of the people for culture and expanding economic opportunities made a diverse cultural life possible. Efforts on the parts of the state and local governments to promote cultural activities brought these services to an increasing number of citizens in the 1960s.

Economic and educational developments expanded, creating new opportunities for white-collar work. Rising standards of living made advanced education possible for the children of a growing number of families. An additional stimulus was the slogan "knowledge is power," adopted by the labour movement.

There was virtual unanimity among Finland's political parties with regard to cultural policies. Differences of opinion arising over priorities and use of state funds by no means indicated serious conflict. A willingness to compromise permitted passage of bills without causing any major discord. Thus a programme was passed to upgrade scientific and scholarly research and instruction in universities and other institutions of higher learning. The aim here was to bring Finnish facilities up to international standards by the 1980s. In the mid 1960s a large-scale school reform was undertaken, providing for the eventual unification of elementary school, junior secondary school, and middle school. All children between the ages of 7 and 15 will attend the new comprehensive school.

The following statistics depict the growing interest in education at all levels. In the 1930s participants in adult education programmes numbered some 20,000. By the middle of the 1950s this figure had increased to 50,000. Some ten years later, in 1966, it had swollen to nearly 150,000. At the beginning of the 1920s there were only 32,000 pupils attending secondary schools. Approximately one-twentieth of those completing the compulsory course had an opportunity to continue their studies. The corresponding figures after the Second World War were 77,000 and one-twelfth. The desire for further education and the opportunities to take advantage of it increased during the 1950s. By the middle of that decade 134,000 pupils attended secondary schools, or 13 % of the eligible age group. The breakthrough occurred in the mid 1960s when every fifth pupil who completed the compulsory course entered secondary school, i.e. 268,000.

Wider access to institutions of higher learning was a natural outgrowth of the expansion of the secondary school system. New institutions were founded to meet the need. In 1966 six universities and more than ten colleges were in operation. An additional five institutes of higher learning were on the drawing board. In 1920 there were a total of 3,300 students in the University of Helsinki, the University of

Technology, and the newly founded Åbo Akademi combined. In 1938–39 there were 9,000 students in these three and the University of Turku, which had opened its doors in 1922. In 1955–56 17,000 students attended institutes of higher learning and in 1966–67 there were 46,500. In 1920 there was one student in Finland for every 1,000 inhabitants, while in 1967 there were 10, i.e. more than in any other western European country.

The increase in the number of civil servants alone was not sufficient to account for the increased demand for higher learning. In 1939 there were 50,000 officials in the basic salary classification and in the mid 1960s this number had doubled, one-third of these officials being women. On the othet hand, industrialization and the growth of the service industries have provided large numbers of jobs for individuals with a higher education. In 1920 there were 10,000 white-collar workers in industry and in 1964 there were 80,000.

6.

Discussion of changes in the Finnish constitution began after the Second World War. The Communists were instrumental in these efforts, proposing far-reaching changes on the model of the people's democracies in eastern Europe. The other parties also called for a review of the existing system both in their new programmes and in practice.

During the period in which the Agrarian Union dominated Finnish policies, attention was focused on the procedure for electing the president, presidential authority, and the term of office. There was considerable support for a more direct method of election and for limitations on the length of the term and on the number of terms a president might serve. The former was based on the fact that most candidates elected according to the established procedure had not received more than one-fifth of the votes cast. Changes were proposed that would give the individual citizen's vote more weight. A two-stage process appeared to be the best way of assuring that the will of the nation was carried out; if none of the candidates received an absolute majority in the first round of voting, a run-off would be held between the two candidates receiving the largest number of votes. This would guarantee that a majority of the electorate had actually voted for the winner.

Discussion concerning limitations on the president's term of office gathered momentum after Urho Kekkonen was elected president for the third time. There were those who sought to limit a single president to two terms in office; some went even further, demanding that an incumbent president be prevented from standing for re-election. Both arguments were heard throughout the 1960s and in the end, Parliament expressed its wish to introduce a direct, two-phase electoral process.

A need arose for legislation regularizing the status of political parties once the party system became an established part of democracy in Finland. This discussion also began in the 1950s although the "party act" was not passed until 1968. A proposed reform of the election legislation under discussion at the same time required that registered parties alone would have the right to put up candidates. Under such legislation the parties would assume an even greater role in Finnish politics, particularly since they would obtain a virtual monopoly on the formation of cabinets. As a result, democracy within the parties and the principles observed in the selection of candidates became the subject of public discussion in the 1960s. Since suffrage in parliamentary elections was universal and equal, the same principle should apply in the selection of the party's candidates.

The number of party members was another issue involved in efforts to expand democracy. Party membership should in some way correspond to the number of votes obtained in elections in order to safeguard democracy. Statistics on party membership are not accurate. In comparing them the methods used by party organizations must be taken into consideration. If membership is computed on the basis of dues paid to local organizations, the statistics are somewhat more reliable. If organizations of women and young people are included on the membership lists, the figures are of course higher. In 1939 the Agrarian Union had 37,000 members, the Social Democrats 33,000, and the Conservative party 11,000. In 1962 the Union announced that it had 272,000 members. In parliamentary elections held the same year the party received 528,000 votes. The corresponding figures for the Social Democratic party were 80,000 and 449,000, for the Conservati-

240

ves 86,000 and 347,000, for the Swedish People's party 56,000 and 148,000, and for the SKDL 150,000 and 507,000. In general, one out of every three members of the Social Democratic party has taken part in voting within the party. According to the new legislation, one party member, participating in voting within the party, represents 20 citizens who cast their votes for Social Democrats. This ratio would have applied in selecting the party's candidates for the 1966 parliamentary elections. The 1906 election act stipulated that one candidate could be chosen for every 30 qualified voters in an election district who formed an association of electors.

In 1954 a decision was made to hold parliamentary elections every fourth year instead of every third year. The aim here was to provide an opportunity to carry out long-range programmes as broad-based parliamentary governments became more frequent. Experience had also shown that a longer term reduces the pressure to compete. Two-year terms meant that representatives merely lived from election to election. Proposals were also made to adopt the British practice of dissolving parliament before the end of term. If the Finnish government could make use of this procedure and dissolved Parliament at what it termed an opportune time, there was reason to believe that the worst aspects of an election campaign might be eliminated.

Sufficient experience was not obtained in the first half of the 1960s to judge the merits of the new system. No single government lasted throughout the parliamentary term of office, although there were fewer crises in 1962–1966. The cabinet formed in the latter year was the first coalition durable enough to last until the next elections. Parliament was dissolved prematurely in conjunction with the note crisis. The government and the president forced through what they considered essential legislation by threatening to dissolve Parliament, although use of the advantages of the British system has rarely been made. The ruling parties have not sought to dissolve Parliament when such action might promote their own policies.

7

In 1961 6 % of the population of the United States was involved in agriculture, forestry, and fishing – the so-called primary occupations. The corresponding percentage for Sweden was 14 and for Finland 35. 35 % of the population of the United States was involved in the processing industries, 45 % in Sweden, and 32 % in Finland. In the same year 59 % of the U.S. population earned a living in the service industries, in Sweden 41, and in Finland 33.

A comparison of the number of people involved in primary occupations in Finland and Sweden illustrates the favouritism shown toward agriculture in the former. In 1900 one-half the Swedish population was involved in agriculture and forestry while two-thirds of the Finnish population earned a living in these occupations. As late as 1960 half the Finnish population was still working in these three basic fields, a figure that held true in Sweden sixty years before. Industrialization, however, proceeded apace in postwar Finland. By 1966 the percentage involved in the three primary occupations had declined to 28 %, while the number employed in the processing industries had risen to 34 % and in the services to 38 %.

Although strong party ties were traditional in Finland, industrialization and membership in trade unions meant that those who migrated from the countryside to population centres also changed their politics. This trend was of particular significance for the Agrarian Union, which had built its support on the ideals of Santeri Alkio and was almost entirely dependent on the backing of the farming population. Mechanization released large numbers of able-bodied individuals from agriculture. The rate was as high as 30,000 a year in periods when change was most rapid in the 1960s. Agrarian Union leaders had to consider what steps were necessary to guarantee the party's future. Thought had to be given to the future applicability of Alkio's ideals. As early as 1949 Johannes Virolainen had taken up this subject in a publication entitled the *Rural View of Life*. New goals were set out in discussions within the party in the 1950s. They were summarized by Virolainen in a work that appeared in 1961, *The Leading Ideals of the Agrarian Union*. After a lengthy controversy, the Union decided to change its name to the Centre party and approve a programme that would continue to appeal to its supporters even after they had migrated to the towns and entered new occupations.

Along with the more profound attempt to keep up with the times on the part of the Agrarians, other parties reviewed their programmes and adopted new names. In 1950 the Conservatives changed the name of their organization from the National Coalition party to the National Coalition and the Finnish People's party became the Liberal People's party. The former opposition within the Social Democratic party became the Socialist Union of Workers and Smallholders (TPSL) and took up a position between the SKDL and the mother party. Veikko Vennamo (born 1913) left the Agrarian Union to found the Small Farmers' party, which later became the Finnish Rural party. He was elected the party's only representative to Parliament in 1966.

In addition to a reassessment of foreign policy, the Social Democrats changed many details in their programme in 1963 and 1966 in order to keep up with the times. Revision was mainly concerned with economic and cultural planning. Far-reaching demands for more social security were also made.

Discussion within the Finnish Communist party focused primarily on the justification for violent revolution and the dictatorship of the proletariat and the prospects for the establishment of a new social order in Finland. By the mid 1960s, opinion within the party was split between the more radical wing that favoured violent revolution and a more moderate group. While the latter persisted in its support of revolutionary goals, its members were willing to work with the Social Democrats for tactical reasons. Cooperation was aimed at helping the working class and forging a united opposition against the non-socialist parties in the cabinet. Both parties of the left considered suppressing a long-standing conflict which had disrupted work in the trade union movement, and in banks, cooperative enterprises, and athletics.

Parliamentary elections – with the exception of those held under extraordinary circumstances in 1919, 1930 and 1945 – show that on the whole, party support has remained constant from one decade to another. Party loyalty oftens appears to be a national characteristic. Finns are slow to accept change, and therefore back what seems reliable and familiar.

No one party in Finland could take credit for either the new jobs or the educational opportunities created by industrialization or for the increase in social security. Since there were no parties that saw any advantage in opposing social and cultural reform, considerable unanimity prevailed. As early as the 1966 elections economic difficulties and unemployment provided fertile ground for radical groups, particularly those outside the cabinet. This was especially true in the developing areas, although no startling upsets occurred.

The use of impartial opinion polls in drafting party programmes was adopted by all parties in the early 1960s. Here again, no one party succeeded in gaining the edge over its rivals. As the role of the head of state in foreign affairs continued to grow during the Kekkonen era, the course of world politics and predictions concerning Finland's foreign policy were primarily important in choosing presidential electors. Neither did changes in party leadership made before the mid 1960s have any appreciable influence on the voters' choice in multi-party Finland.

Parliamentary election campaigns in Finland were long fought with speeches, debates, personal encounters, and articles in the press. Use of radio in campaigns began after the Second World War and television took its place in the 1960s. As the latter grew more widespread, the significance of both public meetings and personal encounters declined. Television saved the people a lot of trouble and succeeded in capturing the attention of an ever larger percentage of the electorate.

The more prosperous newspapers also benefited from technological improvements. Gathering the news, printing, and distribution accelerated, subscription and advertising services were intensified, and profits increased. These developments made more "elegant" papers possible and this in itself attracted subscribers and advertisers. Papers with limited circulations were unable to exploit these advantages. Their ability to compete with the larger national papers as sources of news was seriously impaired. Their numbers of course diminished. The rich became richer, the poor poorer. This trend was disastrous for political papers, especially those of the left. Despite the risks that were obviously involved, new papers were founded to serve a multitude of ends: everything from politics to profits. In 1919 there were 340 newspapers and magazines; this number had grown to over 2,000 by 1964.

The rapid expansion of radio and television restricted the ability of the printed word to shape public opinion, but did not deny it influence entirely. The press was influential in determining party support in the mid 1960s, although the circulation of daily papers representing these parties did not correspond to the votes obtained in the elections.

In the mid 1960s the Agrarian Union had 14 daily papers with a combined circulation of 300,000. The party received 500,000 votes in the 1966 elections. The Conservative party had 13 papers, 380,000 subscribers, and received 325,000 votes. The total circulation of the 12 papers representing the Swedish People's party was 145,000; 135,000 citizens cast their votes for this party. There were 11 Social Democratic papers and 115,000 subscribers. The principal party organ alone had 36,500 subscribers and the party received 645,000 votes. The People's Democrats had 7 papers with a circulation of 110,000. The main party organ, *Kansan Uutiset*, accounted for half this figure. 500,000 voters were cast for the party. *Suomen Uutiset,* the only paper operated by the Small Farmers' party, printed 6,500 numbers, while the party attracted 25,000 voters. The combined circulation of newspapers operated by the three largest parties was 525,000. These parties pulled in 1,650,000 votes, i.e. one for every three subscribers. The corresponding figure for the Social Democrats was six, and barely one for the Conservatives and the Swedish People's party.

Circulations for certain urban national papers provides evidence of voter independence. The *Aamulehti* in Tampere had a circulation of over 90,000 while the Conservative party obtained only 33,000 votes in the North Häme electoral district. Circulation of the organ of the same party in Vaasa was 55,000. The Conservatives attracted only 32,500 votes in this electoral district. The Agrarian party operated the principal paper in Kuopio: *Savon Sanomat* with a circulation of 55,000. In Jyväskylä the *Keski-Suomalainen* had a circulation of 50,000. The party received 37,000 votes in the former area and 33,000 in the latter.

Certain independent papers such as *Helsingin Sanomat* and *Turun Sanomat* forged ahead of the party dailies. The former printed 260,000 papers in 1966 and the latter 80,000. The concentration of subscriptions in the hands of a few dailies in the capital and in provincial centres encouraged the development of paid political advertising. Since this proved expensive for both parties and individual candidates, effective advertising methods had to be considered. Large scale political advertising came into its own in the 1960s. Its probable effect was largely within election alliances, in terms of the distribution of votes, although skilful advertising of individual candidates did benefit the parties indirectly.

The most important development in the field of communication with regard to election campaigns was of course the development of radio and television. The growth of these two media was explosive. There were 300,000 radio licences granted in 1938. This number doubled in the following decade. In 1958 there were 1,140,000 radio licences and more than 1,600,000 in 1966. The first television licences were issued in 1958, although there were more than 820,000 by 1966. Equal access to radio and television was provided for all the parties in Parliament. Party leaders prepared for appearances with care and studied ways of promoting their own parties at the expense of the others, including live broadcasts, in which proving the errors or misrepresentations of one's opponents was impossible.

Television brought the election campaign into the home. Personal encounters between representatives of several different parties and the voters was thereby achieved. None of the traditional forms could have provided this. Public meetings, debates, the press, campaign literature, circulars, photographs, and even efforts to persuade individuals could never have the same effect. Television freed election campaigns from the bonds created by decades of politics. Rapid changes in the balance of power became possible and evidence for this assertion was provided by the outcome of the 1966 election.

Both hard campaigning and rather indefinite promises characterized the 1966 campaign. The Social Democrats emerged the victors, increasing their representation from 38 to 55 seats. The TPSL increased its representation from 2 to 7 through a successful alliance with the People's Democrats. The Small Farmers' party elected its first M.P. The People's Democrats, the Conservatives, the Centre party, (formerly the Agrarian Union) and the Liberal People's party (formerly the Finnish People's party) suffered the greatest losses. Their representation declined from 47 to 41, 32–26, 53–49 and 14–9, respectively.

The result was a major upheaval in Parliament. The non-socialist majority was now socialist, the latter having an edge of 103–97. In many ways the 1966 elections were a turning point in domestic politics. The parliamentary prerequisites for continued Agrarian leadership were now lacking and cooperation between Social Democrats and People's Democrats denied the party access to cabinet-level positions of leadership.

Index of Persons

248